Presented To:

_____

From:

_____

Date:

_____

DARE
to
Believe

DARE
to
Believe

THE TRUE POWER OF FAITH TO WALK
IN DIVINE HEALING AND MIRACLES

BECKY DVORAK

DESTINY IMAGE® PUBLISHERS, INC.

P.O. Box 310, Shippensburg, PA 17257-0310

"Promoting Inspired Lives."

This book and all other Destiny Image, Revival Press, MercyPlace,

Fresh Bread, Destiny Image Fiction, and Treasure House books are

available at Christian bookstores and distributors worldwide.

For a U.S. bookstore nearest you, call **1-800-722-6774.**

For more information on foreign distributors, call **717-532-3040.**

Reach us on the Internet: **www.destinyimage.com.**

ISBN 13 TP: 978-0-7684-4097-3

ISBN 13 Ebook: 978-0-7684-8869-2

For Worldwide Distribution, Printed in the U.S.A.

To protect the privacy of a few individuals certain names have been changed.

DEDICATION

THIS BOOK IS DEDICATED first to my Heavenly Father, who gave me so much; to the Holy Spirit, who has led me every step of the way; and to my Lord Jesus Christ, who healed and delivered everyone in this book by the shedding of His most precious blood. I love You, Father! I love You, Holy Spirit! I love You, Jesus!

Then I want to thank my fun and loving husband, David, for a life filled and overflowing with adventures together. We have seen our Lord Jesus do the most amazing and unexplainable miracles for us, in us, and through us during these past 32 years of marriage, and I believe the best is yet to come!

I pray that the words in this book would become a legacy of faith to pass on to our children: Annie and her husband Adam, Micah and his wife Rebecca, Aaron and his wife Deisy, Ricardo, Jorge, Joaquin, Andres, and Marcos— and to our grandchildren; Addison, Jeremiah, Olivia, and the other little ones who have not been born yet.

I thank all of you for your love and support and for being my family. You are a special gift from God to me. I love every one of you very much!

To my parents, who endured all of my growing up years—you raised a brave and adventurous girl. I will always cherish you in my heart.

To my dear friend, Linda Ryan, who has accompanied me on numerous ministry trips around the world, I say, thank you for being willing and faithful to intercede during all the conferences and seminars and to help me minister to the long lines of sick and hurting people. Our friendship is centered on Jesus!

ACKNOWLEDGEMENTS

To MY HUSBAND, David, thank you for believing in me, for giving me the gift of time to write this work, for listening to me as I read and reread to you what I wrote, and for sharing with me your wise counsel.

And to the Destiny Image team, I thank you for presenting this message to the world with a spirit of excellence.

ENDORSEMENTS

I have known Becky Dvorak for almost 20 years. I have watched her walk by faith and grow in her understanding and practice of healing and press forward boldly to do whatever God asks her to do, whatever the cost. It has been an honor and privilege to travel together as one of her intercessors and see the Lord use her mightily in healing, miracles, and deliverance. She is an anointed and powerful Bible teacher with a heart on fire for God. She hears the Lord clearly and regularly steps out in faith to follow His leading. Her desire to teach and empower the Body of Christ worldwide inspires everyone who hears her. God is continually increasing her gifts and blessing His ministry through her.

As Becky has prayed for people around the world, I have witnessed God open their blind eyes and deaf ears. I have seen Him heal countless backs, knees, shoulders, feet, and teeth. I have seen tumors healed and limbs straightened and strengthened. These accounts are not exaggerations, but the truthful testimony of God's faithfulness and healing power. Becky will rejoice as all the glory goes to God as she continues to follow His lead.

Linda Scott Ryan
Greater Works Ministry
St. Paul, Minnesota

I have known Becky Dvorak since 2004. I thank the Lord that I have had the chance to travel and to do the work of the ministry with her for all these years.

I traveled with this great servant of God from the Northern to Southern part of my country, Tanzania, from the Maasai to the Nyakyusa people groups. I have been blessed to see how the Lord has been using her mightily. She teaches the Word of God in a powerful way, and not only does she teach the people theoretically, but she also shows them how to put into practice and live out that Word. Lessons like "Knowing Who You Are in Christ," "The Holy Spirit," and "Dare to Believe," along with many other teachings about healing, have changed the lives of many people everywhere we went.

As her interpreter, I witnessed many miracles the Lord performed through her ministry. I've seen people come rolling, crawling, and walking with hands and feet bound together, and I've seen them leave upright and free after she prayed for them. I've seen blind eyes opened, deaf ears healed, short limbs grown out, tumors healed, and many other sicknesses and diseases healed. I give glory to our God for using His servant.

God Bless You!

Pastor Piniel Lucumay
Tanzania, Africa

Becky is one of our mighty servants of God with the gift of healing. She not only teaches, but also demonstrates and teaches you how to minister healing through the Holy Spirit. Some of my co-workers and I have served with her ministry in Shanghai, Changsha, and Xinyang Cities (Mainland China) with many Churches since 2008. I praise our Lord to have her demonstrate and witness to us the power of the Holy Spirit and to help many to truly understand and experience God's powerful blessings on us!

Those who have not experienced the Holy Spirit's divine power, who have been unaware of their true identity as God's children, and who are suffering from physical pains and illness must have a good look at this book and learn from her gifted experience.

Albert Chang
Twin City Bay Church
Shanghai, China

For many years, my husband and I have been encouraged and blessed by the incredible stories, testimonies, and miracles of God through Becky and David's missionary ministry. You will find that Becky's book, *Dare to Believe*, is not only an account of their life's journey and amazing miracles, but it is an actual dare! A dare and challenge to study the Bible, to understand the Scriptures—what they mean for us in our everyday lives— and to believe that God still does the miraculous if we dare to believe!

Terry Maston
The CENTER Church
Granada Hills, California

I see the manifestations of the Kingdom of God with power, touching the physical bodies and the hearts of the people—these words describe David and Becky Dvorak.

The experience of knowing them and seeing them minister in the power of God has been edifying for our congregation. Their lives and the teachings that they have imparted to us have challenged the hearts of those who know them and have heard them to search for a life filled with the anointing of the Holy Spirit and manifest the power of God to bless the people.

Pastor Enrique Rodas González
Iglesia Verbo Antigua, Guatemala

CONTENTS

FOREWORD 17

PREFACE 19

INTRODUCTION 21

CHAPTER 1   REDEEMED FROM THE CURSE 23

CHAPTER 2   HEALINGS AND MIRACLES 65

CHAPTER 3   RESOLVING DOUBTS AND QUESTIONS 77

CHAPTER 4   HOW TO RECEIVE HEALING 109

CHAPTER 5   BY THE BLOOD AND OUR TESTIMONY 123

CHAPTER 6   A SPECIAL ROD 135

CHAPTER 7   POWER FROM ON HIGH 143

CHAPTER 8   A SPECIAL TOUCH 153

CHAPTER 9   FAITH PRINCIPALS IN JESUS' LIFE 157

CHAPTER 10   FAITH PRINCIPALS FOR HEALINGS AND MIRACLES 161

CHAPTER 11   MARCOS 175

CHAPTER 12   ANDRES 195

CHAPTER 13   RICARDO 201

CHAPTER 14   SIPERONI 205

CHAPTER 15   OTHER HEALING TESTIMONIES 209

CHAPTER 16   CHILDLIKE FAITH 283

CHAPTER 17   COMMISSIONED TO HEAL 295

CHAPTER 18   SIGNS AND WONDERS POINT TO JESUS 303

CHAPTER 19   THE ARK AND HIS PROMISE 307

                ANSWERS TO REVIEW QUESTIONS 311

                FAITH ASSIGNMENTS 321

FOREWORD

THE BOOK YOU ARE HOLDING, *Dare to Believe*, is a wonderful account of God's unconditional love for you. I really believe that as you read this manuscript, you will understand in a greater dimension the sacrifice of Jesus on the Cross—which provides for us everything the Father has promised to us in the New Covenant of grace!

Learn to *believe* and *receive* God's healing for your life. The presentation that Becky Dvorak provides is a wonderful description of what redemption is all about and what Jesus did to provide all of us with so great a salvation.

Becky and her husband, David, have pioneered the LIFE Homes in Guatemala. Since 1994, they have been faithfully serving the Lord by rescuing abandoned street children and HIV babies. The team that they have trained and mentored and the property that has been developed and maintained are not only a testimony of God's assignment that they carry in their hearts, but also a testimony of their faithful diligence to pursue God's purposes and *dare to believe*.

I believe that the accounts of miracles, and the amazing stories that Becky relates will not only encourage you and give you more reason to give God praise, but also help you position yourself for God's miracles and victory for your personal life. Get ready to *receive* as you *dare to believe*. Enjoy!

Keith Hershey
Founder, Mutual Faith Ministries Int'l
Mission Hills, CA

PREFACE

I ONCE TOLD a Christian woman that she needed to exercise her authority over satan and the attack of cancer against her son's body. She was very puzzled by this statement and wondered how she was to do such a thing. My desire for this book is to teach people how to do just that. I will be covering topics such as the authority we have in Jesus Christ; how He redeemed us from the curse of sin, sickness, and disease; where that curse originated from; and how to put our faith into action to attain our miracle.

He really cares about you! It doesn't matter how hopeless the situation looks. He is able to heal you, and more importantly, He is willing to heal you in spirit, soul, and body.

I have listened to countless numbers of people as they told me that the sickness or disease attacking their bodies was a blessing in disguise from God or that God was using it to teach them some deep truth about His goodness or that it was their cross to bear for His glory. I pray that I am able to shed the light of truth on such gross misconceptions about God in this area. God is good, and every good and perfect gift comes from Him. There isn't anything good about sickness and disease. He is not the one responsible for these afflictions, but He can deliver us from them.

If you are suffering, I want to lead you down the path of healing and deliverance that is found only in Jesus Christ.

If I were to describe myself, I would say I am like a spoon that God uses to stir people's faith. I like to go beyond theology in the Word and discover the purpose of its meaning for today. I want to teach you how to access and apply His healing power to your everyday life. I want to impart the secret of empowering your life by entering into His presence. And I pray that the personal testimonies will proclaim His abundant goodness toward you and me. I'm sending forth a clear challenge that God is who He says He is and that He will do exactly as His Word says. I encourage you to *dare to believe.*

Behind this book is a life filled with tears, trials, and victorious triumphs that can only be manifested for His glory. Much time has been spent with the Lord, and that has been for my good. This book has been stirring within my spirit for quite some time, and I believe now is the time to share it with you.

I pray that your spiritual eyes will be enlightened to the endless possibilities that you possess in Him. I pray that you will be challenged to the very core of your being to trust Him for what seems impossible and to allow His glory to shine forth through your life. May you experience the empowering of the Holy Spirit with magnificent signs and wonders that will glorify your Heavenly Father and win a lost and dying world to the saving grace of our Lord Jesus Christ. *Dare to believe!*

INTRODUCTION

DARING TO BELIEVE GOD is a matter of the heart. It is a quality decision that happens when a heart is truly surrendered to the grace of God that abounds toward us and not against us. It comes from the revelation of the Living Word—the revelation that it is no longer about doing good works to appease God to gain His favor, but about confidently relying on the power of the costly blood of Jesus Christ, which purchased our redemption from the curse of sin, sickness, disease, and every other form of the curse that attempts to overtake us. This divine understanding of God and His Word comes from time spent with the Spirit of God. In the secret place, He releases the true power of faith to walk in divine healing and miracles. This bold, but child-like faith put into action manifests the presence of God's glory around us. And those things which were deemed impossible become possible.

Once I was sharing with a group of Bible students, and I was stirring their faith with personal testimonies of healing and miracles. One of these students spoke up and said, "You make it sound as if you and David walk in healing and miracles on a daily basis."

I replied to him; "Yes." And I say to those who are holding this book, "That's as it should be, and it can be for you as well."

I admonish you, whoever you are, that it matters not what you have or have not done in the past. It matters not what you have or have not said in the past.

Today is a new day; today is your day of salvation. Jesus Christ paid the price in full with His blood for the forgiveness of all of your wrong-doing and for your deliverance from every attack that satan has launched against you and your loved ones. He took upon His physical body all sickness and all disease so that you can receive His free gift of divine healing today. *Dare to believe!*

CHAPTER 1

REDEEMED FROM THE CURSE

A YOUNG COUPLE WAITED with anticipation for the birth of their first born child, and on November 17, 2010, a beautiful baby boy was born into this world. What started out as a celebration of life, very quickly turned into a life-threatening emergency as their newborn son was struggling to breathe his first breaths. Everything was happening so fast, and their baby was now being transported to another hospital.

Upon their arrival, the medical staff worked hard to stabilize the baby. Afterward, the head physician spoke with the couple and gave them the diagnosis, Meconium Aspiration Syndrome, and told them their baby was in critical condition.

They were both exhausted after a long night of labor and now in shock after all that had taken place. The situation was not good, and the reports were bad; this was not how they had imagined this day would be.

But they were not alone, nor were they without hope. They were Christians, and they knew the Word. The word of faith was in them. They had been taught that they had covenant rights with their heavenly Father for the healing of their baby through the blood of Jesus. But would they dare to believe what they had been taught? Could their faith in God's Word over-ride the negative reports, their five senses, and their human reasoning? And would they put their faith into action and exercise those covenant rights? Did they possess the power that it takes to fight their enemy and take back the very breath of life that satan was trying to steal from their son?

This testimony is about our first grandson, Jeremiah. And his parents did dare to believe; they put their faith into action, they stood on the promise of healing for their baby, and they obtained that promise; he is alive and well.

I remember being in the intensive care ward with our son, Micah, Jeremiah's father, and despite the numbers we were or were not seeing on the machines that Jeremiah was connected to, our son Micah stood firm on the Word of God, and he was quietly speaking words of faith, declaring words of life and healing over his son.

How could this Christian couple stand firm in their faith in God and His Word for the healing of their baby? What exactly had they been taught that gave them such confidence in their God? I am going to give you the keys that unlock the true power of faith to walk in divine healing and miracles for you, your family, and for those around you.

Before we can exercise the true power of faith to walk in divine healing and miracles, we need to believe that God is willing and able to heal us. In order to believe this, we need to be fully convinced. We need to eliminate all doubt and hidden unbelief from our hearts that God's divine healing is for today and that it is for everyone and anyone who will believe and receive—including you and me.

How do we do this? How do we rid ourselves of doubt and unbelief? We do it by going before the Lord God and asking Him to reveal the truth of divine healing in the Scriptures to us. As the Word says, *"If any of you lacks wisdom, let him ask of God, who gives to all liberally and without reproach, and it will be given to him"* (James 1:5). And, *"So then faith comes by hearing, and hearing by the word of God"* (Rom. 10:17).

There is much to be said and there are so few words to describe all that Jesus Christ did for us in God's plan of redemption. Before meditating on the benefits of His amazing acts of love toward us, we need to examine the curse of sickness and disease and where it originated. We must build a strong foundation in the Word to base our faith upon in order to remove all doubt and confusion from our minds and hearts as to whether or not it is God's will to heal and to deliver all people from all sickness and all disease.

Let's start at the beginning with the first man, Adam. Adam was created in the image of God the Father; God the Son, Jesus Christ; and God the Holy Spirit

> *Then God said, "Let Us make man in Our image, according to Our likeness, let them have dominion over the fish of the sea, over the birds of the air, and over the cattle, over all the earth and over every creeping thing that creeps on the earth"* (Genesis 1:26).

On the sixth day of creation, God created a special being that would be different from the rest of His creation. He created a man, and He created him in His image. As God is, so was the man created. The word *image* means to mirror or reflect.[1] When we look into a mirror, what do we see? We see our image. We see ourselves as we really are. Adam reflected God's image. As God was, so was Adam created. Adam was the first created being created in the mirror image of God. He was created to reflect God's image. And he was created to have dominion over all things and to subdue the Earth.

> *So God created man in His own image in the image of God He created him; male and female He created them. Then God blessed them, and God said to them, "Be fruitful and multiply; fill the earth and subdue it; have dominion over the fish of the sea, over the birds of the air, and over every living thing that moves on the earth"* (Genesis 1:27-28).

Adam was created to be *fruitful,* to be successful, to produce good results at whatever he put his hands to. He was to engage in spiritual *multiplication* and bring increase and add to the goodness of this Earth. He was to make this Earth *full* with the fruit of God's glory. This magnificent creature was created with the God-given ability to *subdue,* overcome, and bring under control anything that would try to disrupt Divine order in the Garden.

As the psalmist wrote, *"You have made him to have dominion over the works of your hands; You have put all things under his feet"* (Ps. 8:6). This word *dominion* means "to govern, to lead, to rule." Of all of God's wonderful creation, Adam was created and elected to rule. *All things were to be under his feet.* This signifies authority. God, Himself authorized humankind, whom He created in His mirror image, with the power to control this Earth—not to abuse, but to subdue. These words *authority, dominion,* and *subdue* are words of power. Adam was ordained to rule. He had been entrusted with great responsibility.

Then God fashioned a perfect bride for Adam from the man's own body, and He presented Eve to him:

> *And the Lord God caused a deep sleep to fall on Adam and he slept; and He took one of his ribs, and closed up the flesh in its place. Then the rib which the Lord God had taken from man He made into a woman, and He brought her to the man. And Adam said: "This is now bone of my bones and flesh of my flesh; she shall be called Woman, because she was taken out of Man"* (Genesis 2:21-23).

Adam represents the Bridegroom (Jesus Christ), while Eve represents the Bride of Christ. This is a beautiful analogy of the union between the Bridegroom, Jesus Christ, and us, the Bride of Christ.

They had perfect fellowship with God, and He would come to talk with them in the cool of the day. Their relationship was authentic, genuine, intimate, and refreshing to the soul. *"And they heard the sound of the Lord God walking in the garden in the cool of the day"* (Gen. 3:8a). Everything was perfect. There was no sin, no sickness, no disease, no sorrow, no shame, and no pain. There was no corruption or interruption between God and people. It was a perfect world. *"Then God saw everything He had made, and indeed it was very good..."* (Gen. 1:31).

— The Fall —

If God created the world to be so good and perfect, then why is it imperfect today? Let's continue on in the Book of Genesis to find out just what went wrong. Most of us have heard about the fall of humanity, when Eve was tempted by the serpent (satan) to eat the fruit of the Tree of the Knowledge of Good and Evil (see Gen. 3). She ate the fruit and gave it to Adam, and he ate of it, too. Let's look closer at what really happened here. This account in Scripture is more than just disobeying Daddy's rules and stealing apples!

I find it interesting that the serpent of old cowardly avoided the governor, Adam, and went instead to the vise-governor, the helper, Eve, in order to set in motion his plan of deception. Let's observe what the serpent (satan) said to Eve and find out why he tempted her.

> *And the serpent said to the woman, "You will not surely die. For God knows that in the day you eat of it your eyes will be opened, and you will be like God, knowing good and evil"* (Genesis 3:4-5).

Satan lied to Eve when he said that she would be like God. He was playing with her identity by twisting words. She was *already* like God. She was created in the mirror image of the Father, Son, and Holy Spirit. But satan was deceiving her into thinking that the knowledge of evil was something to be desired. However, he didn't tell her the end result. I wonder why? She knew what good was, but she did not know evil. As she meditated on what he had said to her, she convinced herself that it would be satisfying to her body and that it would make her wise. She ate of the forbidden fruit and gave it to Adam. Adam could have refused to eat the forbidden fruit, but he didn't. He was just as guilty as Eve (see Gen. 2).

If we want to breakthrough in healing, we need to understand the answers to some important questions. Why did satan tempt Adam and Eve? Why does he bother tempting us today? Who exactly is satan? And what does all of this have to do with being redeemed from the curse of sickness and disease? We need to know more than just the fact that we are redeemed from the curse. We need a deeper understanding of where the curse originated. When we understand who is behind the curse and what the curse really is, it will be easier for us to receive divine healing into our physical bodies.

— Who Is Satan? —

Scripture talks about the fall of lucifer. He was a beautiful angel whom God created. But he deceived himself and became full of pride because of his beauty, and he thought he was greater than God. He even deceived a third of the angels to believe his deceitful lie and convinced them to rebel against God with him. Scripture says that he fell from Heaven (see Isa. 14:12), but before he fell, it says that he was the anointed cherub who covered and that he was in Eden, the Garden of God, as well as on God's holy mountain (see Ezek. 28:13-15). But lucifer was evicted from these places and, more importantly, from God's presence, and his name was changed to satan (the devil). The angels who fell with him are now called demonic spirits. And God has a place prepared for them called hell, the worst part of which is separation from God, Himself. His foolish pride cost him everything; he lost it all (see Isa. 14:12-21; Ezek. 28:12-19; Rev. 12:4,9; 20:10).

> *How you are fallen from heaven, O Lucifer, son of the morning! How you are cut down to the ground, you who weakened the nations* (Isaiah 14:12).

> *You were in Eden, the garden of God; every precious stone was your covering: the sardius, topaz, and diamond, beryl, onyx, and jasper, sapphire, turquoise, and emerald with gold. The workmanship of your timbrels and pipes was prepared for you on the day you were created. You were the anointed cherub who covers; I established you; you were on the holy mountain of God; you walked back and forth in the midst of fiery stones. You were perfect in your ways from the day you were created, till iniquity was found in you* (Ezekiel 28: 13-15).

— Why Did Satan Go After Adam and Eve? —

He was jealous over what he had lost, and he was even more envious of these beings who were created in the mirror image of God. Before lucifer fell, he was created as a beautiful angel (see Ezek. 28:12-19), but he had not been created in the mirror image of God. The first man, Adam, was so special. He was so different from the rest of creation. Not only was he created in the mirror image of God, but he was created to have authority and dominion over all things on this Earth (see Ps. 8:6), and that included satan. Satan wanted Adam's authority and dominion on this Earth, and that's why he tempted Adam and Eve in the Garden of Eden. And as soon as they ate of that forbidden fruit, they handed over their authority and dominion on this Earth to satan. That's what he coveted and pursued, and that's how he got it (see Luke 4:6).

— Why Does Satan Go After Us Today? —

He is venomously envious of us because he knows that we are created in the mirror image of God. He knows that we, as believers in Jesus Christ, have been given back that authority and dominion on this Earth that he stole from Adam and Eve back in the Garden of Eden. When Jesus Christ took our place at Calvary, He restored humanity's original authority on the Earth.

— A Little Lower than Elohim —

> *For You have made him a little lower than the angels, and You have crowned him with glory and honor. You have made him to have dominion over the works of Your hands; You have put all things under his feet* (Psalm 8:5-6).

In Psalm 8:5, the Hebrew word translated in some versions as angels is *Elohim*. *Elohim* is a Hebrew name for God. There is a big difference between angels and God. Let's read from another translation of Psalm 8:5-6.

> *Yet You have made him a little lower than God, and You crown him with glory and majesty! You make him to rule over the works of Your hands; You have put all things under his feet* (NASB).

29

In Psalm 8, the angels are conversing with God concerning humanity and the position that people have been given by God in the realm of all of His creation. I believe Psalm 8:5-6 is a confirmation of Genesis 1:26-28—that God created people in His mirror image and gave them authority and dominion over all things on the Earth.

In searching the word *Elohim*, I have found several definitions. *Elohim* is plural and could be referring to God (God the Father; God the Son, Jesus Christ; and God the Holy Spirit), gods, angels, or heavenly beings.[2] I believe, in this portion of Scripture, *Elohim* is referring to God the Father; God the Son, Jesus Christ; and God the Holy Spirit.

Surely, we as Christians agree that we have not been created a little lower than the gods (false gods) that a large part of the world worships. False gods are made by the hands of people who are deceived by satan. Because I minister to people of different cultures and because of the rise of New Age in the Western World, I want to highlight what the Scriptures say concerning idol worship.

> *"Has a nation changed its gods, which are not gods? But My people have changed their Glory for what does not profit. Be astonished, O heavens, at this, and be horribly afraid; be very desolate," says the Lord. "For My people have committed two evils: They have forsaken Me, the fountain of living waters, and hewn themselves cisterns— broken cisterns that can hold no water. ...Saying to a tree, 'You are my father,' and to a stone, 'You gave birth to me.' For they have turned their back to Me, and not their face. But in the time of their trouble they will say, 'Arise and save us.' But where are your gods that you have made for yourselves? Let them arise, if they can save you in the time of your trouble; for according to the number of your cities are your gods, O Judah"* (Jeremiah 2:11-13, 27-28).

> *They made a calf in Horeb, and worshiped the molded image. Thus they changed their glory into the image of an ox that eats grass* (Psalm 106:19-20).

For since the creation of the world His invisible attributes are clearly seen, being understood by the things that are made, even His eternal power and Godhead, so that they are without excuse, Because although they knew God, they did not glorify Him as God, or were thankful, but became futile in their thoughts, and their foolish hearts were darkened. Professing to be wise, they became fools, and changed the glory of the incorruptible God into an image made like corruptible man—and birds and four-footed beasts and creeping things. Therefore God also gave them up to uncleanness, the lusts of their hearts, to dishonor their bodies among themselves, who exchanged the truth of God for the lie, and worshiped and served the creature, rather than the Creator, who is blessed forever. Amen (Romans 1:20-25).

As a missionary ministering in different cultures, I have seen firsthand multitudes of lost souls bowing before idols, kissing the ground before them, and kissing their feet made of wood and stone. I have seen them religiously prostrate themselves before the temples in freezing cold temperatures, spin wheels, send messages to dead relatives and false gods, and sacrifice animals. I have seen them march for hours upon hours carrying heavy statues to pay penance for their sins, and I've heard them chanting and crying out to false gods that can neither hear them nor help them.

I have also seen many fall prey to the evil trap of New Age because they were searching for something more than dead religious acts. They wanted to experience something real, and satan gave them a poisoned morsel of the supernatural to taste. But they don't realize that without Jesus Christ they miss the banquet feast of the miraculous realm of the Holy Spirit. I have known numerous Christians who have fallen and slipped into the occult world because they fell out of a love relationship with Jesus Christ and lost their way. They have exchanged the glory of Elohim (God the Father; God the Son, Jesus Christ; and God the Holy Spirit) for the image of a false god that was made by human hands and a false religion that does not glorify Jesus Christ.

In their times of trouble, as they cry out to their human-made idols and trinkets and philosophies, they struggle more than we would, because they lack the guidance that comes from an intimate relationship with the one true God who knows all things. Sticks and stones do not hear, nor do they speak! Others are being misguided by literal voices of demonic spirits. Without Jesus Christ, they have no hope, and they can only wish that things were better because they lack the confidence that comes from a close relationship with the one true God who really cares.

Such people live from one day to the next with a deep inner loneliness because they cannot have true relationship with a god that does not exist or with an evil being that only exists for their destruction. They search high and low for something or someone to fill that void in their lives. Tragically, they are deeply deceived and are being misguided by demonic spirits and the father of all lies, satan. He leads them down a very dark and meaningless path that leads to destruction on this Earth and forever in eternity.

We who have discovered the truth and freedom that is only found in Jesus Christ possess a great gift and have inherited a great responsibility, as well. We are to be about our Heavenly Father's business (see Luke 2:49) and win souls for Jesus Christ (see Prov. 11:30).

As Christians, we agree that we have not been made a little lower than false gods. But, what about the possibility that people were created a little lower than angels or heavenly beings? If we were created a little lower than angels or heavenly beings, then satan would have authority over us because satan (lucifer) is a fallen angel. And that would not line up with the Scripture in the New Testament that says we have been given authority over satan and all his works (see Luke 10:19). I personally refuse to be beneath satan!

Many will agree that we have not been created a little lower than fallen angels (satan and demonic spirits), but they've read that we've been created a little lower than angels. Let's look at some Scriptures to see the role angels are to play in regard to people. *"Are not the angels all ministering spirits (servants) sent out in the service [of God for the assistance] of those who are to inherit salvation?"* (Heb. 1:14 AMP). Through this passage we can see that after the creation of people, who were created in the mirror image of the Father, Son, and Holy Spirit (see Gen. 1:26), the assignment of angels changed to include serving God by serving people.

Many people idolize angels, and it's not correct. Angels are created-beings, created by the Creator to serve Him as He decides. We are to worship the Creator and not the creation. They were not created in the mirror image of God, as God chose to create people. Rather, it is the will of God that angels would serve Him by serving people. If we were created a little lower than angels, we would be serving angles, rather than the angles serving God by serving us. But as we read in Hebrews 1:14, angels are servants of God sent out to assist those who inherit salvation. Humans are the ones who inherit salvation. In First Corinthians 6:3, it says that we (Christians) are to judge the angels. If we had been created a little below angels, they would be judging us, not we judging them. When we look closer, the Scriptures are quite clear that we have not been created a little lower than angels.

To clarify, I am not saying that people have been created equal with God the Father; God the Son, Jesus Christ; and God the Holy Spirit. It says that we've been created a *little lower* than God. God is the Creator, and we are His creation. We are fully dependent upon God, while God is independent and above all. We are to reflect His image and walk in His ways.

I've used the example of the sun and the moon to explain this truth to the Maasai Tribe. The sun is the greater light. It is independent and contains all the energy within itself to produce light. While on the other hand, the moon is a powerful light in the darkness, but it has no light within itself. It cannot produce light; it only reflects the light of the sun. It is fully dependent upon the sun to shine light into the darkness. So, it is considered the lesser light. In fact, if it was not for the power of the sun, the moon would not shine in the darkness.

And that's how it is with us. In this simple example, God represents the sun and we (believers in Jesus Christ) represent the moon. We are called to be a light in the darkness, but without our Heavenly Father's Son, Jesus Christ, and His power source, the Holy Spirit, we would not be able to be a light in the darkness. We have no light within ourselves. We are fully dependent upon Him. He is our power source, and our light comes from Him. Like the moon reflects the light of the sun in the darkness, so we reflect the Son in the world. We reflect the light of His mirror image into the spiritual darkness of this Earth.

Our true identity is probably the most important truth that satan tries to conceal from us because he knows that once we start to unveil the truth about who we really are in Christ and who Christ is in us, we become lethal to satan and his kingdom of darkness. Once we start to recognize who we are in Christ, we start to seize our authority over satan, the temptation of sin, and the consequences of living in a fallen world, such as sickness, disease, and every other foul curse that comes our way. In other words, we start to dominate satan and his evil works, instead of him dominating us. It is amazing that satan can identify those who start to comprehend their identity and operate in their authority in Christ.

I remember traveling to the Maasailand in Northern Tanzania for the first time. Before an evening evangelistic campaign, a demon-possessed man whom I had never seen before ran up to me and knelt before me. The demons within him started crying out to me in English (for I did not understand the Maasai language), "Why have you come to torment us?" I was astounded. *How can they perceive when we know who we are in Christ?* I believe it is partly by watching how we start to speak and act. There is also an actual unveiling of the glory of God that takes place in the spirit realm that they identify and that requires them to yield to and admit defeat.

There were other Christians present in that meeting, but the spirits in this man paid no attention to them. Instead, they cried out to the believer who had started to see a glimpse of who she was in Christ. I have no arrogant intentions in sharing this with you. I am certainly not the only Christian who walks in this revelation. This understanding of the Word came through much time abiding with God in His Word, daring to believe His Word is truth, and then acting upon that truth.

In Exodus 34:29-35, Moses came down from the mountain with the second set of stone tablets with the Ten Commandments written on them. After being in God's presence, his face shone so brightly that the Israelites were afraid to come near him, so he covered his face with a veil. There was no doubt in their minds that Moses had been with God. Others can see when we are in God's presence. His reflected light shines brightly through us, and that light penetrates into the darkness of this world. There will be people in our lives (including satan) who will try to convince us to cover up that light of truth within us, but we must not do it. We must let His light shine through us.

The understanding of our true identity in Christ and the position Elohim gave to humankind is of utmost importance. Many Christians do not know who they are in Christ. They have not been taught that they were created in the mirror image of the Father, Son, and Holy Spirit, and they are oblivious to their spiritual rank—*"a little lower than Elohim."* Therefore, they do not enforce their authority in which they are to walk on this Earth. They believe that the promises of God, such as divine healing, will only be fulfilled after they enter into their eternity with Him. They fail to understand that there is no sickness, no disease, no death, no pain, and no sorrow in Heaven to be delivered from, because the physical body is left behind in this world. Only their spirits live on for eternity.

These promises of healing and deliverance were given for use today, while they live on this Earth, so they can live in the divine grace of Jesus Christ. But as long as these believers in Christ take a passive stance toward the attacks of satan, they will never walk in the victory that Christ gave to them and intended for them to use. That's exactly what satan wants, passive, lukewarm Christians who walk in defeat.

Does satan have you hoodwinked so that he and others cannot see Christ within you? It's time to lift the veil of truth and see who you really are. Listen to what the Word of God says:

> *You are of God, little children, and have overcome them, because He who is in you is greater than he who is in the world* (1 John 4:4).

> *Love has been perfected among us in this: that we may have boldness in the day of judgment; because as He is, so are we in this world* (1 John 4:17).

Brethren, the Greater One in us is Jesus Christ, and as He is, so are we in this world. Jesus Christ is all powerful over satan and all his wicked works, and because of the redeeming blood of Jesus Christ, we too are all powerful over satan and all his works. The more time we chose to spend abiding with God and His Word, the stronger His presence becomes in our lives. And the stronger His presence becomes in our lives, the greater His glory will shine through us. Our enemy, satan, recognizes the presence of Jesus Christ, and he will surrender when he sees Him manifested in our lives.

— The Glory Lifted —

Let's return to the Garden of Eden. As soon as Adam and Eve ate the forbidden fruit, their eyes were opened and they knew that they were naked (see Gen. 3:7). This portion of Scripture is talking about more than just being physically naked. These two perfect created beings were crowned in glory and honor (see Ps. 8:5). But as soon as they chose to succumb to temptation and eat of the forbidden fruit, the glory of God, (their covering) lifted off of them. They were now spiritually naked.

What is the glory of God? It is the *habitation* of His manifested presence. A *habitat* is where something naturally grows, like a plant or an animal. Of course, in this case, we are not talking about a natural habitat, but rather a spiritual one. The miraculous supernaturally grows in the habitat of God's manifested presence.

The psalmist wrote, "*He who dwells in the secret place of the Most High shall abide under the shadow of the almighty*" (Ps. 91:1). The word *dwells* means "to live as a resident or to reside."[3] So, we could say, "He who resides in the secret place..." The words *secret place* mean "hiding place."[4] "He who resides in the hiding place..." The word *abiding* means "continuing."[5] "If we reside in the hiding place of the Most High, we shall continue under the shadow of the Almighty." Let's think this through even further. The word *shadow* means "a mirrored image or reflection, shelter, protection, or a shade within clear boundaries."[6]

Thus, we can conclude that, if we reside in the hiding place of the Most High, we will continue in His mirror image or reflection under the clear boundaries of His shade, shelter, and protection of His presence. There is an actual hiding place that we can find when we choose to reside in close fellowship with Him. It's a secret place under the clear boundaries of His shade. It's a place like no other. His presence is tangible, His voice is audible, His love is overwhelming, His grace is unexplainable, His guidance is unmistakably clear, His provision is abundant, and His miraculous power is released all around.

This is what it was like for Adam and Eve before they fell into sin. They resided in the habitation of His manifested presence. And even though they were not equal with God, they had intimate fellowship with Him that caused them to live in the creative shadow of His unlimited, miraculous blessings. They were in God's habitat and lived in His holy environment. Within the clear boundaries of the habitat of the Most High, everything is perfect; there is no corruption, no evil, no lack, no curse, but only blessings. He's the Creator of blessed perfection.

When Adam and Eve chose to willfully disobey God, the habitation of His manifested presence immediately lifted from their presence. Though they tried, they could not cover or make up for what they had done. There is only one way, and it's God's way. Then they heard the sound of God walking in the Garden in the cool of the day. They felt fear for the first time in their lives, and they hid behind the bushes (see Gen. 3:7-8). But as they were to find out, they could not hide from God, and neither can we. *"Where can I go from Your Spirit? Or where can I flee from Your presence?"* (Ps. 139:7).

The Lord then called out to Adam and said, *"Where are you?"* (Gen. 3:9). God is omniscient, all knowing. He wasn't asking Adam to tell him his physical location. He was asking Adam to identify where he was spiritually. God already knew, but Adam needed to confess it.

Imagine what happened to Adam and Eve. Like many people today, they did not know that fear was and is an actual spirit. The spirit of fear seized the opportunity and invaded that Garden with a very real and evil force, and they didn't even understand what they were experiencing because they did not know evil. They were as vulnerable as babies in the midst of ravenous wolves.

About this, Paul wrote, *"For God has not given us a spirit of fear, but of power, and of love and of a sound mind"* (2 Tim. 1:7). A spirit of fear strips people of their power, their love, and their sound mind. Adam and Eve lost everything; in an instant, they lost their identity, their authority, their confidence, their security, their innocence, their love, their peace, and their joy. Most painful of all, they lost their intimate fellowship with God. It was a sad and grievous day. I believe that all of creation in Heaven, on Earth, and in hell felt what had just happened. All the authority and dominion that had been given to Adam in the beginning to rule this Earth very suddenly changed management. At this point in time, sin was introduced into our world and so were the consequences of that sin, which include sickness, disease, and every other curse. On that day, corruption on the Earth and in the physical body was birthed into our world.

Adam and Eve had entered into a fallen state, and there was a chance that they would eat of another tree in the garden, The Tree of Life, and live forever in that fallen state (see Gen 3:22-24). They simply could not stay. Thus, they were evicted from God's Garden, the Garden of Eden, the habitat of God's manifested presence. Adam and Eve no longer lived in a perfect world. As soon as they sinned, the perfect became imperfect. The Earth was now cursed, and their physical bodies were corrupted as a result of willful disobedience to God. The process of deterioration and degeneration began, and eventually their physical bodies died (see Gen. 3:16-19).

— Satan's Character and Motives —

We know that satan deceived Adam and Eve and that he opposes us, but let's look more closely at who he is so that we can understand our opponent. Then we will examine who we are through the sacrifice of Jesus and how we relate to our enemy. The Bible calls satan a thief, and tells us his motives are to steal, to kill and to destroy us.

> *The thief* [satan] *does not come except to steal, and to kill, and to destroy. I* [Jesus] *have come that they may have life, and that they may have it more abundantly* (John 10:10).

The Bible also refers to him as a roaring lion, seeking for someone to devour, saying that he is our adversary. *"Be sober, be vigilant, because your adversary the devil walks about like a roaring lion, seeking whom he may devour"* (1 Pet. 5:8). Jesus also referred to him as the father of all lies:

> *You are of your father the devil, and the desires of your father you want to do. He was a murderer from the beginning, and does not stand in the truth, because there is no truth in him. When he speaks a lie, he speaks from his own resources, for he is a liar and the father of it* (John 8:44).

In Revelation it says that satan deceives the whole Earth:

> *So the great dragon was cast out, that serpent of old, called the devil and satan, who deceives the whole world; he was cast to the earth, and his angels were cast out with him* (Revelation 12:9).

It also says in Revelation that satan is the accuser of the brethren:

> *Then I heard a loud voice saying in heaven, "Now salvation, and strength, and the kingdom of our God, and the power of His Christ have come, for the accuser of our brethren who accused them before our God day and night, has been cast down"* (Revelation 12:10).

We see from these passages that satan is a deceiver and a liar whose ultimate mission is to destroy us by distorting the mirror image of God within us on this Earth so that he can keep us bound to the curse of sin, sickness, and disease. But as we continue on, we will see that Jesus undid the works of satan so that we could walk free from the curse.

— What Jesus Did —

The Bible teaches us that Jesus Christ came to destroy the works of satan.

He who sins is of the devil, for the devil has sinned from the begin-
ning. For this purpose the Son of God was manifested, that He might
destroy the works of the devil (1 John 3:8).

When Jesus first announced Himself as the Messiah, He did it by reading
this passage from the Old Testament, which specifically outlines the curses of the
enemy and the way that Jesus came to break them:

So He came to Nazareth, where He had been brought up. And as
His custom was, he went into the synagogue on the Sabbath day,
and stood up to read. And He was handed the book of the prophet
Isaiah. And when He had opened the book, He found the place
where it was written: "The Spirit of the Lord is upon Me, because
He has anointed Me to preach the gospel to the poor. He has sent
Me to heal the brokenhearted, to preach deliverance to the captives,
and recovery of sight to the blind, to set at liberty those who are
oppressed, to preach the acceptable year of the Lord."

Then He closed the book, and gave it back to the attendant and
sat down. And the eyes of all who were in the synagogue were fixed
on Him. And He began to say to them, "Today this Scripture is
fulfilled in your hearing" (Luke 4:16-21).

Jesus came to undo the works of satan, and the Bible clearly lists what Jesus
came to do. Thus, we can conclude that the works of satan include physical sickness, disease, depression, oppression, possession, poverty, and every other form
of the curse.

In these passages we can clearly see that satan is the source of all sin and all
corruption on this Earth and in our physical bodies. And sin is the cause of all
earthly and bodily corruption, such as sickness, disease, and every other brutal
and cruel curse that results from that original sin.

— God Had a Plan —

Despite the fall of Adam and Eve, God had a plan to redeem people to Himself. God prophesied that satan (the serpent) would bruise the heel of Jesus (foreshadowing the suffering inflicted upon Jesus' body at Calvary), but that Jesus would bruise his head. May it be clearly understood that Jesus willingly gave His life for us at Calvary. He willingly allowed people to brutally wound His body. It's obvious that Jesus had a clear understanding of the power and purpose behind the shedding of His blood, while satan was totally disillusioned, thinking he had crucified our Lord (see Gen. 3:15).

I received further understanding of this portion of Scripture when we first started ministering with the Maasai. When they hunt down a snake, they first hit, crush, or chop off its head. In the Maasailand in Northern Tanzania, the brethren knew that David and I were interceding for and witnessing to the witchdoctors of that area. At first, the brethren had a difficult time with us visiting them, but after they understood our intentions, they said, "Oh, you are going after the head of the snake!" That's what Jesus did with his heel; He crushed satan's head and destroyed his evil power over us.

We can also see a type of this plan of redemption when God clothed Adam and Eve with tunics made of skin (see Gen. 3:21). This was a powerful and prophetic act of God's mercy toward people and a sign of things to come. Just as there was the shedding of blood to make a temporary covering (the tunic of skin) for Adam and Eve, God had an eternal plan to redeem people—and His name was Jesus Christ. Jesus would shed His blood for our eternal redemption. In the New Testament, Jesus is referred to as the Second Adam, and He came down to Earth from Heaven to redeem people to Himself (see Rom. 5:12-21).

What does it mean to be redeemed? The word *redeemed* means "to save from a state of sinfulness and its consequences, recover ownership of by paying a specified sum, to set free, rescue or ransom."[7]

Jesus Christ did all of this at Calvary for us. His redemption set us free from all guilt and shame and rescued us from eternal damnation—from the hell that we so rightly deserve. By His grace and His grace alone, this redemption liberates us from the consequences of those sins, which are sickness, disease, demon-possession, poverty, and all manner of spiritual and physical corruption. Through His grace, He fulfilled the specified payment found written in the Scriptures— His blood.

Everyone has committed sin. We've all thought, said, or done something that we shouldn't have. *"For **all** have sinned and fall short of the glory of God"* (Rom. 3:23). *"If we say that we have no sin, we deceive ourselves, and the truth is not in us"* (1 John 1:8). Because of the fall of Adam and Eve, we were all born into sin. All people, no matter how good or bad they are, need to be redeemed by the blood of Jesus.

— The First Step —

Because the greatest sickness that exists is a spiritual condition and lost souls are condemned to hell, the first step to being redeemed from sin and the curse of sickness and disease is to confess your sins and commit your life to Jesus Christ. *"For God so loved the world that He gave His only begotten Son, that whoever believes in Him should not perish but have everlasting life"* (John 3:16).

Right now, if you have never asked Jesus Christ to be your Lord and Savior, pray this simple prayer and mean it from your heart.

> *Dear Heavenly Father,*
>
> *I come before You in the name of Jesus Christ. I have examined my heart, and I do acknowledge and admit that I have sinned against You and Your Word. Your Word says, in Romans 10:9-10, "If you confess with your mouth, the Lord Jesus and believe in your heart, that God has raised Him from the dead, you will be saved. For with the heart one believes to righteousness, and with the mouth confession is made unto salvation."*
>
> *Father God, I believe in my heart that Jesus Christ is the Son of God. I believe that He died on the cross to save me from my sins,*

*went to hell in my place, rose again three days later, and is alive and
seated at Your right side in Heaven.*

*Jesus, forgive me of all my sins. Thank You, for saving me from sin,
hell, and myself. I ask You to come into my life to be my Lord and
Savior. Thank You for loving me and accepting me just as I am.*

In Jesus' name I pray, amen.

If you've prayed this prayer from your heart, then you've taken the first step
to being redeemed from sin and the curse of sickness and disease. The first and
greatest miracle—salvation—has taken place within your spirit.

Maybe you are a believer in Jesus Christ already and are battling with sickness and disease in your body. Let's make sure that you've dealt with any sin or
unforgiveness within your own heart. Ask the Lord to reveal any offense that you
may be hanging onto. Ask the Lord to forgive you for not dealing with the offense
correctly. Then forgive by faith and release the other person who has hurt you so
that you too can be released. This is a very important step to being free in spirit,
soul, and body. This is not based upon your feelings, but upon pure surrender to
the Word of God.

> *For if you forgive men their trespasses, your Heavenly Father will
> also forgive you. But if you do not forgive men their trespasses, nei-
> ther will your Father forgive your trespasses* (Matthew 6:14-15).

> *If we confess our sins, He is faithful and just to forgive us our sins
> and to cleanse us from all unrighteousness* (1 John 1:9).

— Tribulation and the Thief —

If you have dealt with all unforgiveness, yet still are not well, it is possible that
this sickness or disease attacking your body is a direct attack from the enemy,
satan. The Word teaches us that in this world we will have tribulation. We will
face difficult times. But Jesus also said that we can *"be of good cheer,"* because He

has overcome the world (John 16:33). He overcame the world at Calvary. He did not tell us to be of good cheer because we are being attacked, but because He overcame. And because He conquered the enemy, we now have hope to overcome the attack in His victory. It's in His victory alone that we have reason to be hopeful, to be full of confidence and thanksgiving, knowing that we too will overcome.

Jesus said, *"The thief does not come except to steal, and to kill, and to destroy, I have come that they may have life, and that they may have it more abundantly"* (John 10:10). As we discussed before, satan comes to steal, to kill, and to destroy. Sickness and disease steal from us and our loved ones. They steal our time, our resources, our peace, our joy, our health, our strength, and even our lives. They kill and destroy us and our loved ones—our hopes, our dreams, our desires, and our future.

But Jesus came that we may have life and life more abundantly. The abundant life is not living with sickness and disease. If it was, we would not visit doctors and take medications to make us feel better. If we truly believed that sickness and disease were part of living the abundant life, we would want to remain in that abundant state. But it obviously is not living in abundance. Every good and perfect gift comes from God (see James 1:17). Health and healing are good and perfect gifts, not sickness and disease.

— Blessings and Curses —

Let us look briefly at blessings and curses. The definition of *blessing* is "something promoting or contributing to happiness, well-being, or prosperity."[8] God desires that we walk in His blessings, but the decision is ours. *"Beloved, I pray that you may prosper in all things and be in health, just as your soul prospers"* (3 John 2).

The blessings and curses are found in the Book of Deuteronomy chapter 28. (Please read the entire chapter, which is found in the Old Testament of the Bible.) Let's first start with the blessings of God found in Deuteronomy 28:1-14.

> *Now it shall come to pass, if you diligently obey the voice of the Lord your God, to observe carefully all His commandments which I*

command you today, that the Lord your God will set you high above all nations of the earth. And all these blessings shall come upon you and overtake you, because you obey the voice of the Lord your God (Deuteronomy 28:1-2).

Notice that it says, *"...If you diligently obey..."*; this promise of blessing is purely conditional. The Israelites had a choice to make. If they chose to obey— not just obey, but *diligently* obey—the voice of the Lord their God, then all the blessings listed in verses 1-14 would come upon them. Not only would they come upon them, but the Bible says the blessings would *overtake* them. This promise of blessing was for the nation as a whole and for the individuals also. God gave them the key to living the blessed life.

We can clearly see that the blessings come through obedience to His ways. Let's read the list of blessings in Deuteronomy 28:3-13 and ponder upon the Word:

1. Dominion, Authority, and Identity

+ God will set us high above all nations (dominion).

+ We shall be the head and not the tail, above and not beneath (authority).

+ The people shall see that we are called by the name of the Lord (identity), and they shall be afraid of us (authority).

2. Divine Favor

+ Wherever we are (city or country) we will be blessed (divine favor). No matter the location or the surroundings, we will be blessed because the promise of blessings starts within the heart, a decision to love God and to follow after His ways.

+ The Lord will establish us as a holy people onto Himself (divine favor).

3. Divine Prosperity

+ The Lord will open to us His good treasure (unlimited supply of blessing).

+ God will bless us with children, good harvest, and increase in livestock.

+ Our needs (basket and kneading bowl) will be met abundantly.

+ Our travels will be blessed (in our comings and goings).

+ Our work (the work of our hands) and the fruit of our labor will be blessed.

+ We shall be the lenders to many nations and not borrowers.

+ Even our weather will be blessed (rain in its season).

4. Divine Protection

+ We will have divine protection from our enemies.

The blessings under the old covenant were obtained by strict adherence to the Law of Moses and through sacrifices. But since Jesus Christ became the Supreme Sacrifice for all, these blessings (including divine healing) are now obtained through a new covenant of His grace (see Rom. 5:15). Grace is unmerited favor, something that we did not earn or deserve, but that was freely given to us to receive. The new covenant of grace made the old covenant obsolete (see Heb. 8:13). If all these blessings came upon the people under the old covenant, consider how blessed we are to be under the new covenant. No longer do we need to sacrifice, but we believe and receive by faith.

Since we no longer live under the old covenant, let's turn to the new covenant or the New Testament to find out what the greatest commandment is.

> *Jesus said to him, "'You shall love the Lord your God with all your heart, with all your soul, and with all your mind.' This is the first and great commandment. And the second is like it: 'You shall love*

your neighbor as yourself.' On these two commandments hang all the law and the Prophets" (Matthew 22:37-40).

The greatest commandment in the New Testament is loving God with our whole selves. When our whole selves—our hearts, souls, and minds—are involved in our relationship with the Lord, a transformation takes place, starting from within. That inward change affects our outward or physical beings and those around us as well. When we become enveloped in the love of God, our faith becomes fully activated to receive His blessings that are promised to us in His Word.

Paul explained this when he wrote, *"For in Christ Jesus neither circumcision nor uncircumcision avails anything, but faith working through love"* (Gal. 5:6). Faith does not work through the law, but by the love of God only.

> *If you abide in Me, and My words abide in you, you will ask what you desire, and it shall be done for you. By this My Father is glorified, that you bear much fruit; so you will be My disciples* (John 15:7-8).

The key to manifesting the blessings of God in our daily lives is abiding, dwelling, and actually residing in the habitation of His manifested presence. When we choose to reside in the secret hiding place of the Most High—continuing to reflect His mirror image and living under the clear boundaries of His shade, shelter, and protection that are found only in His presence—the blessings of God will come upon us and overtake us.

Keeping in mind the theme that we are discussing in this book—divine healings and miracles—we can see that the blessing of the miraculous supernaturally grows in the habitat of God's manifested presence. Those who desire a miracle from God must chose to reside in the habitat of His manifested presence where miracles naturally grow.

Now, let's look at the curses. The definition of *curse* is "to bring evil upon or to afflict."[9] Deuteronomy 28:15-68 talks about the curses.

*But it shall come to pass, **if** you do not obey the voice of the Lord your God, to observe carefully all His commandments and His statues which I command you today, that all these curses will come upon you and overtake you (Deuteronomy 28:15).*

Again, the Israelites were given a free choice; they could choose to obey or to disobey. But *if* they chose to disobey, they were forewarned about what would happen. It would be up to the individual people to make the choice. If they chose to obey, they would live in the blessings of God. If they chose to disobey, they would live in the curses. Just as the blessings of God would overtake the obedient, so too, the curses would overtake the disobedient. There would be no escape from the curses except to repent from a rebellious heart.

Just as it was for the Israelites back then, so it is for us today. If we do not love God with all of our hearts, souls, and minds, if He doesn't hold first place in our lives, and if we do not love others as ourselves (if we are holding onto grudges, are unkind, are critical, are disrespectful to others, are dishonest, and so forth), then we may be opening ourselves up to the curses in this life.

Knowing this, why would we willingly subject ourselves to a curse? Deuteronomy 28 tells us what the curses include. No matter where the cursed were, evil came upon them, and they were afflicted in spirit, soul, and body. Their offspring, their crops, their livestock, their daily provision, their businesses were all cursed. It's amazingly dreadful, but at the same time, it is an eye-opener as to what the Lord calls the curse. Many of the things that people consider "blessings in disguise from the Lord" to teach them lessons in patience and suffering are really part of a curse. Terrible and incurable diseases are listed in the curse, and these horrific diseases would pursue them until they perished.

We must read the curses and each make our choice. The blessings are conditional; we've been given the responsibility of free choice, but hopefully now that we've seen the difference between the blessings and the curses, we will be able to make a wise choice.

— Redeemed From Sickness and Disease —

Jesus redeemed us from the curse of sickness and disease. As I mentioned previously, to be *redeemed* means "to be delivered or rescued from something." Jesus delivered and rescued us from *all* sickness and disease. *Redeemed* also means "to be repurchased, or recovery of something by payment." Jesus Christ repurchased healing for our physical bodies by the payment of His blood. Let's keep this definition fresh in our minds as we read how Jesus Christ redeemed us from sin, sickness, disease, and every other form of the curse by the shedding of His most precious blood.

There are seven places recorded throughout the story of His crucifixion where Jesus willingly shed His blood for us.

1. In the Garden of Gethsemane

Jesus knew that His appointed time was at hand. As He prayed in the Garden of Gethsemane, His mind, will, and emotions were in great agony with the foreknowledge of the suffering He was about to endure for us, that He sweat great drops of blood. He was entering into His destiny—becoming the Supreme Sacrifice for us. Our Lamb of God was about to be painfully slaughtered because of our willful disobedience against God and His ways. At this moment in time, He overcame the temptation to give into the will of human flesh, surrendered all to the will of the Father, and offered His life by His redeeming blood.

Maybe you are in the middle of a ragging battle to give up and to give in to the sickness or disease that is attacking your physical body. I pray that your faith will be strengthened, that you willfully chose to glorify God with your human will, chose life, and overcome this deathly attack.

> *And He was withdrawn from them about a stone's throw, and He knelt down and prayed, saying, "Father, if it is Your will, remove this cup from Me; nevertheless not My will, but Yours, be done." Then an angel appeared to Him from heaven, strengthening Him. And being*

in agony, He prayed more earnestly. And His sweat became like great drops of blood falling down to the ground (Luke 22:41-44).

2. The Plucking of His Beard

Then, having arrested Him, they led Him and brought Him into the high priest's house. But Peter followed at a distance. …Now the men who held Jesus mocked Him and beat Him. And having blindfolded Him, they struck Him on the face and asked Him, saying, "Prophesy! Who is it that struck You?" And many other things they blasphemously spoke against Him (Luke 22:54,63-65).

I gave my back to those who struck Me, and My cheeks to those who plucked out the beard; I did not hide My face from shame and spitting (Isaiah 50:6).

Jesus was shamed, disgraced, dishonored, and humiliated for us and because of us. He willingly allowed them to rip His beard from His face, and along with His beard came pieces of His flesh. He was literally going to "lose face" or be shamed because of our sin. And again, the Lamb of God gave us the redeeming gift of His blood.

During a vision that God gave me (that I share more in depth in Chapter 16, "Childlike Faith") I saw Jesus being whipped. I walked up to touch His face, but as soon as my hand touched His face, He blurred His face from my view. He spoke to me in an audible voice and said, "Becky, you could not stand to see My face at this point in time; by My stripes you are healed."

Perhaps something terrible has happened in your past; maybe you were the victim or you were the cause. Either way, it is preventing you from receiving the power in His blood for your healing to manifest. I want to encourage you that Jesus took your shame so that you can stand before Him shameless.

3. By His Stripes

Then he released Barabbas to them; and when he had scourged Jesus, he delivered Him to be crucified (Matthew 27:26).

Surely He has borne our griefs (sicknesses, weaknesses, and distresses) and carried our sorrows and pains [of punishment], yet we [ignorantly] considered Him stricken, smitten, and afflicted by God [as if with leprosy]. But He was wounded for our transgression, He was bruised for our guilt and iniquities; the chastisement [needful to obtain] peace and well-being for us was upon Him, and with the stripes [that wounded] Him we are healed and made whole (Isaiah 53:4-5 AMP).

By His *stripes*, the bloody wounds that were inflicted upon His body by the whipping He received, we were healed. Jesus was whipped severely, almost to the point of death, so that we could be healed. But it was not His time yet to die. Our health and well-being were so important to Him that He offered His back and allowed them to brutally whip Him with a leather strap embedded with sharp pieces of metal and bones that literally tore his flesh from His body with each strike. With each crack of the flesh-ripping whip, He repurchased healing for every sickness and every disease, known or unknown, that ever was, is, or is to come.

In the vision I mentioned earlier, I saw Him at the whipping post being brutally whipped for my healing. I will never forget what I saw and heard. There are no words to justly describe that scene, but during it all, our eyes were fixed on one another. The Lamb of God lovingly gave us His blood to restore healing to us—the ones He loves.

> *For God so loved the world that He gave His only begotten Son, that whoever believes in Him should not perish but have everlasting life. For God did not send His Son into the world to condemn the world, but that the world through Him might be saved* (John 3:16-17).

4. The Crown of Thorns

Then the soldiers of the governor took Jesus into the Praetorium and gathered the whole garrison around Him. And they stripped Him and put a scarlet robe on Him. When they had twisted a crown of thorns, they put it on His head, and a reed in His right hand. And they bowed the knee before Him and mocked Him, saying, "Hail, King of the Jews!" Then they spat on Him, and took the reed and struck Him on the head. Then when they had mocked Him, they took the robe off Him, put His own clothes on Him, and led Him away to be crucified (Matthew 27:27-31).

Thorns are symbolic of the curse. After the fall of Adam and Eve, the ground became cursed with thorns and thistles. God said to Adam,

…Cursed is the ground for your sake; in toil you shall eat of it all the days of your life. Both thorns and thistles it shall bring forth for you, and you shall eat the herb of the field (Genesis 3:17-18).

After Jesus was scourged, the Roman soldiers mocked our King and fashioned a crown of thorns for Him, and He willingly allowed them to push those large, thick thorns into His skull. Then they beat upon His head, causing Him severe pain, and again the Lamb of God willingly bowed His head and gave His Blood for us. I believe this crowning of thorns is symbolic of being crowned as "the Curse." And the Blood on this accursed crown removes the power of the curse that was caused by our sin. Thus, we no longer need to suffer the consequences of sin, and we are free from all sickness and disease.

5. The Nailing of His Hands

And He, bearing His cross, went out to a place called the Place of a Skull, which is called in Hebrew, Golgotha, where they crucified

Him, and two others with Him, one of either side, and Jesus in the center (John 19:17-18).

There was the shedding of His Blood as they nailed His hands to the Cross. Those precious hands that reached out and healed all those who came to Him were now being willfully nailed to that wooden cross. Our precious Lamb of God willingly opened His healing hands and gave of His blood freely so that we could be healed and so that we could also extend His healing power through our willing hands as well.

6. *The Nailing of His Feet*

Our Lamb of God willingly walked to Golgotha, to offer His blood as a sacrifice on that wooden altar so that we could walk in His authority, have dominion, subdue the Earth, and be free from all forms of the curse, including sickness and disease.

7. *The Piercing of His Side*

But when they came to Jesus and saw that He was already dead, they did not break His legs. But one of the soldiers pierced His side with a spear, and immediately blood and water came out. ...For these things were done that the Scripture should be fulfilled, "Not one of His bones shall be broken." And again another Scripture says, "They shall look on Him whom they pierced" (John 19:33-34,36-37).

As they pierced His side, the last of His blood and water gushed out from His body with a great force. This great force is the power in His blood that He gave to us, the spiritual Body of Christ, who have been born-again by the living water, Jesus Christ.

God's Plan of Redemption was very thorough; He willingly shed His Blood for us so that we could be completely and perfectly free from all sin and from all consequences of sin, sickness, disease, and every other form of the curse.

— He Became the Curse —

*Then they journeyed from Mount Hor by the Way of the Red Sea
to go around the land of Edom; and the soul of the people became
very discouraged on the way. And the people spoke against God
and against Moses: "Why have you brought us up out of Egypt to
die in the wilderness? For there is no food and no water, and our
soul loathes this worthless bread." So the Lord sent fiery serpents
among the people, and they bit the people; and many of the people
of Israel died. Therefore the people came to Moses, and said, "We
have sinned, for we have spoken against the Lord and against you;
pray to the Lord that He take away the serpents from us." So Moses
prayed for the people. Then the Lord said to Moses, "Make a fiery
serpent, and set it on a pole; and it shall be that everyone who is bitten, when he looks at it, shall live." So Moses made a bronze serpent,
and put it on a pole; and so it was, if a serpent had bitten anyone,
when he looked at the bronze serpent, he lived* (Numbers 21:4-9).

The Israelites had sinned against God and Moses. They were discontented,
and they complained about everything, so God permitted a plague of fiery serpents to be released among the people. They bit them, and many people died.
Then the Israelites, in the midst of their crisis, called out to God through Moses
for His deliverance. God responded and instructed Moses to fashion a fiery serpent and to set it up on a pole. If anyone who was bitten by a serpent looked at
the bronze serpent, then that person would be healed. What God instructed
Moses to do not only delivered the Israelites, but also served as a prophetic sign
of God's plan of redemption through Jesus Christ at Calvary. *"And as Moses lifted
up the serpent in the wilderness, even so must the Son of Man be lifted up"* (John
3:14).

Jesus Christ redeemed us. He delivered and rescued us from *all* forms of sickness and disease. He repurchased healing and health for our physical bodies by
the payment of His blood at Calvary. *"Who Himself bore our sins in His own body
on the tree, that we, having died to sins, might live for righteousness—by whose stripes*

you were healed" (1 Pet. 2:24). The truth of the matter is that we have already been healed. Now, we need to learn how to activate the promise of His healing power in our lives today.

The crowning of thorns symbolized when Jesus Christ was crowned as "the Curse":

> *When they had twisted a crown of thorns, they put it on His head, and a reed in His right hand, and they bowed the knee before Him and mocked Him, saying, "Hail King of the Jews"* (Matthew 27:29).

> *Christ has redeemed us from the curse of the law, having become a curse for us (for it is written, "Cursed is everyone who hangs on a tree"), that the blessings of Abraham might come upon the Gentiles in Christ Jesus, that we might receive the promise of the Spirit through faith* (Galatians 3:13-14).

When Jesus Christ hung upon the Cross, He not only bore our sin and the consequences of that sin—including all sickness and disease and every other curse—upon His body, but He actually *became* sin, sickness, disease, and every other curse for us. Every debilitating sickness and disease, in their worst form, came upon Him. Every pain, sorrow, and injustice, in their most perverted state, clung to Him. All grief, loneliness, and abandonment fell upon Him. These curses not only came upon Him, but they also clung to Him, and He actually transformed into the curse for us. In the natural, those standing nearby could not even recognize Him as being human any more.

> *[For many the Servant of God became an object of horror; many were astonished at Him.] His face and His whole appearance were marred more than any man's, and His form beyond that of the sons of men—but just as many were astonished at Him* (Isaiah 52:14 AMP).

The One who was blessed transformed into the cursed. In becoming the curse, He endured the most painful event of all, separation from the Father. His Heavenly Father's presence was lifted from Him. Forever they had been one in spirit, and now they were separated. The Father could no longer look upon His Son, because His Son had become the curse for all wickedness. And in deep anguish and despair, He cried out, *"My God, My God, why have You forsaken Me?"* (Matt. 27:46). To be *forsaken* means to be abandoned, deserted, or disowned, to have another's back turned on a person. Jesus was forsaken for us and because of us.

Because He became the curse for us, we've been redeemed. We've been rescued from the consequences of every sin. He repurchased healing and deliverance from *all* sickness and disease for us. *"I know that whatever God does, it shall be forever. Nothing can be added to it, and nothing taken from it. God does it, that men should fear before Him"* (Eccles. 3:14). *"Jesus Christ is the same yesterday, today, and forever"* (Heb. 13:8).

— A Swindler, Not! —

Jesus Christ willingly fulfilled His Father's will and plan of redemption for us. He knew full well the price that He would pay to redeem us from sin and the results of sin, which are sickness, disease, and every other heinous form of the curse. Jesus Christ also willingly fulfilled the law and His Father's will and plan of redemption for us as a man and not as God. He was not a swindler. He did not cheat. He did not use His God powers to escape the dreadful pain and suffering that He would endure at Calvary.

Let this mind be in you which was also in Christ Jesus, who, being in the form of God, did not consider it robbery to be equal with God, but made Himself of no reputation, taking the form of a servant, and coming in the likeness of men. And being found in appearance as a man, He humbled Himself and became obedient to the point of death, even the death of the cross (Philippians 2:5-8).

He took upon His physical body every type of arthritis, tumor, cancer, and asthma; every excruciating pain, sickness, and disease; known or unknown; that ever was, is, or will be. He did this not as God, but as a man would, so that we could be delivered and healed from it all. God did not cheat! He could have used His God powers and commanded the pain and torture to cease with the power of His words, but He didn't utter a word. He did not deceive us. A swindler, He is not!

> *He was oppressed and He was afflicted, yet He opened not His mouth; He was led as a lamb to the slaughter, and as a sheep before its shearers is silent, so He opened not His mouth* (Isaiah 53:7).

> *The place in the Scripture which He read was this: "He was led as a sheep to the slaughter; and as a lamb before its shearer is silent, so He opened not His mouth. In His humiliation His justice was taken away, and who will declare His generation? For His life is taken from the earth"* (Acts 8:32-33).

> *Who, when He was reviled, did not revile in return; when He suffered, He did not threaten, but committed Himself to Him who judges righteously* (1 Peter 2:23).

— Paid in Full —

Jesus Christ, by His grace alone, paid for us the price in full with His own blood so that we could be forgiven of sin and be free from the consequences of that sin—*all* sickness, disease, and every other form of the curse. *"For He made Him who knew no sin to be sin for us, that we might become the righteousness of God in Him"* (2 Cor. 5:21). *"Who Himself bore our sins in His own body on the tree, that we, having died to sins, might live for righteousness—by whose stripes you were healed"* (1 Pet. 2:24).

When Jesus said, *"It is finished!"* (John 19:30), He was declaring that the Plan of Redemption was complete. He willingly shed His blood seven different times during the crucifixion. Seven is a very significant number in the Bible. It represents the completion of something, and in this case, it signifies the completed work of redemption. Nothing was left undone. He conquered satan and all of his evil works.

Jesus paid the debt for all sin and for all sinners and for the results of that sin—corruption in the Earth and in our physical bodies through sickness and disease. He finished what He came to do on this Earth. He willingly and unselfishly erased our debt with His precious blood by His grace, His unmerited favor toward us; it is a free gift to anyone who will believe and receive.

One of the redemptive names of God is Jehovah-Rapha. When translated, it means, "I am the Lord your Physician" or *"I am the Lord who heals you"* (Exod. 15:26). This is not a name that someone else gave to Him, but a name God prophetically spoke about Himself. With confidence in His Word, we can go boldly to our Jehovah-Rapha, our Lord Jesus Christ, and receive the healing and deliverance that He recovered by the payment of His shed blood at Calvary. The price has been paid in full!

— Exceedingly Far More Powerful —

What Jesus did at Calvary for us is exceedingly far more powerful than the wicked consequences that humankind suffered from the fall of Adam and Eve. According to the Word, there is no comparison (see Rom. 5:15). He superseded the curse. He did away with it completely, and there is total freedom from the curse for those who choose to believe and receive His free gift of grace.

> *But God's free gift is not at all to be compared to the trespass [His grace is out of all proportion to the fall of man]. For if many died through one man's falling away (his lapse, his offense), much more profusely did God's grace and the free gift [that comes] through the undeserved favor of one Man Jesus Christ abound and overflow to and for [the benefit of] many* (Romans 5:15 AMP).

We've been released from the power of the curse. We do not need to live lives dominated by the accursed things in this world any longer. He gave us authority and dominion over the curse. He set us free from sin and the consequences of sin. We deserve eternity in hell, but instead He offers us eternity with Him in Heaven. In place of the curse of sickness and disease, He offers us divine health and healing. Instead of poverty, He offers prosperity in spirit, soul, and body. He offers all of this and more, and it's free, paid in full, for anyone and everyone who will receive this divine gift of grace.

— The Glory Returned —

After the redeeming power in His blood was released to undo the curse, Jesus died, and three days later, He rose again from the dead, giving us eternal life with Him by conquering death itself. Jesus Christ is alive. He gave us the power of His redemption in His resurrection. And as He ascended into Heaven, He gave to His Church the promise of the power of the Holy Spirit. On the day of Pentecost, they were all filled with the Holy Spirit.

When the Day of Pentecost had fully come, they were all with one accord in one place. And suddenly there came a sound from heaven, as of a rushing mighty wind, and it filled the whole house where they were sitting. Then there appeared to them divided tongues, as of fire, and one sat upon each of them. And they were all filled with the Holy Spirit and began to speak with other tongues, as the Spirit gave them utterance (Acts 2:1-4).

That same Spirit that raised Christ from the dead now dwells within the spirit of every true believer in Jesus Christ. His Holy Spirit is the manifested glory of His presence within us. And when we choose to dwell in the habitation of His manifested presence, that resurrecting power of the Holy Spirit, by the redeeming power of the blood of Jesus Christ, is released and activated in us and through us, and all things become possible.

Then, the same day at evening, being the first day of the week, when the doors were shut where the disciples were assembled, for fear of the Jews, Jesus came and stood in the midst, ad said to them, "Peace be with you." Now when He had said this, He showed them His hands and His side. Then the disciples were glad when they saw the Lord. Then Jesus said to them again, "Peace to you! As the Father has sent

Me, I also send you." And when He has said this, He breathed on them, and said to them, "Receive the Holy Spirit" (John 20:19-22).

But you shall receive power when the Holy Spirit has come upon you; and you shall be witnesses to Me in Jerusalem, and in all Judea and Samaria, and to the end of the earth (Acts 1:8).

— Confidence in Him —

But Christ came as High Priest of the good things to come, with the greater and more perfect tabernacle not made with hands, that is, not of this creation. Not with the blood of goats and calves, but with His own Blood He entered the Most Holy Place once for all, having obtained eternal redemption (Hebrews 9:11-12).

As I continue to examine the power of His blood and enter into a deeper understanding of how we've been redeemed from the curse of sin, sickness, and disease; and as I ponder and meditate upon the new covenant of grace that we have been given in Jesus Christ; I have found myself in His presence, boldly daring to stand against pain, sickness, disease, and even death for the sake of others and for myself. We have an eternal blood covenant with the Father that cannot be changed or erased.

For we do not have a High Priest who cannot sympathize with our weaknesses, but was in all points tempted as we are, yet without sin. Let us therefore come boldly to the throne of grace, that we may obtain mercy and find grace to help in the time of need (Hebrews 4:15-16).

Now this is the confidence that we have in Him, that if we ask anything according to His will, He hears us. And if we know that He hears us, whatever we ask, we know that we have the petitions that we have asked of Him (John 5:14-15).

We have studied the curse, what it is, where it originated from, and who is responsible for the curse. We have specifically focused in on two of the consequences of the curse of the original sin—sickness and disease—and how the curse and these consequences are affecting the inhabitants upon the Earth today. More importantly, we have formed a scriptural foundation on which we can confidently stand upon with the revelation knowledge that Jesus Christ redeemed us from the curse of sin, sickness, and disease so that we can boldly obtain divine healing for our physical bodies.

As I travel around the world teaching others how to activate the healing power of the Holy Spirit in their lives, I meet many people with severe physical needs who are struggling with doubt and unresolved questions concerning healing. I would like to address some of these issues in the next few chapters. I pray that the words of this book will encourage your heart to seek after God, to confidently trust in the power of His blood, and to put your faith in His Word into action. Claim what is rightfully yours in the name of Jesus Christ and *dare to believe!*

— Endnotes —

1. *The Free Dictionary by Farlex*, s.v. "image"; www.thefreedictionary.com/image; accessed September 24, 2011.

2. *Blue Letter Bible*, s.v. "elohiym" (Strong # 430); www.blueletterbible.org/lang/lexicon/lexicon.cfm?
Strongs=H430&t=KJV; accessed September 24, 2011.

3. *The Free Dictionary by Farlex*, s.v. "dwell"; www.thefreedictionary.com/dwells; accessed August 25, 2011.

4. *The New Strong's Exhaustive Concordance of the Bible* (Nashville, Thomas Nelson, 1984), Hebrew # 5643, 5641.

5. *The Free Dictionary by Farlex*, s.v. "abiding"; www.thefreedictionary.com/abiding; accessed August 25, 2011.

6. *Ibid.*, s.v. "shadow"; www.thefreedictionary.com/shadow; accessed August 25, 2011.

7. *Ibid.*, s.v. "redeemed"; www.thefreedictionary.com/redeemed; accessed August 25, 2011.

8. *American Heritage Dictionary*, s.v. "blessing"; www.answers.com/topic/blessing; accessed August 25, 2011.

9. *Ibid.*, s.v. "curse"; www.answers.com/topic/curse; accessed August 25, 2011.

REVIEW QUESTIONS

1. According to Genesis 1:26-28, Adam and Eve were created in the image of God. What does the word *image* mean?

2. In Psalm 8:6, it says that all things were to be under people's feet. What does this signify?

3. What was it that satan wanted from Adam?

4. *Elohim* is a Hebrew word for?

5. Since the creation of humanity, what is the assignment of angels?

6. What is the most important truth that satan tries to hide from Christians?

7. What is the glory of God?

8. What were the results of the sin of Adam and Eve?

9. Despite the fall of Adam and Eve, God had a plan. What was it?

10. What does the word *redeemed* mean?

11. What is the definition of *grace?*

12. Who is the thief and what did he come to do?

13. What do sickness and disease do?

14. What did Jesus come to give us?

15. Every good and perfect gift comes from God. What are two good and perfect gifts?

16. What is the definition of a *blessing?*

17. What is the key to manifesting the blessings of God in your life?

18. How do we believe and receive the blessings of God in our lives?

19. What is the definition of a *curse?*

20. List the seven ways Jesus shed His Blood for us.

21. What did Jesus become for us?

22. Jesus Christ willing fulfilled the law and His Father's Plan of Redemption not as God, but *how?*

23. What is the Holy Spirit within us?

24. What do we have with God that cannot be erased?

CHAPTER 2

HEALINGS
AND MIRACLES

My desire is not only to stir people's faith to believe God for their own miracles, but to equip them to minister healing to others as well. In the next several chapters, we are going to be looking at different aspects of divine healing. In this chapter, we are going to study two different avenues of receiving healing, the difference between healings and miracles, and the most common methods of divine healings.

— Two Avenues to Receive Healing —

There are two ways we can receive healing as Christians—through gifts of the Holy Spirit or through activating our own faith. Paul talked about the gifts of the Spirit for healing when he wrote, *"to another faith by the same Spirit, to another gifts of healings by the same Spirit, to another by the working of miracles..."* (1 Cor. 12:9-10). These spiritual gifts are given to people, as the Holy Spirit wills, to minister divine healings and miracles to others in need. There are people who clearly have a supernatural gift of faith to believe God for the impossible, and they have a continual flow of fabulous testimonies of God's supernatural interventions. There are others who have a divine gift of healing upon their lives, and God uses them in this supernatural gift to minister healing to sick people, while others walk in a supernatural gift of miracles, and breathtaking miracles or unexplainable events happen around them.

However, we do not necessarily need to have the gifts of the Spirit for healing in order to receive supernatural healing. Jesus included healing as one of the signs that would follow *all believers*. In other words, healing can also manifest by activating our faith in God and His Word.

> *And these signs will follow those who believe; in My name they will cast out demons; they will speak with new tongues; they will take up serpents; and if they drink anything deadly, it will by no means hurt them; they will lay hands on the sick, and they will recover* (Mark 16:17-18).

God, in His great mercy, did not leave anyone out of the picture. He said that by faith *all believers* in Jesus Christ can lay hands on the sick and they will recover. *All believers* in Jesus who choose to activate their faith for healing can minister healing.

As you study the Scriptures concerning your authority over sickness and disease, your faith will become stronger, and you will be able to receive healing for yourself and release it to others as well. The Holy Spirit is moving mightily throughout the whole Earth, teaching the Body of Christ how to activate faith for divine healing and to use this powerful tool to win the lost for Jesus Christ.

— Spiritual Gifts for Healing —

> *...to another faith by the same Spirit, to another gifts of healings by the same Spirit, to another the working of miracles, to another prophecy, to another discerning of spirits, to another different kinds of tongues, to another the interpretation of tongues. But one and the same spirit works all these things, distributing to each one individually as He wills* (1 Corinthians 12:9-11).

The late Kenneth Hagin wrote a book called *The Holy Spirit and His Gifts*, explaining in detail the gifts of the Holy Spirit.[1] I studied out of this book years ago and found it very helpful. I would recommend it to anyone who desires to have a greater understanding of the gifts of the Holy Spirit. Here, we will only be focusing on the Gift of Faith, Gifts of Healings, and the Working of Miracles.

— The Gift of Faith —

This is a special kind of faith that is given, as the Holy Spirit wills or desires, in order for an individual to receive a miracle from God. We've all been given a measure of faith to use in our everyday lives (see Rom 12:3), but the Gift of Faith is an extraordinary, supernatural type of faith.

Let's look at a biblical example. Shadrach, Meshach, and Abed-Nego were given the Gift of Faith. Though they were thrown into the fiery furnace, they did not burn to death, and they did not even have the smell of smoke on them (see Dan. 3). It took a divine gift of the Holy Spirit, a gift of supernatural and extraordinary faith, to overcome the fear of death and the spirit of death in order to overcome this deadly situation. Even the guards outside of the fiery furnace died instantly from the heat of the flames, but not Shadrach, Meshach, and Abed-Nego! They first put their natural faith in God, and then they turned the situation over to Him. Thus they were given a Gift of Faith to overcome death. Even those outside of the fiery furnace could see from a distance that Jesus Christ was with them. One truth that I pray will resound in this book is that God honors faith.

Here's another example from my own life. After our son Marcos was raised from the dead (this story is told in Chapter 11) and while we were battling one impossible situation after another, our faith remained unshakable. We could look death in the eye and not be moved. This was a special kind of faith that the Holy Spirit gave to us so that we could receive our series of miracles from God for Marcos. We were like Shadrach, Meshach, and Abed-Nego in the beginning of the battle, and we exercised our everyday faith in Jesus Christ at first. God honored our faith, and at some point in time, we were given a supernatural kind of faith to do what we did. Everyone who was looking from the outside of our fiery furnace could see that Jesus was walking with us in the midst of the flames.

— The Gifts of Healings —

The Gifts of Healings (notice this is plural) are manifested through a person to another sick person. A person with the Gifts of Healings may pray over people for many different reasons and see them healed, but that same person will see particular types of healings manifested over and over while ministering to others.

For example, I have ministered healing over people for many different sicknesses and diseases and they are healed, but I continue to see certain types of healings manifest over and over again in greater number than other type of healings; the terminally ill or injured are healed, paralytics are set free, barren women conceive, and deaf people are healed.

My friend Linda Ryan has a gift with the elderly in the area of backs, arthritis, and migraines being healed more than other types of healings in her ministry. It's as if God brings people with these specific types of sickness and disease our way to minister healing to them.

— The Working of Miracles —

The Working of Miracles is working out performing or doing a miracle by the power of the Holy Spirit working through the individual. There are many examples in the Bible for us to understand this Gift of the Spirit. But I will name just a few—the creation of the world (see Gen. 1), the parting of the Red Sea (see Exod. 14:15-31), and the feeding of the 5,000 with a boys lunch (see John 6:5-14). In each of these examples, the supernatural power of God manifested into the physical realm and miraculous events took place. And in each event, the power of the spoken word was released, then the manifested presence of God broke loose into the physical realm, and the miraculous came into being.

Here's another example from our battle for Marcos' life. Without my knowledge, our son Marcos had been pronounced dead in the hospital. At that same time, while I was praying in my bedroom, God spoke to me in an audible voice and told me to rebuke the spirit of death that was over Marcos at that very moment. I did, and he came back to life. I was praying in the Spirit, the power of the spoken word was being released, and then the manifested presence of God broke loose into physical realm. I could hear His voice audibly calling me by name and instructing me on what I needed to do, and then the miraculous event came into being and our son came back to life. (You can read more about this amazing testimony in Chapter 11.)

We will study the healings and miracles that Jesus performed in the Book of Luke in Chapter 10, "Faith Principals for Healings and Miracles."

— Miracles vs. Progressive Healings —

It is important to understand the difference between miracles and progressive healings, especially if we are going to be ministering divine healing to others, so that we can encourage those in the Word when their healing is taking time to manifest.

Now, let's examine the difference between miracles and healings. Miracles are instant. Physical changes start to happen immediately. When Jesus healed the man with the withered hand instantly, it was an example of a miracle (see Luke 6:6-11). When our adopted son, Andres, was a toddler, one of his legs was much shorter than the other, and it was causing him great difficulty with walking. One day, while he was lying on the changing table, I received the revelation that I could speak to his leg and release a miracle. I commanded it in Jesus' name to grow evenly with the other leg, and it did instantly in front of my eyes. I stood Andres up on the floor, and he immediately started to walk normally. (Read about Andres' testimony in Chapter 12.)

Unlike miracles, progressive healings don't happen instantly or all at once. Rather, it's a process to obtain the total manifested healing. Little by little the healing manifests as the individual stands firm in faith in God and His Word and ignores the natural realm of the five senses and human reasoning. None-the-less, such healing is still miraculous. Jesus healed a blind man in this way, using a two-step process to release his complete healing (see Mark 8:22-26).

I have experienced this sort of healing in Andres' life as well. Andres was born with many physical challenges. One of his main challenges was that he was severely autistic. He use to scream and tantrum for hours at a time, would constantly spin around in circles, and suffered from many other autistic behaviors. My husband and I put our faith into action, and we started to take our authority in the name of Jesus over abnormal behaviors. One by one, the autistic behaviors started to fall away. He no longer screams and tantrums, he doesn't spin in circles anymore, he can look people in the eye, and he can start and carry on a conversation. It didn't happen all at once, but was progressive in nature. He was healed of one abnormal behavior after another.

In the end, whether a healing comes instantly or progressively, it is still only possible by the supernatural power and grace of God.

— Common Methods of Healing in the Bible —

Now let's examine some of the most common methods of healing utilized by Jesus and His followers in the Bible. Though God can heal in any way He chooses, these examples give us a framework from which to start.

The Laying on of Hands

According to Mark 16:15-18, all believers in Jesus Christ are commanded to go into all the world and to lay hands on the sick, with the promise that they will recover. We should all be ministering the healing power of the Holy Spirit by the laying on of hands. The laying on of hands for healing is a point of contact between the receiver and the divine Healer, God. Jesus demonstrated this when He healed two blind men by the laying on of hands (see Matt. 9:27-31).

Once during a healing conference, I was led to pray for an elderly blind woman. I asked her what she wanted, and she said that she wanted to see. So I laid my hands over her eyes and released the healing power of the Holy Spirit to flow through my hands into her eyes. Instantly she received that healing power and was completely healed; now she sees perfectly.

Anointing With Oil

Jesus sent out the 12 disciples by twos with authority to preach the Word, cast out demons, and anoint the sick with oil so that they would be healed (see Mark 6:7,12-13). This is how we are to evangelize the world; it demonstrates God's compassion and power to the lost and readies their hearts to receive Him as Lord and Savior.

Anointing with oil is not used only for the unbeliever, but also within the Church, specifically for those who need the added strength of someone stronger in the faith. God has instructed the sick to call upon the elders and have the elders anoint them with oil and pray for their healing (see James 5:14).

The healing power isn't in the oil; it doesn't possess magical powers. In the natural realm, it's an act of obedience to the Word of the Lord and a point of contact for the receiver. In the spirit realm, it's a symbol of the Holy Spirit. The act of anointing is a symbolic act of releasing the power of the Holy Spirit for healing.

Once, after a Church service, two young boys came forward together for healing. I anointed them with oil; this was their point of contact between the power of the Holy Spirit and their needs. I prayed, and they were both instantly healed. One had been deaf, and the other was sick with a fever and stomach problems.

— The Power of Faith —

In Acts 14:8-10, a man who had been crippled from his mother's womb heard Paul speaking. Paul saw that this man had faith to be healed, and he commanded him to stand to his feet. The man put his faith into action and leaped to his feet and walked. We read in Exodus 7:8-12 how God taught Moses and Aaron to cast Aaron's special rod before the pharaoh and let it become a serpent. We've all been given a special rod—faith. It's our choice to not only speak the Word of God, but to put it into action and allow it to become the miracle that we need.

(See Chapter 6, "A Special Rod.") I saw this manifest in my own life while ministering healing to a man with a paralyzed arm. I told him to lift up his arm by faith; when he did, he was instantly healed.

— The Power of the Word of God —

Once when Jesus taught in the synagogue, a man with a withered hand was present. Jesus told the man to stretch forth his hand, and when he did, it was healed (see Luke 6:6-11). The Word of God in Jesus' teaching released the healing power. There is great power in the Word of God, and it produces whatever is studied or taught. When people teach on faith and healing, that is what manifests.

Once I was teaching about faith and healing, and there was a man with a withered hand listening attentively to the message. I did not even know he was there. But his faith was so stirred that his withered hand was healed as he heard the message. No one laid hands on him, no one anointed him with oil; he was simply healed by the power of his faith in the Word of God.

— The Power of the Spoken Word —

When Jesus commanded a deaf and dumb spirit to come out of a boy, using the power of the spoken word, the boy was delivered and healed (see Mark 9:25). In Mark 11:23, Jesus taught His followers (including us) to speak to the mountains in their lives so that they would be removed. We are to use the creative force of the tongue, take authority over the problem, and speak into existence what we need. If we need healing, then we speak words of life, healing, health, and strength.

On numerous occasions I have been asked to pray for individuals who were both deaf and mute. So, with the power of my words, I would command a deaf and mute spirit to leave the person and then command the person's ears to be opened. Time and time again, these individuals could hear immediately. And when I would ask them to repeat something after me, they would begin to speak. Often times, I only needed to command the deaf ears to be opened, and they would be able to hear and speak immediately. It's a joyful event to witness! To clarify, when I say that I *commanded*, it doesn't mean I was shouting. It simply means I was speaking with the authority that I've been given in Jesus Christ. Many times this is done with a whispering tone. Volume does not equal authority.

— Obedience —

The Old Testament prophet Elisha told Naaman to go and dip seven times in the Jordan River so that he would be healed of leprosy. At first Naaman was furious, but then he did as he was told, and he came up healed of leprosy after he dipped in the Jordan for the seventh time (see 2 Kings 5:1-14). As we discussed previously, Deuteronomy 28:1-2 teaches that, if we diligently *obey* the voice of the Lord and observe carefully all His commandments, blessings of God will not only come upon us, but will overtake us.

I have seen this work in my own life. Once I was very sick with typhoid, and I heard the Lord say to me, "Get up and get dressed." I obeyed, and the blessing of healing came upon me. All typhoid symptoms were immediately gone, and I regained my physical strength. (You can read this testimony in Chapter 16, "Childlike Faith.")

— Prayer Clothes —

The Bible records that God worked unusual miracles through the apostle Paul, so that even handkerchiefs or aprons were brought from his body to the sick and they were healed and delivered of diseases and demonic spirits (see Acts 19:11-12).

Often times, during our healing services, people will bring cloths of all sorts. I will release a healing anointing over them, and the people will take them home and place them on their loved ones who are sick. When they do this, the healing anointing is released into their physical bodies. Also, when visiting the sick in their homes or in the hospitals, I have often silently prayed a healing anointing over their pillows so that as they lay their heads on them the healing power of the

Holy Spirit will be released. Once I was impressed by the Lord to lay my hands on someone's pillow and intercede; later that person had a serious heart attack while sleeping, but did not die.

Just because we may not understand something in the Bible does not mean that it is foolish. I have learned to have a high respect for the things of God. I have seen the most amazing miracles all around the world, and they did not happen through me reasoning according to my own understand, but through simply believing what God's Word says, even when it seems unbelievable.

But God has chosen the foolish things of the world to put to shame the wise, and God has chosen the weak things of the world to put to shame the things which are mighty (1 Corinthians 1:27).

In the next chapter, we will resolve doubts and questions concerning healing.

— Endnote —

1. Kenneth E. Hagin, *The Holy Spirit and His Gifts* (Tulsa, OK: Faith Library Publications, 1991).

REVIEW QUESTIONS

1. What are the two avenues to receive healing?

2. What is the Gift of Faith?

3. What is the Gifts of Healings?

4. What is the Working of Miracles?

5. What is the difference between a miracle and progressive healing?

6. What are the more common methods of healing in the Bible?

CHAPTER 3

RESOLVING DOUBTS
AND QUESTIONS

THIS CHAPTER COVERS different topics concerning healing that I believe will help people to receive healing for themselves and to minister healing to others. But I want to preface this chapter by stating first that I realize that many people are suffering great emotional pain from the loss of loved ones, while others are standing on the front lines battling against death itself. In no way am I condemning or judging such people. I do not believe condemnation is of God (see Rom. 8:1). But I do believe that iron is to sharpen iron (see Prov. 27:17) and that we are to strengthen and encourage one another in the faith (see Col. 2:2). With that in mind, let's dig into some of the most common questions regarding healing.

— Why Am I Sick? —

For those struggling with illnesses and diseases of various kinds, this is the foremost question. Though we don't always know the answer, and this is not an exhaustive list, the Word has given us many clues about why people do sometimes get sick.

Tribulation in this World

I have told you these things, so that in Me you may have [perfect] peace and confidence. In the world you have tribulation and trials and distress and frustration; but be of good cheer [take courage; be confident, certain, undaunted]! For I have overcome the world. [I have deprived it of power to harm you and have conquered it for you] (John 16:33 AMP).

The Lord says that we will pass through difficult times in this life. We live in a fallen and imperfect world filled with corruption. But in the midst of it all, He says that we must be of good cheer, not because of the difficulty we are facing, but because He overcame this difficult situation for us at Calvary, and in Him we can be healed.

The Enemy Seeks to Destroy

Be well balanced (temperate, sober of mind), be vigilant and cautious at all times; for that enemy of yours, the devil, roams around like a lion roaring [in fierce hunger], seeking someone to seize upon and devour (1 Peter 5:8 AMP).

Many of us have found ourselves at some time in the midst of a battlefield, and we didn't know why. We or our family members were suffering one serious attack after another, and we could not figure out the reason. Many are unaware of the reality that our enemy, satan, is consumed with the obsession to destroy us and our loved ones. If we allow the enemy to devour us, he will! He is out to steal, to kill, and to destroy us; that's his mission (see John 10:10). He will keep on attacking until we make him stop.

We need to become very aware of what is happening around us and learn how to overcome the attacks of satan. Even though the enemy is attacking and seeking to destroy us, we do not need to live lives of despair because greater is He (Jesus) who lives within us than he (satan) who is in the world (see 1 John 4:4).

The greater One living within us is Jesus, and He has triumphed over all attacks of the enemy.

A Lack of Teaching

Hosea 4:6 says, *"My people are destroyed for a lack of knowledge…."* This is as true today as it was when it was written. Many people have not been taught that the Lord desires to heal them. Some have been taught that the Lord heals only a few select people or, worse yet, that the Lord puts sickness and disease upon people to teach them a lesson in patience and endurance or to test their faithfulness toward Him. All of these are wrong doctrines not supported in Scripture. When we break free of wrong teaching and discover the truth in the Bible that Jesus wants to heal us, we are freed to receive that healing. Through the remainder of this book, my heart's desire is to teach just that and to answer questions raised by these wrong doctrines regarding healing.

Disobedience or Sin

> *But it shall come to pass, if you do not obey the voice of the Lord your God, to observe carefully all of His commandments and His statutes which I command you today, that all these curses will come upon you and overtake you* (Deuteronomy 28:15).

Disobedience and sin are one and the same; they open the doors of our lives to their consequences—sickness, disease, and every other form of the curse. (See Chapter 1, "Redeemed from the Curse.")

Once David and I were out in a village, and a Christian woman came running over to ask us to come quickly to minister healing to her daughter, who was dying from an asthma attack. When we arrived, we found her lying on the ground, gasping for breath. I rebuked a spirit of death and the asthma and released the Spirit of Life to flow through her. I wasn't seeing the quick results that were needed. Then I found a religious trinket in her hand and took it away from her; the attack stopped immediately and she began breathing normally again. Through the help of an interpreter, I witnessed to her about Jesus Christ, but she refused to receive Him as Lord and Savior. Instead she picked up the trinket again, and the asthma attack immediately started up again full force, like when we first found her. She refused Jesus Christ and clung to a human-made religious image that could not hear or help her. She disobeyed the first commandment, *"You shall have no other gods before Me"* (Exod. 20:3).

Another time, David and I were ministering in a different village when we came across a little boy who could not walk. Once the trinkets from the witch-doctor were removed, however, he was set free and could walk!

The occult world in all forms is rebellion toward God, and we cannot mingle in witchcraft or satanic practices in any shape or form and believe for a miracle from God. It does not work! It matters not what culture we are from, we need to rid ourselves and our homes of all satanic and New Age books, movies, games, jewelry, trinkets, statues, pictures, and the like. Both black and white magic are of the same antichrist spirit—of satan—and they need to be renounced and removed immediately in the name of Jesus!

Back in 1994, our first year living in Guatemala City, Guatemala, my husband had befriended two young men in the neighborhood. Unfortunately, one was tragically shot and killed. A short time later, the other young man who had survived the situation came to the door and gave David a gift to say thank you. It was a Mayan idol that he had found in a river. We were new to Guatemala, and we were just learning the language. So we were not able to communicate very well yet in order to explain to him about idols.

We had some errands to run that afternoon before our three children came home from school so we left the idol on the table to show our children and to discuss with them what the Bible says about such things. We had no intentions of keeping this idol; we were just going to show our children what one was. However, it took us longer to get home then we had anticipated, and our children got home before us. When they walked into the kitchen, they saw this idol sitting on the table. Upset at the thought that we might be considering keeping it, our son Micah went and found a hammer and smashed the idol to bits! I always thanked the Lord for such a strong son who wouldn't even allow the presence of such an ungodly thing to be in his home. We need to examine what is in our homes, what the origin of certain things is, and be willing to cleanse our homes of such items.

— Premature Death —

Let's talk about a very difficult subject: premature death. Premature death is when death occurs before the average life expectancy. I believe the Bible offers some answers for this very difficult and painful topic.

As we have read previously, Jesus said: "*The thief does not come except to steal, to kill, and to destroy. I have come that they may have life, and that they may have it more abundantly*" (John 10:10). Satan is the thief; he comes to steal, to kill, and to destroy. Sickness, disease, and premature death rob people of their time, joy, peace, and resources. Sickness, disease, and premature death kill people and their loved ones and destroy their hopes, dreams, and future. The one responsible for all of this destruction is the thief, satan.

Thankfully, that is not the end of the story. Jesus came to give life and life in abundance; He is the giver of life, not only eternal life, but also life over premature death—abundant, healthy life over sickness and disease while living on this Earth. When people are sick and diseased, are they living in abundance? No. They are fighting to survive. They are fighting against sickness, pain, death, hopelessness, and depression.

> *In as much then as the children have partaken of flesh and blood, He Himself likewise share in the same, that through death He might destroy him who had the power of death, that is the devil, and release those who through fear of death were all their lifetime subject to bondage* (Hebrews 2:14-15).

Jesus Christ broke the bondage in these Scriptures. He suffered for us at Calvary. He bore upon His body *all* sickness and disease and the fear of death. He became the curse for us so that we could be free from sickness and disease on this Earth. (See Chapter 1, "Redeemed From the Curse.")

Recently I watched a movie in which a mother was trying to explain to her older child why their baby had passed away. She said that God must have needed the baby more in Heaven than on the Earth. Sounds like a sweet and harmless thing to say to a child, but is it scriptural? And is it really harmless to say such things?

In my studies, I have not found this explanation to be scriptural; in fact, I have found such statements to be harmful to the hearer. Who would want to serve a God who harmed a loved one? We do an injustice to the hearer when we ignorantly say that it was God's will and plan to snatch away a loved one by a tragic accident or by a slow and painful death—knowing that those left behind would suffer great pain and loss. The Word says that the truth will set us free (see John 8:32). The truth is the best way to handle premature death. It allows for a healthy closure in the midst of a difficult situation.

I hope that we can uncover and discover the truth in the Scriptures in this chapter together. Now let's look at some Scriptures that tell us what God's plan is for the death of His children:

> To everything there is a season, a time for every purpose under heaven: A time to be born, and a time to die; a time to plant, and a time to pluck what is planted (Ecclesiastes 3:1-2).

> You shall come to your grave in a full age, like a shock of corn comes in its season (Job 5:26).

> You take away their breath, they die, and return to the dust (Psalm 104:29).

Now let's consider a biblical example. In Deuteronomy 34, after fulfilling his life calling, Moses climbed the mountain and died. He knew his time was done. Moses was 120 years old when he died, and his eyes were not dim nor his natural vigor abated. He did not die of a horrible disease, nor was his body all decrepit and worn out from old age, daily life, or the work of the ministry. We too can live full lives like Moses and be strong and in good health until the Lord takes our breath away, in our old age, to be with Him. Clearly we can see in the Scripture that premature death or death from any sort of disease is not God's will for His children.

— Willing to Heal —

Another question many people have about healing is whether God is *willing* to heal them? They know He can, but they're not sure if He *wants to.* A leprous man in the Bible had the same question.

> *And it happened when He was in a certain city, that behold, a man who was full of leprosy saw Jesus; and he fell on his face and implored Him, saying, "Lord, if You are willing, You can make me clean." Then He put out His hand and touched him, saying, "I am willing; be cleansed." And immediately the leprosy left him* (Luke 5:12-13).

This man was asking an honest question. He didn't know the will of God, and Jesus answered his honest question. He said, *"I am willing; be cleansed."* Those who, like this man, are unsure that the Lord wants to heal them can be at peace, because He does want to heal them. (See Chapter 1, "Redeemed From the Curse.")

Often times I hear people pray powerful prayers for healing, only to end with the statement, *"If it be Thy will."* When this statement is used in this manner, it negates everything that was just prayed. No longer is it a question asking God to clarify His will concerning healing; rather, it has turned into a statement of doubt. No faith is being activated. The doubt lies in the fact that they are not certain that the Lord will heal them. However, if it was not Jesus' will to heal everyone all the time, then what He did for us at Calvary would be in vain, and we know that's not true.

If we are not seeing the results we desire, it's not because God is withholding it from us. He is ever constant and true to His Word. The problem lies within us, and we need to be willing to look into that mirror and examine ourselves very carefully in order to deal with the issues that may be preventing our answer from manifesting.

— Reasons for No Healing or Lost Healing —

Another common question that people raise is why some people are not healed and why others are initially healed, but then seem to lose their healing over time. Following are some of the most common explanations for why people do not receive the breakthrough they desire.

Lack of Knowledge Concerning Healing

As mentioned previously, there are many misconceptions concerning healing. People need to be taught the fundamentals of divine healing found in the Bible so that they can have a firm foundation to stand against sickness and disease. *"My people are destroyed for a lack of knowledge"* (Hos. 4:6a).

Lack of Faith for Healing

> *But let him ask in faith, with no doubting, for he who doubts is like a wave of the sea driven and tossed by the wind. For let not that man suppose that he will receive anything from the Lord; He is a double-minded man, unstable in all his ways* (James 1:6-8).

If people do not have a sound, biblical understanding of what the Bible teaches concerning healing, when they are attacked with sickness and disease and find themselves dealing with pain and other symptoms, they will struggle with doubt and unbelief, and they will have a difficult time attaining the healing that is rightfully theirs.

Need for a Change of Confession

Death and life are in the power of the tongue, and they who indulge in it shall eat the fruit of it [for death or life] (Proverbs 18:21 AMP).

Indeed, we put bits in horses' mouths that they may obey us, and we turn their whole body. Look also at ships: although they are so large and are driven by fierce winds, they are turned by a very small rudder wherever the pilot desires. Even so the tongue is a little member and boasts great things. See how great a forest a little fire kindles! And the tongue is a fire, a world of iniquity. The tongue is so set among our members that it defiles the whole body, and sets on fire the course of nature; and it is set on fire by hell. ...Out of the same mouth proceed blessings and cursing. My brethren, these things ought not to be so (James 3:3-6,10).

Our confession controls every area of our lives, and that includes the health of our bodies. If we desire healing, then we need to speak words of healing. We need to get a handle on our tongues. Every word we speak is producing either life or death. We must listen to what comes out of our mouths and correct any faithless words. If we continue to speak words of sickness and death, then that is what we will have.

Don't claim the sickness as yours! For example, when you say things like "my cancer," you've accepted it into your body, you've laid claim to or taken ownership of it. You do not want the cancer; it's not yours. It's a foreign and unnatural object attacking your body; you are fighting against it, and it has to leave!

I know this goes against what the world teaches. The world counsels people to accept the illness and not be in denial. But the Lord's ways are not our ways. This response is not being in denial, but exercising our authority and covenant rights with the Father according to the Word of God. It is dominating that cancer in the name of Jesus. If we will change negative speech patterns to words full of life, health, and strength, then our physical bodies will start to line up with our positive, faith-filled words.

There is power in every word that is spoken. When we are standing in faith for healing, we will need to make a radical change in the way we speak. We will have to choose to speak words of life and healing while ignoring all physical symptoms. (This is discussed in further detail in Chapter 5, "The Blood and Our Testimony.")

A friend spoke with me after he heard me teach on this very subject. He had recently lost his father to prostate cancer and was fighting with some doubt and confusion concerning divine healing, but after hearing the message, he was set free. His father was a Christian man, and God had used him mightily. My friend shared with me about his father's horrible struggle with cancer; even though he said he was standing in faith against that attack from satan, he had died. His death obviously brought doubt and confusion to family and friends about God's will concerning healing.

But after hearing the message about the power of our words, that there is literal life and death in the tongue, the truth about his father's situation was revealed to him. He said he remembered the day very clearly when his father took him aside and revealed his true confession about the cancerous attack that was killing his body. He told him that he needed to make sure to have his prostate checked regularly so that he would not have *"what he had."*

I'm not saying there is anything wrong with doctors and having physicals; those things are just fine. But I am calling attention to the power of our words. Often times we do not realize what is coming out of our mouths. His father, without understanding the power of his words, took ownership of the cancer attacking his body. Even though recognizing the truth hurt my friend, it also set him free at the same time. There was a restoration of his confidence in God's Word concerning healing. He was able to put a closure to his doubts, and that is very important for those of us who remain.

Sin Issues That Need to Be Dealt With

Then Jesus went into the temple of God and drove out all those who bought and sold in the temple, and overturned the tables of the moneychangers and the seats of those who sold doves. And He said to them, "It is written, 'My house shall be called a house of prayer,' but you have made it a den of thieves.' " Then the blind and the lame came to Him in the temple, and He healed them (Matthew 21:12-14).

Jesus drove out the spirit of mammon from the temple. We cannot serve two masters at the same time; either we serve God or we serve mammon. He even drove out and overturned the seats of those who sold doves.

No one can serve two masters; for either he will hate the one and love the other, or else he will be loyal to the one and despise the other. You cannot serve God and mammon (Matthew 6:24).

I find that very interesting. He drove out and overturned the seats of those who sold doves in the temple. A dove in Scripture represents the Holy Spirit. I believe this means that when Jesus was cleansing the temple from all wickedness, He kicked out the religious spirits—those who had wrong motives and were misusing the things of God. The Holy Spirit is God's free gift to those who believe in Jesus Christ, and satan is always trying to imitate the things of God in the form of religion. The true things of the Holy Spirit cannot be bought or sold.

People with the spirit of religion appear to do all the right things and even say all the right things, but their hearts are far from the Lord. The Pharisees always pretended to be religious, but Jesus called them "whitewashed tombs" because they were spiritually dead (see Matt. 23:27).

First, Jesus cleansed the temple spiritually, and then He healed the blind and the lame. For many people, their temples need a spiritual cleansing from sin before the power of the true dove (the Holy Spirit) can be released and received for physical healing.

Or do you not know that your body is a temple of the Holy Spirit Who is in you, Whom you have from God, and you are not your own? (1 Corinthians 6:19)

Expectations About How God Will Heal

In Second Kings 5:1-14, the prophet Elisha told Naaman to dip in the Jordan River seven times so that he would be healed of leprosy. Naaman's initial response was anger because he was expecting to be healed in a certain way, but eventually he did what he was told to do, and he was healed.

Sometimes people who do not receive their healing were expecting to be healed a certain way and ended up becoming angry, embarrassed, and full of pride, eventually refusing to cooperate with the Lord.

God, who is all knowing, is fully aware of the depth of our problems. He sees beyond the surface or the physical symptoms. Often times, the root of a sickness and disease is caused by a spiritual problem, and He wants to pull up the weed seeds in our lives that are causing the problems. Usually, this is a process; it takes time to allow Him to weed our spiritual gardens so that we can be healed in spirit, soul, and body.

I have met many women with serious eating disorders. They desire instant healing, a quick fix, but God wants to deal with the heart of the matter and take them through the process of deliverance so that they can be free from past hurts, which is often the cause of the eating disorder. Sometimes they don't want to face their past, and they will rebel against God and refuse His ways. Therefore, they remain in the same state with the same problems.

Therefore strengthen the hands which hang down, and the feeble knees, and make straight paths for your feet, so that what is lame may not be dislocated, but rather be healed. Pursue peace with all men, and holiness, without which no one will see the Lord: looking diligently lest anyone fall short of the grace of God; lest any root of bitterness springing up cause trouble, and by this many become defiled; lest there be any fornicator or profane person like Esau, who for one morsel of food sold his birthright. For you know that afterward, when he wanted to inherit the blessing, he was rejected, for he found no place for repentance, though he sought it diligently with tears (Hebrews 12:12-17).

But, I also know others who have chosen to deal with past injustices and have forgiven those who don't deserve to be forgiven. Now they are completely free from the bondage of past hurts and are healed of eating disorders and other physical ailments because they surrendered to God and allowed Him to heal them in spirit, soul, and body. We must not allow unforgiveness to rob us of our birthright! Healing is part of our birthright when we receive Jesus Christ as our Lord and Savior.

Wrong Motives for Healing

You ask and do not receive, because you ask amiss, that you may spend it on your pleasures (James 4:3).

Once I had a woman come forward in the healing line. When I asked her what she needed, she responded by saying that she wanted a complete "makeover." She wanted a new body, no excess fat, no wrinkles, a new head of hair, a brand new set of teeth; her list went on and on. Her requests had nothing to do with health issues, but a desire to look like a young woman again. This woman was struggling to accept the fact that she was growing older, and more than a physical makeover, she needed an inner healing of her emotions in order to make a quality decision to age with grace. Make no mistake, I am a firm believer that we can be physically healthy in our old age, but there isn't anything wrong with having gray hair!

Lack of Encouragement and Support From Others

In Exodus 17:8-16, while Moses stood on the top of the hill—with Aaron and Hur at his side and his up-raised hands holding the rod of God—Joshua and the Israelites prevailed over the Amalekites. But when Moses' arms became heavy and tired, he would lower his arms and the Amalekites would prevail. He needed help and extra strength to support Joshua on the battlefield so that Joshua would win the battle.

> *But Moses' hands became heavy; so they took a stone and put it under him, and he sat on it. And Aaron and Hur supported his hands, one on one side, and the other on the other side; and his hands were steady until the going down of the sun. So Joshua defeated Amalek and his people with the edge of the sword (Exodus 17:12-13).*

If Joshua's success on the battlefield depended upon Moses support on the mountain top, then what was Moses doing? First, Moses climbed up to the mountaintop. In the New Testament we often find Jesus going to the mountaintop to spend time with the Father. This was the key to the success of Jesus' ministry on this Earth. Before Jesus' greatest battle on this Earth, Calvary, He prayed and interceded for strength (see Luke 22:41-44). Those who were with Him were sleeping and could not stay awake to pray, so as He prayed, the Father sent an angle to minister strength to Jesus. Moses too was on the mountaintop with his arms held high, interceding for Joshua on the battlefield. Joshua was fighting a difficult battle, and he could not win this battle on his own. He needed the support of others, and that is what Moses was doing. But even Moses needed help to support Joshua, and Aaron and Hur came along side of Moses to be that extra strength and support. One of the most important points in this account is that it takes a faithful and strong support team to win certain battles.

When people are in the midst of the battle against life and death, they need the support and encouragement of others to not give up, but to continue on and fight until the victory, until their miracle manifests.

We can learn several faith principals from this encounter in Scripture:

+ Moses stood on top of the hill. He did not allow the enemy, Amalek, to defeat and overtake Joshua. He made a decision and was willing to fight the battle in the supernatural realm.

✦ Aaron and Hur climbed to the top of the mountain with Moses. There is power in unity.

Two are better than one, because they have a good reward for their labor. For if they fall, one will lift up his companion. But woe to him who is alone when he falls, for he has no one to help him up. Again, if two lie down together, they will keep warm; but how can one be warm alone? Though one may be overpowered by another, two can withstand him. And a threefold cord is not quickly broken (Ecclesiastes 4:9-12).

✦ Aaron and Hur put a stone under Moses and he sat on it.

Behold, I lay in Zion a chief cornerstone, elect, precious, and he who believes on Him (Jesus Christ) will by no means be put to shame (1 Peter 2:6).

When we encounter people who need healing, we may need to lead them to Jesus Christ (our Chief Cornerstone) first and then teach them and encourage them concerning healing. If they are already believers in Jesus, we need to build them up in the faith to stand upon their Chief Cornerstone, Jesus Christ, and their covenant rights through the blood of Jesus Christ.

✦ Aaron and Hur held up Moses' arms when they became heavy and difficult to hold up.

We need to become like Aaron and Hur and be willing to join a team and to help fight the battle with those who are struggling. We need to stand in the gap and fight for them and with them so that they can overcome.

✦ Joshua defeated the enemy with the edge of the sword because of the support of Moses, Aaron, and Hur.

For the word of God is living and powerful, and sharper than any two-edged sword, piercing even to the division of soul and spirit, and of joints and marrow, and is a discerner of the thoughts and intents of the heart (Hebrews 4:12).

With the support of others, use the power of the spoken Word of God to defeat the enemy, sickness, disease, and premature death. (See Chapter 6, "A Special Rod" for more on this.)

Struggles With the Past

Many people do not receive healing because they are struggling with their past and do not really believe that God can forgive and heal them because of their many past sins. This issue is powerfully addressed in this vision recorded in Zechariah:

> *Then he showed me Joshua the high priest standing before the Angel of the Lord, and satan standing at his right hand to oppose him. And the Lord said to satan, "The Lord rebuke you, satan! The Lord who has chosen Jerusalem rebuke you! Is this not a brand plucked from the fire?" Now Joshua was clothed with filthy garments, and was standing before the Angel. Then He answered and spoke to those who stood before Him, saying, "Take away the filthy garments from him," And to him He said, "See, I have removed your iniquity from you, and I will clothe you with rich robes." And I said, "Let them put a clean turban on his head." So they put a clean turban on his head, and they put the clothes on him. And the angel of the Lord stood by* (Zechariah 3:1-5).

Here Joshua the high priest is standing before the Angel of the Lord, and satan is condemning him. What does the Lord do? He rebukes satan! And He says to remove the filthy garments from Joshua the high priest. The filthy garments represent sin, the old sinful nature, the carnal person. And then the Lord says to Joshua the high priest, *"See, I have removed your iniquity from you, and I will clothe you with rich robes."*

In Hebrew, *iniquity* means "perversity, depravity, sins, and faults."[1] And in Isaiah 53:5 it says that Jesus was bruised (beaten) for our iniquity (perversity, depravity, sins, and faults).

Some are standing before the throne of God requesting physical healing, but the enemy, satan, is whispering lies in their ears, bringing up their past failures, and it's causing them to doubt God's forgiveness, and they are struggling with guilt and condemnation. We cannot be confident that we are going to receive anything from the Lord when we are struggling like this.

In this passage, the Lord then says to Joshua the high priest that He will clothe him with rich robes. The rich robes represent salvation by the blood of Jesus.

> *I will greatly rejoice in the Lord, My soul shall be joyful in my God; For He has clothed me with the garments of salvation, He has covered me with the robe of righteousness, as a bridegroom decks himself with ornaments, and as a bride adorns herself with her jewels* (Isaiah 61:10).

> *In Him we have redemption through His Blood, the forgiveness of sins, according to the riches of His grace* (Ephesians 1:7).

> *If we confess our sins, He is faithful and just to forgive us our sins and to cleanse us from all unrighteousness* (1 John 1:9).

If we have asked the Lord to forgive us of past sins, then we are forgiven. The enemy can no longer hold our past against us because we are covered with the most costly, exquisite, powerful robe that exists—the blood of Jesus!

Then the Lord said to put a clean turban on Joshua the high priest. The clean turban represents the transformation with the mind of Christ, or the Word of God.

And do not be conformed to this world, but be transformed by the renewing of your mind, that you may prove what is that good and acceptable and perfect will of God (Romans 12:2).

that He might sanctify and cleanse it with the washing of water by the word (Ephesians 5:26).

God wants to replace our old thoughts, our old ways of doing things, by transforming our minds with the Word of God. As we turn to God and His Word, we will begin to trust Him and believe His Word; no longer will we struggle with guilt and condemnation from our past sins and failures. Then we will be able to go boldly before God concerning physical healing or anything else that we have need of.

Now this is the confidence that we have in Him, that if we ask anything according to His will, He hears us, And if we know that He hears us, whatever we ask, we know that we have the petitions that we have asked of Him (1 John 5:14-15).

Perceptions of God as Being Evil

Some people may have a difficult time seeing God as loving and good because they were brought up in abusive situations as children, and they see Father God as being harsh and mean, like their abusive parents were. Because of the abuse, they struggle to be able to receive anything good from anyone, including God. They believe the lies that have been spoken over them that they are not worthy or not capable of being loved. These hurting individuals need both deliverance and healing in spirit, soul, and body. *"For I will restore health to you and heal you of your wounds,' says the Lord..."* (Jer. 30:17).

Refusal to Change Bad Habits or Sinful Behaviors

Sometimes people receive healing, but then lose their healing later. This has caused many to question the validity of the healing or the goodness of God.

However, I think often this loss of healing comes through the choices that the individuals make after they receive their healing. Jesus even warned a man He had healed about this:

> *Afterward Jesus found him in the temple, and said to him, "See, you have been made well. Sin no more, lest a worse thing come upon you"* (John 5:14).

> *Your own wickedness will correct you, and your backslidings will reprove you...* (Jeremiah 2:19).

Here is a true story about a puppy that was given a second chance, which will help to illustrate the importance of changing negative habits and sinful behaviors. One of our Labradors had a litter of puppies, and they were running all over the place.

On a particular day, I had some errands that I needed to do in the city. Before getting into the car, I walked around and made sure that there weren't any children or toys behind the vehicle, but I didn't think to check under the vehicle for puppies. As I proceeded to back up the car, I realized that I had run over one of the puppies who had decided to take a nap in the shade under the car. It was not a good situation; the puppy was seriously injured and about to die. I felt terrible. The children were crying, and my husband was upset.

A little later, as I was driving down the road with tears running down my face, I said to the Lord, "I feel so bad about running over the puppy; please heal the puppy." The older boys in the children's home had carried the puppy off to spend his last moments with them. My husband assumed the puppy had died and that they had buried him out in the woods. But several hours later, when I returned home from running my errands in the city, I was surprised and thrilled to find that the puppy was just fine. It was as if nothing had happened to it! When I saw my husband, I made a comment about the puppy, and he was just as surprised as I was that he was alive and well.

God cares about everything we care about, and I believe He heard my prayers and the children's prayers for that puppy. I know He healed that puppy. There is no way he could have survived otherwise. That puppy needed a miracle, and for the sake of the children, God gave him a second chance.

One would think that puppy would have realized that the size and weight of that vehicle did him harm and that, no matter how pleasurable the cool of the shade felt to him, it was dangerous to sleep under that car. But he didn't learn his lesson, nor did he appreciate the gift of being given a second chance to live. It was as if he had no understanding of such things!

A few weeks later, I had to leave the country, and now our son, needed to run some errands in the city. As he backed up the car, he realized that he had run over the same puppy who could not resist the dangerous habit of sleeping in the cool of the shade under that car. A worse thing came upon him, and it cost him his life.

What could possibly be the point of sharing a sad story about a puppy in a book about healing? Amazingly enough, many people act like that puppy. God miraculously heals them and gives them a second chance to live life, but they take His mercy for granted and return to dangerous habits and sinful behaviors, only to have a worse thing come upon them, and it costs them their lives.

The Enemy Steals the Healing

As we've read, *"The thief does not come except to steal, and to kill, and to destroy"* (John 10:10a). The enemy is a thief. He only comes to steal, to kill, and to destroy, and he is the father of all lies (see John 8:44). Sometimes when people seem to lose their healings, it is not because of sin issues in their lives, but because satan is trying to steal their healing. He will go whole-heartedly after those who have been healed, because he fears the power of their testimony. He knows that a living testimony is a powerful weapon against him and his darkness. He is fully aware of the lost souls at stake. He doesn't want to lose those lost souls to Jesus. So, he tries to silence those who obtain their healing with weapons of taunting fear and doubt. He even puts physical symptoms back on those who were healed to see if they will bow to him and accept the sickness or disease back; but we must not allow him to do this.

After Lazarus was miraculously raised from the dead, satan moved through the chief priests to try and have him put to death because he feared his living testimony (see John 12:10-11). Lazarus' testimony was spreading like wildfire, and many people were turning to Jesus because of it. Satan wanted to snuff out the flames. He is afraid of the impact that our living testimonies will have on his kingdom of darkness! But we need not fear! The Word teaches us that we have the Greater One, Jesus Christ, living within us (see 1 John 4:4). (Read how we overcame our wicked encounter with him in Chapter 11, "Marcos.")

Weak in Faith and Vulnerable to Attack

"Be sober, be vigilant; because your adversary the devil walks about like a roaring lion, seeking whom he may devour" (1 Pet. 5:8). A lion in the wild will hunt, attack, and devour a vulnerable prey first. It will go after a young, weak, or injured animal or one that has strayed away from the safety of the herd rather than taking on a strong animal. Vulnerable prey for satan are those who have moved away from God and His Word; those who are weak in relationship with God; those who have not taken the time to study the Word; those who have carelessly strayed away from the Body of Christ, are dabbling in the things of the world, and are no longer living out the Word. They've become weak in the faith and are vulnerable to attack. Because such people are vulnerable, they easily lose their healing to satan's attack. They easily believe his lies that they have not been healed and, as a result, accept back the disease into their bodies.

Fear That the Sickness Will Return

Inasmuch then as the children have partaken of flesh and blood, He Himself likewise shared in the same, that through death He might destroy him who had the power of death, that is, the devil, and release those who through fear of death were all their lifetime subject to bondage (Hebrews 2:14-15).

For the thing I greatly feared has come upon me, and what I dreaded has happened to me (Job 3:25).

For God has not given us a spirit of fear, but of power and love and of a sound mind (2 Timothy 1:7).

Fear is a very powerful and controlling force. It is actually an evil spirit. I believe the spirit of fear is often an actual forerunner to serious sickness and disease and premature death. Fear is the opposite of faith; faith and fear do not operate together. Fear is a lack of trust in God and His Word, and the Word actually says that fear is bondage.

Many are living in a prison within themselves, being tormented with a fear of death. This fear steals the very life out of them. But there is hope. His name is Jesus Christ, and those who are living in extreme fear can be delivered from this curse. To find freedom, we must simply repent and surrender our lives to Jesus Christ. We must fill ourselves to overflowing with the Word of God until His thoughts and ways manifest in our lives. And we must continue to live lives that are centered in His Word so that we will be free. Mediate and ponder upon the following verse, which shows the path forward:

But as for me; I would seek God, and to God I would commit my cause who does great things, and unsearchable, marvelous things without number (Job 5:8-9).

We must seek God, commit our cause to Him, and meditate on His greatness.

— Authority Over All Sickness and Disease —

Many have wondered, *Do we really have authority over all sickness and disease?* This is a good question, and it has a great answer. Yes, we really have been given authority and dominion over *all* sickness and disease. We have dominion over every living thing that moves on this Earth. That includes every sickness and disease, because they are caused by microscopic organisms that are actually living and moving. They enter our bodies, and that is how we become sick.

> *Then God blessed them and God said to them, "Be fruitful and mul-*
> *tiply; fill the earth and subdue it; have dominion over the fish of the*
> *sea, over the birds of the air, and over **every** living thing that moves*
> *on the earth" (Genesis 1:28).*

> *Behold, I give you the authority to trample on serpents and scorpi-*
> *ons, and over **all** the power of the enemy, and nothing shall by any*
> *means hurt you (Luke 10:19).*

We have authority over all the power of the enemy (satan) and over his works, including all sickness and disease. In this section, I want to examine in depth some of the common questions and objections that people have regarding the assertion that believers have authority over all sickness and disease.

What About Medications and Medical Treatments?

Personally, I believe that those who are struggling with not taking medication or receiving medical treatments should take the medication or receive the medical treatments. If it's a struggle, then they are not built up in the faith yet, and they are dealing with fear and doubt. In the meantime, as they receive medical treatment, they should continue to study the Word concerning healing until their faith is strong and all doubt is removed from their hearts. Each of us will know in our own hearts when we're ready to step out in this.

> *But let him ask in faith, with no doubting, for he who doubts is like a*
> *wave of the sea driven and tossed by the wind. For let not that man*
> *suppose that he will receive anything from the Lord; He is a double-*
> *minded man, unstable in all his ways (James 1:6-8).*

What Is Misplaced Faith?

Have you ever considered what you put your trust in? It grieves my heart at times to realize how much faith I have put unknowingly in certain things. For example, it's been a very long day of ministry; my flesh is tired, and my head is starting to hurt. What do I do? I go to the medicine cabinet, swallow a little pill for the pain, and go to sleep, never even thinking to take my authority in the name of Jesus over a headache.

I'm not saying that medicine is bad, because it's not. I just want to open our spiritual eyes of understanding about misplaced faith. Instead of putting my trust in God, the Creator of my body, I have misplaced my faith and trusted completely in a little pill to heal me. All of my faith is resting in that little pill instead of in the Creator of the universe.

I have a friend who was talking to his sister, and she started insisting that he was going to suffer from high blood pressure because everyone else in their family was suffering from it. This man was healthy and strong, and his blood pressure was normal. At first, he rebuked such a negative thought, but later on that night, he found himself starting to meditate on his sister's negative words. He started to worry about it, and within a few days, he started to feel tightness within his chest and was feeling ill. He scheduled an appointment with a doctor. The doctor ran several tests and told him that he didn't have anything to worry about because he had a very strong heart and everything was normal. As he was driving home from the doctor's office, he was thanking the Lord for the good report. Then he heard the Lord say to him, "It's sad that you trusted the word of a doctor over My Word." The man had misplaced his faith; he trusted the doctor's word more than the Word of the Lord. He quickly repented after receiving the revelation from the Lord about his misplaced faith.

After receiving the healing power of the Holy Spirit into their bodies, people often put so much attention on future test results for a confirmation of their healing that they lose their focus on the Lord and His Word. They are overtaken with fear and worry because they have misplaced their faith, and they become totally consumed with test results, trusting less and less in the promises of God.

If the first test result turns out negative, they are completely devastated and often give up altogether. This is misplaced faith; we are to trust the Word of the Lord over test results, even when the complete healing takes time to manifest.

Once at one of our meetings, a woman came forward for healing. She didn't feel anything as she was being prayed for, so she assumed she was not healed and left the altar the same way as she came. She had misplaced her faith and trusted her five senses over the Lord and His Word. I've had people come up to me and say that they had all these other well-known people pray over them for healing and nothing happened, and they look at me and say, "Now, you try." These people have misplaced their faith, and are seeking the ability of people, not God.

It is very important that we trust in the Lord and in His Word. His Word says that by the whippings Jesus received, we are healed. It doesn't matter if we feel something or not when we are being ministered to for healing. Our faith is not to be in supernatural sensations or in our natural five senses, but in Jesus Christ and His Word. Medicine is a good thing, but when we trust more in medicine than the Lord—who gave people the wisdom to know how to make medicine in the first place—then we have placed our trust in the wrong things. When we are at peace only after hearing a good report from the doctor or receiving a good test result, then we have misplaced our faith. *"Some trust in chariots, and some in horses; but we will remember the name of the Lord our God"* (Ps. 20:7).

What About Paul's Thorn in the Flesh?

*And lest I should be exalted above measure by the abundance of the revelations, a **thorn in the flesh** was given to me, a messenger of satan to buffet me, lest I be exalted above measure. Concerning this thing I pleaded with the Lord three times that it might depart from me. And He said to me, "My grace is sufficient for you, for My strength is made perfect in weakness." Therefore most gladly I will rather boast in my infirmities, that at the power of Christ may rest upon me. Therefore I take pleasure in infirmities, in reproaches, in* *needs, in persecutions, in distresses, for Christ's sake. For when I am weak, then I am strong* (2 Corinthians 12:7-10).

This phrase *"thorn in the flesh"* is never used to represent sickness and disease. It always tells us exactly what it is in the context of the verse. In the passage above, Paul's thorn in the flesh was a messenger of satan, a demonic spirit sent to buffet him. *Buffet* means "one attack after another."

References to *a thorn in the flesh, a thorn in the side,* or *thorns or irritants in the eye* occur in several other places in Scripture as well. In each place, the passage makes clear who or what is being referred to. In Numbers 33:55, it is *"the inhabitants of Canaan"*; in Joshua 23:13, *"the nations of their enemies"*; and in Second Samuel 23:6, *"the sons of rebellion."* All of these are physical enemies, or in the case of Second Corinthians 12, spiritual enemies. What they are *not* referring to is illness in any form.

Many people believe that God has given them *a thorn in the flesh*—by which they mean a sickness or disease intended to teach them patience and endurance and to draw them closer to God. This is a lie from satan. This belief turns many away from God. They blame Him and see Him as being mean, uncaring, and unloving as a father. They do not want anything to do with Him. Yet as we can see in the above Scriptures, the phrase *a thorn in the flesh* never was used in Scripture to refer to sickness and disease. Rather, Jesus Christ came to give us life and life in abundance (see John 10:10).

Are We To Bear a Cross of Infirmity?

Many people believe that God has given them a "cross of infirmity" to bear, but is this Scriptural? In the Book of Mark, it talks about taking up a cross:

And when He had called the people to Him, with His disciples also, He said to them, "Whoever desires to come after Me, let him deny himself, and take up his cross, and follow Me. For whoever desires to save his life will lose it, but whoever loses his life for My sake and the gospel's will save it" (Mark 8:34-35).

The meaning of the phrase *"take up his cross"* in this portion of Scripture is not referring to bearing sickness and disease in our physical bodies, but rather to self-denial of fleshly wants and desires in exchange for His will and plan for our lives.

God has not given us a cross of infirmity to bear. He does not put sickness and disease in our bodies to teach us patience and endurance, to teach us to value life, to draw us closer to Him, to give us the opportunity to witness to the other patients and medical staff, so that we would die and give another the opportunity to live by donating organs, or to pay for past sins. All of these ideas are tragically wrong. Certainly often when people are very ill they do cross-examine their lives and discover what is and is not important, and they start to get their lives in order. But the fact remains the same: God does not put sickness and disease in our bodies. Sickness and disease are part of the curse, and God is not the source of the curse. He is the solution to the curse.

I am a mother of eight children. I also have one son-in-law, two daughters-in-law, and a few grandchildren and foster children. I love all of my children. I desire to be close to every one of them. But I would never even think about breaking one of their arms to get their attention or causing some tragic accident to draw them closer to me. I would never think of sticking their hands in the fire to teach them that fire burns; in fact, I taught my children to stay away from such people. If I, being human, wouldn't do such cruel things to my children, then why would we think God would do such cruel things to us? (See Matthew 7:11.)

Jesus Christ bore all sin, sickness, and disease in His body for us so that we could be forgiven, delivered, and healed while we walk on this Earth (see Isa. 53:4-5). Salvation is a free gift to those who will surrender. It is not won by works, good deeds, or acts of suffering. Rather, deliverance and healing, like salvation, are acquired by faith in Him and His Word of grace.

Is God a Teaser?

May it be clearly understood: God does not tease us with healing. He does not heal us one day and take it away the next; that is not God's doing, but the work of satan.

One woman's father teased her terribly as a child with food. He would give her something sweet, like fudge, to eat. And after he saw her enjoying what he had given, he would take it away. This wasn't a fun, little game; it was done with a mean, taunting spirit. The woman developed an eating disorder as food became a comfort to her. Strangely enough, she ended up losing her ability to taste.

I prayed for her for healing, and she was instantly healed, only later to lose her healing. As we further investigated the situation, our sister admitted that when she returned home, she returned to old behavior patterns. She ate excessive amounts of sweets and then verbally beat herself for having done so. The next morning she could no longer taste food again.

Praying for insight, as I ministered to her about root issues, I shared the situation with my husband. He did not know the background information about this woman's father, but only the outward manifestation, and he unknowingly said, "God does not tease!" When I heard those words, I knew what the root of the problem was. She had been comparing Father God to her earthly father. I continued to encourage her in the Word and felt impressed to give her the verse Hebrews 11:11. I told her she needed to be like Sarah who conceived her miracle (Isaac) because she judged God faithful.

> *By faith Sarah herself also received strength to conceive seed, and she bore a child when she was past the age, because she judged Him faithful who had promised (Hebrews 11:11).*

God does not dangle healing in front of us to see if we will take a bite and then pull it away from us again. He is not cruel, but loving, and He suffered greatly at Calvary to undo the works of satan so that we could be healed.

> *The Lord also will be a refuge for the oppressed, a refuge in times of trouble. And those who know Your name will put their trust in You; for You, Lord, have not forsaken those who seek You (Psalm 9:9-10).*

I hope that this section of questions has helped to shed the light of truth on an area of your life that may have been preventing your healing from coming forth. I would like to end this chapter with a word of prayer for you. Please lay your hand on your body and let's pray.

Dear Heavenly Father,

I thank You for revealing the truth to my friends concerning the different strongholds that the enemy has had that have prevented their healings from coming forth. In Jesus' name, I renounce you, satan, and all of your tactics against these people. I rebuke a spirit of infirmity, a spirit of fear, a spirit of death, and any other hindering spirit that is controlling their lives. Right now, my friends, I release the power of that same Spirit that raised Christ from the dead, the Holy Spirit, the Spirit of Life. I release His healing power to flow into your bodies in Jesus' name. No weapon formed against you shall prosper. I command your bodies to line up to the Word of God, and I boldly declare that by His stripes you are healed. I command all pain and all swelling to cease, all broken, sprained or strained body parts to be whole in Jesus' name. I speak into existence new blood, new cells, new organs, and new systems. I declare that this newly created body works together in harmony to produce life and life in abundance. I renounce every negative report that stands in contrary to the Word of God. I speak life and strength to dead and weak body parts, knowing that with my God all things are possible. I rebuke the spirit of doubt and unbelief from whispering lies into your ears, and I command every lying tongue (whether human or spirit) to be silenced against you, my friends, in Jesus' name. I release the Spirit of Peace, Love, and Joy to enter into your domain. Lord, I give You praise and honor as my friends fulfill their destiny that You created them for.

In Jesus' name, amen.

Together we resolved many doubts and questions concerning healing. Now we are going to examine motives of the heart that need to change in order for us to receive divine healing by faith, how to receive healing in the Word, and how to overcome the natural realm of our five senses and human reasoning, especially when physical healing takes time to manifest.

— Endnote —

1. *Blue Letter Bible*, s.v. "avon" (Strong #5771); www.blueletterbible.org/lang/lexicon/lexicon.cfm?strongs=H5771; accessed September 24, 2011.

REVIEW QUESTIONS

1. What is the best way to handle premature death? Why?

2. What is God's plan for the death of His children?

3. What is the difference between the leprous man's words, "*Lord, if it by Thy will, You can make me clean,*" and the common statement we hear today, "If it be Thy will"?

4. If people do not have a sound, biblical understanding of what the Bible teaches concerning healing, when they are attacked with pains and symptoms of sickness and disease they will struggle with *what?*

5. What controls every area of our lives, including the health of our bodies?

6. Before Jesus healed the blind and the lame in the temple, He had to do *what? And what does this mean for us?*

7. Often the root of sickness and disease is *what* type of a problem?

8. How did Aaron and Hur support Moses in the battle against the Amalekites? How did this affect Joshua? And what does this mean to us?

9. In the account of Joshua the High Priest from Zechariah 3:1-5, what do the filthy garments, the rich robes, and the clean turban represent? And what does this mean for us?

10. An individual who grew up in an abusive family situation often needs?

11. What is the moral of the puppy story?

12. Why was satan afraid of Lazarus' resurrection and healing?

13. Who is a vulnerable prey for satan?

14. Who is often an actual forerunner to serious sickness and disease?

CHAPTER 4

HOW TO
RECEIVE HEALING

BEFORE WE CAN STAND in faith for physical healing, we need to be fully convinced that it is God's will to heal us *all the time* and of *everything*. Until we know and understand what God's will is, there is nothing to base our faith upon. It is important that our minds are renewed with the Word of God. As the apostle Paul wrote:

> So then faith comes by hearing, and hearing by the Word of God (Romans 10:17).

> And do not be conformed to this world, but be transformed by the renewing of your mind, that you may prove what is that good and acceptable and perfect will of God (Romans 12:2).

— Necessary Changes of the Heart —

Many people are not correctly positioned in their hearts to receive healing. The Lord gave me the following list in a dream of the attitudes of that heart that we need to cultivate. I believe it will help and bless you.

1. We Need to Be Humble

Like Jairus, we need to humble ourselves, fall down at the feet of Jesus, and make our requests known (see Luke 8:41). Acknowledging that He is our Lord and Savior and our source for healing, we must invite His healing power into our homes, just as Jarius did.

2. We Need to Seek

We need to seek and find out, as the leprous man did, what the will of the Lord is concerning healing (see Luke 5:12-13). We need to study the Word of God for ourselves. As we read about the actual healing in His Word, our faith will be stirred to believe.

3. We Need to Press Into His Presence

Just as the woman with the issue of blood pressed into Jesus' presence and touched the very heart of Him, we need to enter into His manifested presence (see Luke 8:43-48).

4. We Need to Be Fully Persuaded

Abraham was fully persuaded, and we need to be, too. We need to rid ourselves of all doubt and unbelief regarding whether or not it's God's will to heal us. Like Abraham, we need to call those things that are not as though they are while ignoring the realm of the five senses and all human reasoning (see Rom. 4:13-22).

5. We Need to Judge God Faithful

Like Sarah, we need to come to the realization that God is faithful (see Heb 11:11). The more we allow His presence to manifest in us while we are in His Word, the more we will know Him and learn to trust Him. We too will judge Him faithful to keep His promises to us.

6. We Need to Be Obedient

As Naaman discovered, obedience is a must (see 2 Kings 5:1-14). Whatever God instructs us to do, we must do it! And we must do it with a submissive attitude, knowing who He is and who we are in Him.

7. We Need to Put Our Faith into Action

Immediately, we need to put our faith into action, as the man with the withered hand did, and watch what happens! The healing may be instant, or it may be progressive in nature; either way, it is miraculous. But it will only start after we put our faith into action (see Luke 6:6-10).

8. We May Need to Find Support

We may need to do as the paralytic man did and rely on friends of like-faith to support us while we obtain our healing (see Luke 5:17-26).

— How to Receive Healing From the Word of God —

The Word of God must be a mainstay to those seeking divine healing. In it we find God's truth about His will and purpose and about the situations in our lives. Only in His Word do we find an accurate lens through which to see life.

Study the Word of God

The Bible itself says, *"My son, give attention to My words, incline your ear to My sayings"* (Prov. 4:20) and *"So then Faith comes by hearing, and hearing by the Word of God"* (Rom. 10:17).

We must study and keep on studying the Word of God concerning healing until the Word becomes more real to us than our present situations. We must consume ourselves with the Word so that it speaks louder than the pain, the symptoms, or any negative report. Praying and fasting over the Word, we must ask the Holy Spirit to give us the divine revelation of its meaning within our own hearts. He desires for us to understand how to activate His Word in our lives. And once we receive our healings, we need to continue to study the healing Scriptures and learn to speak words of health and life over ourselves so that we can live sustained lives of divine health.

I have had to literally force my mind to be silent. I have had to fight my flesh to stay in His presence in the Word in order to overcome my mind, negative thoughts, physical pain, and symptoms, but the power of the Word works.

Focus on the Word of God, Not on the Symptoms

Do not let them depart from your eyes; keep them in the midst of your heart (Proverbs 4:21).

This Book of the Law shall not depart from your mouth, but you shall meditate in it day and night, that you may observe to do according to all that is written in it. For then you will make your way prosperous, and then you will have good success (Joshua 1:8).

We must not focus on the sickness, pain, and symptoms, but rather on the Word. We must speak the Word and glorify God with our words, not the sickness. We must thank the Lord that His healing power has been received into our physical bodies and that He is faithful and true to keep His Word. Telling everyone we see that we are in pain or not feeling well is not taking a posture of faith. It will only bear negative fruit. And we must stay away from people who would draw us into a realm of unbelief. If those around us are asking us how we are feeling, we can find creative ways to express a faith-filled response and not allow ourselves to be drawn into negative, faithless conversation. Words have power! Our healings are in the confession of our tongues. Some people's words are preventing their healings from manifesting.

Stand Firm in Faith in the Word of God

For they are life to those who find them, and health to all their flesh (Proverbs 4:22).

Therefore take up the whole armor of God, that you may be able to withstand in the evil day, and having done all to stand (Ephesians 6:13).

If we will stand firm in our faith and do and say what the Word of God teaches, regardless of what is happening in the physical realm, then we will see our healings come to pass. It is that simple.

— Overcoming the Realm of Our Five Senses —

Genesis chapters 15-18 and 21 tell the story of the man we now refer to as the "father of faith." God made a covenant with a man named Abram, who was married to a barren woman named Sarai. The Word of the Lord came to Abram in a vision promising Abram great reward through many generations, but Abram was childless (see Gen. 15:1). Abram could not even envision himself as ever having a child; he had no hope of being a father. Basically his response to the Lord was, "I see myself childless" (see Gen. 15:2).

A very important step in receiving a promise from God is being able to envision that promise fulfilled before it even happens—that's faith. Abram did not have the vision of faith to be a father; he lacked hope. Thus, he started reasoning with the present circumstances in his life and figured that Eliezer of Damascus, a servant in his house, would be his heir. In response, God said that Eliezer wasn't his heir, but that one from Abram's own body would become his heir (see Gen. 15:4). Then God took him on a spiritual journey, brought him outside, and told him to look up at the stars and count them if he could. God was giving Abram the vision that he lacked. There were too many stars for him to count, and God told Abram, "That's how many descendants you will have" (see Gen. 15:5).

When a vision is truly from God, it's much bigger than we are. It's something we cannot obtain on our own. That's why it's called a miracle; it's not brought about by our own strength, but by faith in His. This was a very important lesson that Abram had to learn, and he learned it the hard way before He understood.

Sarai also could not see herself ever having a child. She, like Abram, had no hope, and instead of seeing God as her hope, she blamed Him for her barrenness. Sizing up the situation in the natural and using her five senses and human understanding as her guide, she came up with a plan of her own. Abram agreed and conceived a child with her maidservant, Hagar (see Gen. 16). This plan was not God's plan; it was conceived of the flesh, not by faith, and it gave no glory to God. Sarai too had a hard lesson to learn, for now she was despised in the eyes of her maidservant.

Even though God gave us the gifts of brilliant minds, the ability to think things through, and our five senses to walk in the natural realm—these gifts were never intended to take His place. Our human reasoning and our five senses are to be guided and controlled by faith in God and His Word, not the other way around. As we can learn from this example of Abram and Sarai, human reasoning and our five senses can be the source of great troubles for us. God has a much better way called faith.

Abram was 86 years old when Hagar bore his son, Ismael. Thirteen years later, the Lord appeared to Abram, when he was 99 years old and said, *"I am Almighty God; walk before Me and be blameless. And I will make My covenant between Me and you, and will multiply you exceedingly"* (Gen. 17:1-2). He restored Abram to Himself and re-birthed a vision in him. God knew the power of the spoken word, and He needed Abram to release His creative power into the situation, so He changed his name from Abram to Abraham. *Abraham* means "the father of many nations." So whenever Abraham spoke his name, he was prophetically declaring that he was the father of many nations. The spoken word has the power to create or to destroy. The Lord also changed Sarai's name to Sarah, saying that she would bear a son, that she would be a mother of nations, and that kings of peoples would come from her womb that once was barren. God loves to bring forth the possible from the impossible. It gives Him all the glory and leads many to His everlasting Kingdom.

Sarah had a decision to make in this miracle as well. When she first heard the prophetic message from God's messengers that she would bear a child, she laughed with doubt and unbelief. When the messengers asked why she laughed, she lied and denied that she had laughed, but they corrected her. God knows what's in our hearts, and our hearts need to be rid of all doubt and unbelief in order to conceive a miracle. Doubt and unbelief are like spiritual weeds, and they choke the Word of the Lord from manifesting miracles.

Most of us remember that Sarah laughed at the prophetic word spoken by God's messengers, but Abraham also laughed with doubt and unbelief when he first heard the Word of the Lord (see Gen. 17:17-19). He actually fell on his face and laughed! He started reasoning in his heart once again about their ages; he was now 100 years old and Sarah was 90 years old. Sarah was past childbearing years. Those were the facts of life; all human reasoning shouted at this couple that this was impossible. Abraham actually was bidding with God that He would bring the blessing through his son, Ishmael. God said no; He wouldn't do that. He was going to bring about His promise to Abraham by the way of faith and not according to the fleshly ways of people.

In response to Abraham's human reasoning, God said to him, *"Is anything too hard for the Lord? At the appointed time I will return to you, according to the time of life, and Sarah shall have a son"* (Gen. 18:14). Abraham made the decision to trust God. He chose to ignore and negate the five senses and all human understanding and made a quality decision of faith to trust in God's faithfulness. This time he did not take into account his age or his aged body, the lack of his physical strength, or that Sarah was an elderly, barren women. He chose to trust completely in the God of the impossible and considered the greatness of His God.

Romans 4:12-35 tells us of Abraham's faith:

> (as it is written, "I have made you a father of many nations") in the presence of Him whom he believed, even God, who gives life to the dead and calls those things which do not exist as though they did;

...And not being weak in faith, he did not consider his own body, already dead (since he was about a hundred years old), and the deadness of Sarah's womb, and being fully convinced that what He had promised He was also able to perform (Romans 4:17,19-20).

Sarah too lined herself up with the promise of God that she would bear Abraham's son in her old age. God's promise did come to pass, just as He said it would. She conceived a child at the age of 90 by her own faith, and that barren womb miraculously bore a son.

By faith Sarah herself also received strength to conceive seed, and she bore a child when she was past the age, because she judged Him faithful who had promised (Hebrews 11:11).

He took away her shame and sorrow and gave her a baby son named Isaac. *Isaac* means "laughter." Her laughter of doubt and unbelief that she had been questioned about earlier was transformed by His miraculous power. God had not forgotten her; He restored her joy.

Faith Principals From Abraham's Life:

+ He was not weak in faith.

+ He did not consider his own body.

+ He did not consider the deadness of Sarah's womb.

+ He did not waiver at the promise of God through unbelief.

+ He was strengthened in faith.

+ He gave glory to God.

+ He was fully convinced.

Faith Principals From Sarah's Life:

+ By faith Sarah received strength to conceive and bear a child in her old age.

+ She judged God faithful to His promise to her.

This is one of the most challenging areas in regard to healing; that is why it is imperative to study the Word of God. We have been trained ever since we were born to rely on our five senses. When we are standing in faith for healing, we need to learn to deny the five senses and all human reasoning. We will have to choose to say no to what we see, hear, smell, taste, and feel and to stand our ground against all negative reports by trusting completely in the Word of God.

When we take the faith principals from Abraham and Sarah's example listed above and faithfully put them into practice, our miracles will manifest. (See Chapter 11, "Marcos" for a real life example of this concept.)

— When Healing Takes Time to Manifest —

Many people struggle to know how to respond when their healings do not manifest immediately. Here are some keys to walking out a progressive healing:

1. Submit and Resist

James 4:7 gives us the first key: *"Therefore submit to God. Resist the devil and he will flee from you."*

+ Submit to God.

+ Resist the devil.

+ The devil will flee from you. (See Chapter 7, "Power From on High," specifically the testimony at the end of the chapter.)

Submission is a matter of the heart; it's having the right attitude toward God and His Word. We can obey God and still not be submissive because obedience is an act, while submission is an attitude. Resisting is also a matter of the heart.

In this case, it's a decision to refuse to surrender to the enemy's thoughts of doubt and unbelief toward God and His Word. When we submit to God and resist the devil, he will flee from us.

2. Draw Near to God

The next verse in James goes on to say: *"Draw near to God and He will draw near to you. Cleanse your hands, you sinners; and purify your hearts, you double-minded"* (James 4:8).

+ We draw near to God.

+ He will then draw near to us.

+ We sanctify ourselves.

When we choose to draw near to God, we make the decision to give Him first place in our lives and to develop a holy, intimate relationship with Him. This goes beyond the realm of salvation or even seeking His blessings. This is entering into a true fellowship with Him. In order to enter into fellowship with Him, we need to be willing to deny ourselves of ungodly desires, sins, and even self. Sin and self separate us from God; that's why it says to purify our hearts. God perceives the intentions of the heart; a rebellious heart repels Him, but a pure and undefiled heart toward Him is very alluring and desirable. He will draw near to a tender heart.

God's purpose in creating humankind in His mirror image was to have fellowship with beings like Him. We can draw as close to Him as we desire to. The more we enter into His presence, the more real He becomes to us. He becomes the One we run to first with all our joys and sorrows. We will find ourselves communing with Him throughout the whole day about everything. And He will speak to us in our dreams and give us visions. We will find such a strong fellowship with Him in His Word, which will become so alive to us. This type of encounter with Him is exciting. It's the cure for doubt and unbelief. In that place, the manifested presence of God His blessings will start to overtake us.

3. Be Patient

Therefore be patient, brethren, until the coming of the Lord. See how the farmer waits for the precious fruit of the earth, waiting patiently for it until it receives the early and latter rain. You also be patient. Establish your hearts, for the coming of the Lord is at hand (James 5:7-8).

One of the most important things next to developing our relationship to the Lord is to develop patience and remain patient, being fully persuaded that we will receive our miracles from God. Perhaps, along with the healing, He desires to develop in us a character of strong faith that can endure the test of time.

Consider the example of the farmer. He waits patiently for harvest time. But while waiting patiently (not being full of doubt and fear of crop failure), he waters and fertilizes the desired harvest, even though he does not see any results in the very beginning. He's confident that if the conditions are right, he will reap a bountiful harvest.

We need to see ourselves as the farmer and our desired harvest is our miracle. Just like a farmer, we need to water and fertilize that seed that has been planted in our hearts with words of hope, expectancy, and thankfulness for His faithfulness to us and our needs. And sometimes we need to be willing to pull a few weeds of doubt and unbelief from the soil of our hearts so that our desired harvest will not be choked. And we need to put our faith into action and plan for and expect to harvest our miracle. We need to use the power of our God-given imagination and allow ourselves to plan what we will do when our miracle manifests. Miracles can be compared to plants; some take longer to grow and to develop than others.

4. Be Strong in the Lord

Finally, my brethren, be strong in the Lord and in the power of His might. Put on the whole armor of God, that you may be able to stand against the wiles of the devil. For we do not wrestle against flesh and blood, but against principalities, against powers, against the rulers of the darkness of this age, against spiritual hosts of wickedness in the heavenly places. Therefore take up the whole armor of God, that you may be able to withstand in the evil day, and having done all, to stand. Stand therefore, having girded your waist with the truth, having put on the breastplate of righteousness, and having shod your feet with the preparation of the gospel of peace, above all, taking the shield of faith with which you will be able to quench all the fiery darts of the wicked one. And take the helmet of salvation, and the sword of the Spirit, which is the word of God; praying always with all prayer and supplication in the Spirit, being watchful to this end with all perseverance and supplication for all the saints (Ephesians 6:10-18).

The key to this portion of Scripture is in verse 10: "*Be strong in the Lord.*" How do we become strong in the Lord? By developing our relationship with the Lord—going beyond salvation and becoming His friends. We begin to develop our knowledge in the Word concerning healing. But it's not enough to just study the Word; we need to put it into action on a daily basis. And lastly, we need to put on the whole armor of God, not just the parts that we are comfortable or familiar with. Let's learn to use them and apply them to every situation.

No matter how long it takes, no matter what others may say, we must persevere and move forward with God and His Word. The enemy's grip will start to loosen up, and when it does, we must not let our guard down, but push all the harder and we will win! Our healings will manifest.

We studied in this chapter the attitudes of the heart that need to be changed in order to receive our healing, how to receive divine healing from the Word of God, overcoming the realm of the five senses, and what to do when our healing takes time to manifest. Now, we are going to study how to live in the realm of the victorious by the power in the blood of Jesus and by the word of our testimony according to Revelation 12:11.

REVIEW QUESTIONS

1. What do you need to be before you can stand in faith for physical healing?

2. What are eight changes of the heart needed to receive healing by faith?

3. List three steps to receiving healing from the Word of God.

4. What spiritual weeds choke out the Word of God from manifesting miracles?

5. What should our human reasoning and our five senses be guided and controlled by?

6. What four things should you do while your healing is taking time to manifest?

CHAPTER 5

BY THE BLOOD
AND OUR TESTIMONY

HOW DO WE OVERCOME sickness, disease, and premature death? That's what we will learn in this chapter. In the Book of Revelation it says, "*And they overcame him by the Blood of the Lamb and by the word of their testimony, and they did not love their lives to the death*" (Rev. 12:11). Let's examine further these two keys to victory—the blood of the Lamb and the word of our testimony:

— The Blood of the Lamb —

Surely He has borne our griefs (sicknesses, weaknesses, and distresses) and carried our sorrows and pains [of punishment], yet we [ignorantly] considered Him stricken, smitten, and afflicted by God [as if with leprosy]. But He was wounded for our transgression, He was bruised for our guilt and iniquities; the chastisement [needful to obtain] peace and well-being for us was upon Him, and with the stripes [that wounded] Him we are healed and made whole (Isaiah 53:4-5 AMP).

Who Himself bore our sins in His own body on the tree, that we,
having died to sins, might live for righteousness—by whose stripes
you were healed (1 Peter 2:24).

We can overcome sickness, disease, and premature death because Jesus shed His blood for us. Jesus Christ redeemed us. He delivered and rescued us from all sickness and disease. He repurchased or recovered, by the payment of His blood, healing and health for our physical bodies. He bore our sickness and disease upon His own body for us so we wouldn't have to. He carried our sorrow and pain. He was afflicted by God on our behalf. He was wounded and bruised for our sin, guilt, and weaknesses. He was punished to regain our peace and well being, and He was whipped so that we could be healed and made whole. God's plan to redeem us is complete and perfect. Our debt has been forgiven; it has been erased from the books because it was paid in full by His blood. Our belief in the power of His blood activates His healing power in our daily lives.

— The Word of Our Testimony —

The next step to overcoming sickness, disease, and premature death is found in the word of our testimony. There is power in our words. Let us go back to the beginning in Genesis and discover how God put this principal into practice when He created our world.

In the beginning God created the heavens and the earth. The earth
was without form, and void; and darkness was on the face of the
deep. And the Spirit of God was hovering over the face of the waters.
Then God said; "Let there be light", and there was light. And God
saw the light, that it was good; and God divided the light from the
darkness (Genesis 1:1-4).

God was preparing to create humankind, but before He could do that, He needed to prepare a place for people to live. In verse 2, it says that the Earth was without form and void and darkness was on the face of the deep. This doesn't sound like a place that could sustain humankind. It sounds rather bleak and hopeless. But the Spirit of God was on the scene, and He was hovering over the face of the waters.

Who is the Spirit of God? He's the Holy Spirit. Who is the Holy Spirit? He's the third part of the Godhead—Father God; Jesus Christ, the Son of God; and the Spirit of God, the Holy Spirit. He's the creative, explosive power of God. And it says that He was hovering over the face of the waters, yet nothing happened. Why not? He was waiting for something.

The word *hover* is a power-filled word; its more than mere waiting for something to happen. It is an action-filled word that describes a waiting with expectancy. It is like a pregnant woman during her time of waiting before she gives birth to the precious miracle within her. She is imagining with the eyes of her spirit this child in her arms; she is planning where her baby will sleep, how she will feed her baby, what her baby will wear, what she will cover her baby with, and she preparing a safe place in her home for her child to live. She is putting her faith into action for the arrival of her child. So too, the Holy Spirit was waiting with expectancy for the creation of the world, the creation of humankind.

The wheels of creativity were turning inside of God. The Father, the Son, and the Holy Spirit were planning for this blessed event, but They knew that, before They could create humankind, They would have to create a very special place for people to live. Great thought was put into the creation of this Earth. The order of every minute detail was thoroughly thought through, discussed, well-planned, and scheduled for production. Not one detail was over-looked. Finally, this plan of creation was ready to be released, and the production manager was in place.

But what was He waiting for? He was waiting for Father God to speak the spoken word, which would release the creative, explosive power of the Holy Spirit to create what Father God spoke. It says in verse three, *"then God said…"* As soon as Father God spoke the words; *"Let there be light."* The creative, explosive power of the Holy Spirit was released and had conceived the Father's words *"Let there be light,"* and this light was delivered. The light shined in the darkness.

This light was not the creation of the sun, moon, and stars. That happens in Genesis 1:14-19 on the fourth day of creation. What was this light? It was the glory of God, the habitat of His manifested presence on the scene.

God created this magnificent Earth and all that is within it with the power of His words.

> **By the word of the Lord** *the heavens were made, and all the host of them by the breath of His mouth. He gathers the waters of the sea together as a heap; He lays up the deep in storehouses. Let all the earth fear the Lord; Let all the inhabitants of the world stand in awe of Him.* **For He spoke, and it was done; He commanded, and it stood fast.** (Psalm 33:6-9)

Did you know that the Holy Spirit is traveling the whole Earth looking for people to do miracles through? And amazingly enough, it matters not who you are, but that your heart is loyal to Him.

> *"For the eyes of the Lord run to and fro throughout the whole earth, to show Himself strong on behalf of those whose heart is loyal to Him* (2 Chronicles 16:9a).

Many are facing situations in their lives that appear to be dark and hopeless. I am writing this to encourage them that with the Spirit of God *there is always hope!* We can create the spiritual atmosphere by verbally inviting Him to hover over our life situations:

> *Sweet Holy Spirit, I invite You to come into my life. I give You free reign to hover over me and my situation. Do what only You can do, and create in my life the miraculous for the glory of my Lord. Teach me how to cooperate with You and to speak those things that will release Your creative, explosive power into my life.*

After we have given a verbal invitation to the Holy Spirit to hover, brood, and incubate over our life situations, then we give Him what He is waiting for and needing from us—our faith-filled words, which will release His creative, explosive power and create the miracles that we so desperately need.

I thank You, sweet Holy Spirit, for releasing in me Your creative, explosive power. I give You glory for the miracle that is taking place within me. I thank You that I am strong and healthy. I give You praise that no sickness, disease, growths, or pains of any sort may remain in my body. I will honor You all the days of my life, and because of Your power flowing through my body, I will fulfill my destiny and will live to a ripe old age, full of strength and health.

As the writer of Hebrews tells us, *"By faith, we understand that the worlds were framed by the word of God, so that the things which are seen were not made of things which are visible"* (Heb. 11:3).

— The Power of Faith-Filled Words —

God created the world through the power of faith-filled words:

In the beginning God created the heavens and the earth. The earth was without form, and void; and darkness was on the face of the deep. And the Spirit of God was hovering over the face of the waters. Then God said; "Let there be light", and there was light. And God saw the light, that it was good; and God divided the light from the darkness (Genesis 1:1-4).

In this passage, we see the follow progression:

+ The Spirit of God was *hovering* over the face of the waters.

+ Then God *said*, "Let there be light."

+ And there *was* light.

+ And God *saw* the light.

This is the perfect example of how a miracle takes place. It's so clear and simple, and yet so very powerful. It's like a four-step process to producing a miracle. First of all, God's manifested presence was on the scene; then God *said*; then there *was*; and then God *saw*. This is so beautifully uncomplicated. Before anything else, we need God's glory, His manifested presence on the scene. We need to learn to discipline ourselves to shut out the unnecessary in our lives and to press into His manifested presence first and foremost, allowing ourselves the joys and the blessings of residing in the habitation of His manifested presence. Our miracles are in His habitat.

Just as God created with the power of His faith-filled words, He's given us that ability as well. We need to speak what we need into being, and as we do these first two steps, our miracles will manifest. They may manifest instantly, or they may be progressive in nature, but either way, what we have need of will manifest. Then we will see with our own eyes the goodness of our God.

We are all living out today what we have spoken over ourselves or what others have spoken over us in the past. We need to listen to and examine what is coming out of our mouths. What have we been speaking? Have we been speaking positive or negative words? If we realize that we have been speaking negative words, then we need to repent for such negative, faithless words and make a conscious effort to start speaking positive, faith-filled words. And we also can take authority and rebuke every negative, curse-filled word that has been spoken over us by others in the name of Jesus.

I know that this is very challenging to change the way in which we speak because we live in such a negative world. Many people do not even know how to speak something positive because they have been so programmed to be negative. But it is possible to change the way in which we speak. If we want to walk in the miraculous realm of the Holy Spirit, it is a must!

> *Death and life are in the power of the tongue, and they who indulge in it shall eat the fruit of it [for death or life]* (Proverbs 18:21 AMP).

> *"As I live," says the Lord, "just as you have spoken in My hearing, so I will do to you"* (Numbers 14:28).

(as it is written, "I have made you a father of many nations") in the presence of Him whom he believed, even God, who gives life to the dead and calls those things which do not exist as though they did (Romans 4:17).

We need to start listening to what we are saying because God is listening to our words and giving to us according to what we are speaking. He says that the power of life and death are in the tongue.

If you are in a battle against premature death, you need to start speaking words full and overflowing with life, healing, and deliverance. If you are speaking about a funeral, that is what you are going to have. If you are in need of a miracle, you need to start declaring those things that do not exist as though they do. If you've been given a death sentence by your doctor and you desire to live and finish your race on this Earth, then you are going to have to become very radical in your faith and speak the opposite of that report. You are going to have to speak to sick and dying body parts and declare that they are recreated and functioning perfectly in the name of Jesus Christ. Declare in the name of Jesus that you will live and not die and that you will complete your race on this Earth. *Dare to believe God and His Word!*

This Book of the Law shall not depart from your mouth, but you shall meditate in it day and night, that you may observe to do according to all that is written in it. For then you will make your way prosperous, and then you will have good success (Joshua 1:8).

His Word is to become the standard in our lives, and we are to *meditate* on it, which means "to utter, speak, devise, plot, muse, and imagine the Word of God."[1] We are to read, study, ponder upon, and speak His Word out loud over ourselves and into life's situations. In the scheme of life, an occasional meditation of His Word isn't enough; we need to make this a daily habit or a lifestyle.

I am not referring to the practices of Eastern religions such as transcendental meditation. This is not of God. TM is dangerous and opens people up to demonic influences and causes all sorts of trouble later on in life. This is not

Biblical meditation, but that of New Age. If you are involved in transcendental meditation you need to stop and repent and return to it no more.

God is the inventor of meditation, and His way is to fill your spirit with His Word by reading, studying, pondering upon its meaning, speaking it out loud, and then doing what it says. This is true Biblical meditation.

— The Language of Healing —

The language of healing is very bold and radical in nature. It does not allow one word of doubt to be taken in or spoken. It will not tolerate doubt! It will not dwell on or consider the word *impossible!* It is birthed from time spent with the Holy Spirit and His Word. The more it is spoken on a consistent basis, the more it produces. And it will eventually lead us to the timeframe of the instant.

Here are some basic examples of the healing language. Take these examples and fashion them to your need of healing.

I Am...

I am healed in the name of Jesus!

I am cancer free in the name of Jesus!

I am free from sickness and disease, in Jesus' name!

I am strong and well, in Jesus' name!

I am free from alcohol, nicotine, caffeine, or any other drug, in Jesus' name!

I Can...

I can do all things through Christ who strengthens me!

In Jesus' name, I can bend my knee!

I can walk, in Jesus' name!

I can see without glasses, in Jesus' name!

I can read and write, in Jesus' name!

I can lose weight and keep it off, in Jesus' name!

I can sleep peacefully without pain, in Jesus' name!

I Will...

I will live, in Jesus' name!

I will fulfill my destiny, in Jesus' name!

I will walk on my own again, in Jesus' name!

I Will Not...

In Jesus' name, I will not receive this sickness or disease into my body!

I will not die before my time, in Jesus' name!

In the name of Jesus, I will not be bound to a wheel chair!

I will not be bedridden, in Jesus' name!

I Rebuke...

I rebuke the spirit of death over my body, in Jesus' name!

I rebuke, in the name of Jesus, every sickness and disease attacking my body!

I rebuke this pain and swelling in my body, in Jesus' name!

I Command...

I command, in Jesus' name, the pain and swelling to cease!

I command you, satan, to release my healing, in Jesus' name!

I command my knee to be recreated, in the mighty name of Jesus!

I command this spine and everything connected to it to be realigned and healed, in Jesus' name!

I command the blood to be washed clean, recreated, and healed, in Jesus' name!

There are many promises for healing in the Scriptures. Here are a few to meditate upon.

> *"For I will restore health to you, and heal you of your wounds," says the Lord* (Jeremiah 30:17).

> *He sent His word and healed them, and delivered them from their destructions* (Psalm 107:20).

> *Therefore I say to you, whatever things you ask when you pray, believe that you receive them, and you will have them* (Mark 11:24).

> *Do not, therefore, fling away your fearless confidence, for it carries a great and glorious compensation of reward. For you have need of steadfast patience and endurance, so that you may perform and fully accomplish the will of God, and thus receive and carry away [and enjoy to the full] what is promised* (Hebrews 10:35-36 AMP).

We've seen how the blood of Jesus and the word of our testimony will cause us to walk in victory. In the next chapter we are going to learn about another spiritual weapon that all believers in Jesus possesses, but may not be aware of it or how to use it. It is called a "Special Rod."

— Endnote —

1. *Blue Letter Bible*, s.v. "hagah" (Strong #1897); www.blueletterbible.org/lang/lexicon/lexicon.cfm?Strongs=H1897&t=KJV; accessed September 26, 2011.

REVIEW QUESTIONS

1. How do we overcome sickness, disease, and premature death?

2. What is the four-step process to producing a miracle?

3. Why is it so important that we are careful with the words we speak?

CHAPTER 6

A SPECIAL ROD

IN THE LAST CHAPTER, we discussed the power of our words. God gave us an example to follow when He created the heavens and the Earth. We learned how the Spirit of God, the Holy Spirit, was hovering, over the face of the waters, waiting for Father God to speak so that His power could be released to create. We also saw how we need to speak faith-filled words over our lives and circumstances so that the creative, explosive power of the Holy Spirit can be released to create what we have need of.

Now, we are going to examine another spiritual weapon that God has given to us. I call this weapon a "Special Rod." Every believer has been equipped with this weapon, but many do not know how to use it or that they even have it. *"My people are destroyed for lack of knowledge"* (Hos. 4:6a).

In Chapter 1, which is the base of this whole book, we learned that, in Genesis 1:26-28, God created humanity in His mirror image and He created humankind to have authority and dominion on this Earth and over all the evil works of satan (see Luke 10:19).

The Book of Exodus holds a story that adds to our understanding of this concept (see Exod. 6:28-7:13).

> *That the Lord spoke to Moses, saying, "I am the Lord. Speak to Pharaoh king of Egypt all that I say to you." But Moses said before*

the Lord, "*Behold, I am of uncircumcised lips, and how shall Pharaoh heed me?*" (Exodus 6:29-30)

God was calling Moses and giving him his life assignment, and Moses responded with excuses of why he thought God must have the wrong man. Moses was looking at things in the natural and forgetting (or just didn't understand) who he was in God. Sound familiar? Most of us respond to God's call on our lives in this manner at first. Let's see how God responds to him.

So the Lord said to Moses: "See, I have made you as God to Pharaoh, and Aaron your brother shall be your prophet (Exodus 7:1).

I think this verse is so exciting and powerful. It sounds like the same message found in Genesis 1:26. This verse is bursting with our identity—who we are in Christ. Moses was created in the mirror image of the Father, Son, and Holy Spirit, and just like a mirror reflects the image in front of it, so he would reflect the mirror image of God before Pharaoh, the king of Egypt.

In this portion of Scripture, Pharaoh represents satan and Egypt represents the world and the world's ways. Moses represents the Chosen One in us—Christ in us. This is exactly what the apostle John meant when he wrote:

Love has been perfected among us in this; that we may have boldness in the day of judgment, because as He is, so are we in this world (1 John 4:17).

We must learn to ask the Holy Spirit to reveal to us how to apply the Scriptures to our daily lives. The Bible is much more than a history book; it's a living book for us, and we are meant to apply it's truths in our everyday lives.

So the Lord said to Moses: "See, I have made you as God to Pharaoh, and Aaron your brother shall be your prophet (Exodus 7:1).

Let us take a closer look at the second half of this Scripture, "*...and Aaron your brother shall be your prophet.*" Prophets (who can be either men or women) are spokespeople for the Lord. Prophets speak a message that comes directly from the heart of the Lord to a specific nation or a specific person or group of people for a specific time. It is God who is doing the speaking, using the mouths of the prophets for His purposes. What does the phrase, "*... and Aaron your brother shall be your prophet,*" represent in this Scripture for us today? It represents the spoken Word of God. God has repeated this same message throughout His Word—we are created in His mirror image, and He has given us power through the spoken word.

Let's continue on with this study, taking with us the symbolism that we are learning:

+ Moses reflects the Chosen One, God in him, before the Pharaoh.

+ And he is taking with him Aaron, his brother—his prophet or the spoken Word of God.

+ Pharaoh represents satan.

+ Egypt represents the world and the world's ways.

— Our Special Rod —

Now we move into the next theme of this teaching, which is that God has given each one of us a powerful, spiritual weapon, and I call it a "Special Rod."

In Exodus 7:8-12 we read that God gave to Aaron a special, miraculous rod to use. He taught Moses and Aaron what it was and how to use it:

> *Then the Lord spoke to Moses and Aaron, saying, "When Pharaoh speaks to you, saying, 'show a miracle for yourselves,' then you shall say to Aaron, 'Take your rod and cast it before Pharaoh, and let it become a serpent'"* (Exodus 7:8-9).

When we are facing difficult and impossible situations, we, like Moses and Aaron, are to take and use our authority that we have in Christ. The Chosen One, Jesus Christ, is living in us so, using the power of the spoken word, we must cast our rod before Pharaoh (satan) and let (allow) it to become a serpent (or whatever the miracle it is we are needing).

Imagine you have a special rod or a staff in your hand, just like Aaron did, and Pharaoh or satan is mocking you and saying, "Show me a miracle." You cast (or throw) your rod out before the Pharaoh (satan), and it starts to transform into the miracle you need, but because of fear and doubt, you run and pick up the rod that you cast down. Will that special rod be able to transform into the miracle that you need? No. Once you cast out your special rod, you need to leave it and allow it to become the miracle that you are seeking and needing.

I started the previous paragraph with the word *imagine*, but we do not need to imagine, because we do have special rods. These special rods are the spoken Word of God put into action or the active, spoken Word of God. All we need to do is release it. God has given us every spiritual weapon we need to overcome in this world. We need to learn how to use the weapons that He has given us.

We "cast" our special rod before the enemy and his attack against our lives by calling those things which do not exist as though they existed already (see Rom. 4:17). We first cast out our special rod by the power of our confession. Our words have the power to create or to destroy life (see Prov. 18:21). And then we need to act according to the words that we have spoken. If we are in a battle against life and death and we choose life (see Deut. 30:19), we must not only speak words of healing and life, but we also should put our faith into action and plan and act like we are going to live.

> But Pharaoh also called the wise men and the sorcerers; so the magicians of Egypt, they also did in like manner with their enchantments. For every man threw down his rod, and they became serpents, But Aaron's rod swallowed up their rods (Exodus 7:11-12).

Why did the enchantments of the magicians of Egypt produce serpents? No matter who people are, believers or non-believers, every word spoken, good or bad, produces life or death. We are creating or destroying all the time with every word that we speak. It's a law that God had set in motion. So even the evil Egyptian magicians could produce serpents, but Aaron's rod swallowed up all the little serpents of the Egyptian magicians. "*You are of God, little children, and have over-come them, because He who is in you is greater than he who is in the world*" (1 John 4:4).

— Where Is He? —

As the Holy Spirit was teaching me about the special rod I had been given, He taught me at the same time how to use it. Just like He did with Moses and Aaron, He will do for us. He wants us to understand how to use our weapons of warfare. He wants us to be victorious. I would like to share a testimony, in order to stir faith, about what happened to me while the Holy Spirit was teaching me how to use this special rod. There are more healing testimonies later on in the book.

One day I went to visit a hospital to encourage and pray for people dying from HIV/AIDS. When I arrived there, I asked the nurse how the patients were doing that day. He looked at me and said, "Sister Becky, they are not doing well. Two men are going to die within a few hours. You need to pray with them." I knew that what he said to me was just a religious response to a difficult situation, but that didn't matter. I received it as an assignment from the Lord.

So, I walked into the room where these two men were dying. They were lying in separate beds, side by side; there were no family members, just me and an unseen visitor (the Holy Spirit).

I walked over to the first bed where a man was lying in a coma, unable to move or to respond to anyone. While I was standing next to him, I looked directly into his eyes that were fixed on the ceiling. I calmly told him that I was a Christian and that I believed in healing. I read the redemptive passages from Isaiah 53:4-5 to the man. I looked him in the eye and asked him if I could pray for him. I saw his left eye twitch. I told him that I saw his eye twitch and that I was going to take that as a "yes!" I laid my hands on his head and rebuked premature death, HIV/AIDS, and everything that was attacking his body in the name of Jesus. I commanded the Spirit of Life back into his body. Immediately, the man sat up and started saying, "I'm healed! I know I'm healed!" He jumped up out of bed, speaking a mile a minute, telling me that he was a Christian, but had not been walking right with Jesus. He kept repeating that he was healed and that he was going to go home, and he left the room.

I walked over to minister to the other man lying in his bed; even though his physical body was in a coma, his spirit was not. And I know that his spirit had seen and heard what had just taken place. He had witnessed a miracle; his spirit was already primed to wake up. As I was ministering to this second man, the nurse walked back into the room. He looked at me and said with panic in his voice, "Where is he?" I looked up at the nurse and told him that I had prayed for him and that he had gotten up out of bed and left the room. The nurse said, "What?" and ran out of the room to look for him. A little while later, the man walked back into the room. I told him that the nurse had been looking for him, and he said to me, "I know. He found me in the cafeteria eating. I was so hungry!" The man continued to talk to me and told me that he was going to go back to his home. I never saw that man again in that place.

Our God is able and willing to do above and beyond that which we can possibly think or imagine. By the way, the second man I ministered to woke up out of the coma and was breathing normally. I led him in a prayer of repentance, and he received Jesus Christ as his Lord and Savior. This man was about to enter into hell, but I woke him up just in time to receive Jesus.

I had discovered that God had given me a special rod, and He was training me how to use it. Put God's Word into action and watch it happen! *Dare to believe!*

In the next chapter we are going to learn how to activate the creative, explosive power of God in our lives so that we can walk in divine healings and miracles on a daily basis.

REVIEW QUESTIONS

1. What is our special rod?

2. Who releases our special rod?

3. How do we cast our special rod before the enemy and his attack against our lives?

4. Give an example.

CHAPTER 7

POWER FROM ON HIGH

IN ORDER TO WALK in the realm of the miraculous, we need to align ourselves
with the Holy Spirit. As we learned earlier, the Holy Spirit is the creative,
explosive power of God. The miraculous is His realm. The Holy Spirit lives and
resides within the spirits of every believer in Jesus Christ. When we are baptized
in the Holy Spirit, we give Him permission to manifest His power in our lives.
It's like lighting a match. That match stick already had the sulfur to produce fire,
but someone needed to strike it so that the fire-producing power can be released.
It's a very simple example of what happens when we are baptized in the Holy
Spirit and His creative, explosive power is released in us.

The baptism of the Holy Spirit is a very powerful spiritual weapon that God
has given to us to overcome the attack of the enemy. I believe this is why satan
has caused such division within the Body of Christ about it. But regardless of the
division, His Word is truth. It's very dangerous to tell God what we will and will
not believe from His Word. Thus, it is important that we study the baptism of
the Holy Spirit from the Scriptures.

— Scriptural Proof for the Baptism of the Spirit —

First, it needs to be clearly understood that the baptism of the Holy Spirit is
for the believer in Jesus Christ only. It says in Luke 5: 37-38,

And no man putteth new wine into old bottles; else the new wine will burst the bottles, and be spilled, and the bottles shall perish. But new wine must be put into new bottles; and both are preserved (KJV).

We are dealing with the creative, explosive power of God; the same power that created the Earth and everything good within it; the same power that raised Christ from the dead (see Rom. 8:11). Such power would literally destroy an un-regenerated spirit or the spirit of someone who has not been born-again in Jesus Christ. We do not play around with the things of God. But as powerful as the Holy Spirit is, His baptism is for any believer in Jesus Christ.

> *But you shall receive power when the Holy Spirit has come upon you; and you shall be witnesses to Me in Jerusalem, and in all Judea and Samaria, and to the end of the earth (Acts 1:8).*

It says that we shall receive power when the Holy Spirit comes upon us. When we are baptized in the Holy Spirit, His power is released in us so that it can be released out of us to others. This power is to be used to minister to others in the realm of the supernatural with signs and wonders following. This supernatural power of the Holy Spirit also equips us to walk in overwhelming victory. We as Christians do not need to live defeated lives. The creative, explosive power of the Holy Spirit is waiting to be released through us.

> *Likewise the Spirit also helps in our weaknesses. For we do not know what we should pray for as we ought, but the Spirit Himself makes intercession for us with groaning which cannot be uttered. Now He who searches the hearts knows what the mind of the Spirit is, because He makes intercession for the saints according to the will of God (Romans 8:26-27).*

Not only has God given us the supernatural power of the Holy Spirit to walk in the miraculous, but He has also given to us His supernatural language to speak things into existence by praying in tongues the perfect will of the Father for every situation. We do not always know how to pray for people and situations, but the Holy Spirit within us does. With the empowerment of the baptism of the Holy

Spirit, we can pray in the Spirit or in tongues and intercede with power on the behalf of others and ourselves.

About tongues, the apostle Paul wrote, *"He who speaks in a tongue edifies himself, but he who prophesies edifies the Church"* (1 Cor. 14:4). When we pray in tongues, it edifies and builds us up. This is a very important tool that needs to be taught to the whole Body of Christ. Imagine how a spirit of depression would flee from the Church!

When we pray in tongues we are promised that we will pray with supernatural power as a mighty rushing river. When we pray in the Spirit, the power of the living water "Jesus Christ" flows from our very beings. And that same Spirit that raised Christ from the dead is releasing the power of the Holy Spirit into every situation.

> *"He who believes in Me, as the Scripture has said, out of his heart will flow rivers of living water." But this He spoke concerning the Spirit, whom those believing in Him would receive; for the Holy Spirit was not yet given, because Jesus was not yet glorified* (John 7:38-39).

The Baptism of the Holy Spirit is for anyone who has received Jesus Christ as their Lord and Savior. This is what the apostle Peter preached immediately following the initial outpouring of the Holy Spirit at Pentecost.

> *Then Peter said to them, "Repent, and let every one of you be baptized in the name of Jesus Christ for the remission of sins; and you shall receive the gift of the Holy Spirit. For the promise is to you and to your children, and to all who are afar off, as many as the Lord our God will call"* (Acts 2:38-39).

Some people say that the Baptism of the Holy Spirit is no longer for today, but this passage in Acts 2 is scriptural proof that it is for today. It says that the promise is to us and to our children and to all who are afar off, meaning this is our inheritance for generations to come.

The evidence that someone has received the baptism of the Holy Spirit is that they will start to speak in tongues. We see this throughout the New Testament:

> And when Paul had laid hands on them, the Holy Spirit came upon them, and they spoke with tongues and prophesied (Acts 19:6).

> And they were all filled with the Holy Spirit and began to speak with other tongues, as the Spirit gave them utterance (Acts 2:4).

Some people find the idea of tongues intimidating. But we do not need to be afraid because we are speaking to God and not to other people. Paul called it "speaking mysteries":

> For he who speaks in a tongue does not speak to men but to God, for no one understand him; however, in the spirit he speaks mysteries (1 Corinthians 14:2).

It is the Father who gives the Holy Spirit to those who ask of Him, and He always gives us good gifts.

> If a son asks for bread from any father among you, will he give him a stone? Or if he asks for a fish, will he give him a serpent instead of a fish? Or if he asks for an egg, will he offer him a scorpion? If you then, being evil, know how to give good gifts to our children, how much more will your Heavenly Father give the Holy Spirit to those who ask Him? (Luke 11:11-13)

We see in the Scriptures that the baptism of the Holy Spirit is for the believer in Jesus Christ only. The purpose of the Baptism of the Holy Spirit is to empower us with His supernatural power to be a witness with signs and wonders following, and we too will receive the benefits of this supernatural power to walk victorious lives. Along with His supernatural power, He has given us a special language to be used to pray the perfect will of the father in every situation, to intercede effectively, and to edify ourselves. The Baptism of the Holy Spirit is part of our inheritance promised to us by Jesus Christ for us and our future generations. The Heavenly Father will give the Holy Spirit to those who ask Him for it.

— Prayer for the Baptism —

Before we pray, here are some instructions. Read through them and then pray through the prayer below.

- Lay your hand on your heart or your forehead.

- Ask the Father for the Baptism of the Holy Spirit in the name of Jesus.

- Expect to speak in other tongues.

- You receive by faith, but just like anything else, you need to put your faith into action. After praying for the baptism, open up your mouth and allow the utterance that is stirring around on the inside of you to come forth. In other words, give voice to what is stirring on the inside of you. The Holy Spirit will not force Himself upon you. You need to cooperate with Him. It's easy, but very powerful.

Dear Heavenly Father,

I am a believer in Jesus Christ, and I ask you in His name for the Baptism of the Holy Spirit, with the evidence of speaking in tongues. I believe and receive from You.

In Jesus' name, amen.

Now open up your mouth, start moving your tongue, and give voice to what is starting to stir in your heart. It won't be anything you recognize. But do not be afraid; just cooperate with the Holy Spirit. In time you will start to learn the importance and the power in this type of prayer.

— The Power of Praying in Tongues —

One night, in the year 2000, at our children's home in Guatemala, something happened that forever solidified in me the importance of praying in tongues. My husband was in the States at the time, and our son, Aaron, and I were home with all of the children. One of the boys from the streets, Victor, had a problem with drug addiction and demonic possession. I do not know what he had done that night, but I think he had taken some type of drug or chemical.

It was nighttime, and the electricity went out; we could literally feel a very evil presence in the atmosphere. Suddenly, something became seriously wrong with Victor. We started to lose him; he was barely breathing, and then I could not tell if he was breathing at all. I took my authority over the situation in the name of Jesus, and I commanded his spirit to start calling out the name of Jesus. Within a minute or two, I could see his tongue starting to move, and we could hear him saying under his breath, "Jesus, Jesus, Jesus…" Then the electricity came back on.

I looked the boy in the eye, and I could see with the discerning of spirits (see 1 Cor 12:10) that he was under the influence of demonic spirits. I knew we were in for another battle. I asked another boy in the home, Antonio, to read Scriptures over Victor while Aaron and I went to tend to the other boys in the home, who were filled with fear at what they had seen and heard taking place.

The electricity went out again. Victor started screaming and going wild and wrapped himself up in a blanket trying to hide and escape from the situation. I ran into the room and started to rebuke the demonic spirit. I asked, "In Jesus' name, who are you?" Immediately, I started to hear many voices talking at the same time, but they were not inside the room or inside the house. They were outside of the house, actually surrounding the house. It sounded like thousands of voices talking at once.

Suddenly, our son, Aaron, who also walks in the gift of discerning of spirits, ran into the room and shouted, "Mom, they (the demonic spirits) are surrounding the house! They are looking in the windows. Some are flying, and others are dragging chains around the house!" As he said this, he also handed me the cell phone. Somehow he had been able to dial his grandfather's home in Minnesota, where his dad, my husband, was staying for a week, and he left a message on the answering machine.

It was all happening so fast. Aaron and I were with Victor, and we both started to tremble with fear. We were now battling head on with the spirit of fear. I was trying with all my might to speak a message to Aaron, but could not speak. We were literally in the spirit realm. I kept trying and finally spoke the following words out to Aaron, who was sitting in a chair right next to me; "Aaron, pray in tongues!"

We both started to pray in tongues and fight what was coming against us. Victor was screaming and was out of control. The cell phone started ringing in my hand, and I could hear my husband, David, calling out my name. His father, who was not a Christian at the time, heard the message on the answering machine and woke David up and told him he needed to hear this message immediately! His father was panicking in Minnesota, standing next to David as David was calling out my name on the phone. David was trying to be calm for the sake of his father, who had no understanding of such things, and he was trying to figure out just who was surrounding our house!

So there I was exercising my authority over an extreme situation, and all I could do was pray in the Spirit or in tongues. David kept asking me to give him an explanation as to what was going on, and I was able to get the following words out, "David, I cannot talk right now!" I continued to pray in tongues, which he could hear, along with Victor screaming in the background and who knows what else he could hear over that phone.

As Aaron and I continued to pray in tongues, all of a sudden the presence of the Holy Spirit overshadowed us and the present situation, and both of us started to laugh at the same time. We laughed so hard that we both had to hold onto our stomachs because they hurt so bad from laughing so hard, and tears were streaming down our faces. As we continued to laugh uncontrollably, all the demonic spirits, starting fleeing as fast as they could! By the power of the Holy Spirit, we laughed in the face of fear and called his bluff. And it was over.

We fought a very difficult battle for Victor. In the midst of the battle, we pulled out our most powerful weapon that Jesus had promised to give us before

He ascended into Heaven, the power of the Holy Spirit (see Acts 1:8). And we overcame the enemy by the blood of the Lamb and by the word of our testimony (see Rev. 2:11).

We have studied about and prayed for the baptism of the Holy Spirit. Our faith was stirred as I shared a personal testimony of the power of the baptism of the Holy Spirit with the evidence of praying in tongues. In the next chapter, we are going to make our way through the crowd and touch the very heart of Jesus.

REVIEW QUESTIONS

1. With whom do we need to align ourselves in order to walk in the realm of the miraculous?

2. Who is the Holy Spirit?

3. According to Acts 1:8, what shall we receive when the Holy Spirit comes upon us?

4. We do not always know how to pray, but when we pray in tongues, what does the Holy Spirit pray through us?

5. What does praying in tongues do for the one praying?

6. Acts 2:38-39 says that the promised Holy Spirit is for *who*?

7. What is the evidence that someone has received the baptism of the Holy Spirit?

8. According to Luke 11:11-13, how does a believer in Jesus Christ receive the Holy Spirit?

CHAPTER 8

A SPECIAL TOUCH

THIS TEACHING IS BASED on one of my favorite women in the Bible. She isn't remembered because she did some valiant act of faith, but because of a special touch.

> *Now a woman, having a flow of blood for twelve years, who had spent all her livelihood on physicians and could not be healed by any, came from behind and touched the boarder of His garment. And immediately her flow of blood stopped. And Jesus said, "Who touched Me?" When all denied it, Peter and those with him said, "Mater, the multitudes throng You and press You, and You say, "Who touched Me?" But Jesus said, "Somebody touched Me, for I perceived power going out from Me." Now when the woman saw that she was not hidden she came trembling; and falling down before Him, she declared to Him the reason she had touched Him and how she was healed immediately. And He said to her, "Daughter, be of good cheer, your faith has made you well. Go in peace" (Luke 8:43-48).*

She had lost everything, including her hope. But somehow she had heard about a man who could heal the sick, and her hope was revived. This woman was dying and she knew it. She was in a desperate situation. This woman was sick and weak. She had been slowly bleeding to death for the past 12 years. Something was seriously wrong with this woman, and the medical profession did not know of a cure for this illness.

She mustered up all the strength she had left and made her way to the man who could heal. There was a large crowd of people, and they were a bit out of hand. As Jesus made His way through the crowd, the people were pulling and jumping on Him. There were so many people with such desperate needs, and they all wanted what He had. How was this weak and dying woman ever going to make her way through this crowd?

With great determination, this desperate woman pushed her way through, and then she saw Him. I believe that at first this woman was like all the rest and wanted what she heard Jesus had to offer—healing. But on her journey to see the Great Healer, something marvelous happened within her. I believe that as she bowed or knelt down in the midst of that chaotic crowd of people and touched the hem of His garment, as the healing power flowed into her body, an even greater miracle took place within her spirit.

Everybody was touching Jesus at that moment. They were out of control and jumping all over Him. They all wanted what He had to offer—healing. That's why Peter and the others responded the way they did when Jesus asked, "Who touched Me?" They were looking at things in the natural realm.

> And Jesus said, "Who touched Me?" when all denied it, Peter and those with him said, "Master, the multitudes throng You and press You, and You say, "Who touched Me?" But Jesus said, "Somebody touched Me, for I perceived power going out from Me" (Luke 8:45-46).

Several years ago I taught this message at a small village church in Guatemala. David and I had just finished teaching that afternoon at a home gathering in a nearby town. Right after we were done ministering at this meeting, we had to rush to make it to the next meeting. We would take turns teaching each week; this particular week it was my turn to teach. I had planned on teaching what I had just taught at the other meeting. But as I walked into that crowded little church, making my way up to the pulpit, for we had arrived just in time for me to stand and teach, I knew in my spirit that God was changing the message that I had planned to teach. He only gave me the following Scriptures as I reached the pulpit—Luke 8:43-48.

I greeted the people and started to read the account of the woman with the issue of blood. As I read the words from verse 45, *"Who touched Me?"* I heard and felt the Holy Spirit whisper in my ear, "touched," and knew exactly what He wanted to say to me and to the people.

There were many people touching Jesus because they wanted what they heard He had to offer—healing. And He wanted to give it to them, as well. Jesus was moved with compassion for the lost people. But I believe something happened within the spirit of this woman as she touched the hem of His garment. In order for her to touch the hem of His garment, she had to bow low or kneel. She had to humble herself, and as she bowed low she came into the realm of His presence.

When we come into the habitation of His manifested presence, something wonderful happens. We touch Him, we touch His presence, and we become united with His presence. *"But he who is joined to the Lord is one spirit with Him"* (1 Cor. 6:17). When we are in the habitation of His manifested presence, we see Him as He really is. And His true love, mercy, and compassion overtake us. In His presence, He heals us from the inside out.

This is what happened to this woman. She came first to be healed. This was it! Either she was going to be healed and live, or she was going to die. She knew it. But she didn't realize all that was going to take place when she touched the hem of His garment. I wonder if we ever really know all that is going to happen as we come into His presence.

I believe that as she touched the hem of His garment, she came into the very presence of His being, and she no longer saw Him as the Great Healer, but as the Messiah. She reached out and touched Him for who He was and no longer for what He had. She touched the very center of His Spirit, and not for what was in His hand. She received the revelation of who He was and saw that He was the only one who could save her, deliver her, and, yes, heal her.

When we are in dire need of healing, we must make our way into the habitation of His manifested presence, into the realm of His glory, and allow Him to do what only He can do—heal us from the inside first. Then what we have need of physically will manifest.

Ever wonder what drew people to Jesus? In the next chapter, we are going to look at the faith principals that guided the life of Jesus, so that we can learn from His example how to live a life of faith.

REVIEW QUESTIONS

1. What happened when the woman with the issue of blood touched the hem of His garment?

2. What happens when we touch Jesus in this manner?

CHAPTER 9

FAITH PRINCIPALS IN JESUS' LIFE

L ET'S TAKE A LOOK at Jesus' life and see what faith principals were guiding His life and ministry. In Luke 4:1-13, we read how Jesus was filled with the Holy Spirit and led by the Spirit into the wilderness, where He was tempted by the devil for 40 days. Jesus fasted for 40 days. Then He was able to overcome every temptation that the enemy tempted Him with by standing firm in His faith in the Word and quoting the Scriptures.

What are the faith principals that we can observe about Jesus in these Scriptures? What gave Him the ability to overcome all temptations of the enemy? Let's look at the individual verses in one of these passages to discover the faith principles guiding Jesus' life.

> *Then Jesus being filled with the Holy Spirit, returned from the Jordan and was led by the Spirit into the wilderness (Luke 4:1).*

— Faith Principles: —

+ Jesus was filled with the Holy Spirit.

+ Jesus was led by the Spirit.

In order for us to walk in the realm of healing and miracles, we to need to be filled with the Holy Spirit, and we need to learn to be led of the Holy Spirit. Healing and miracles are accomplished by the power of the Holy Spirit. The Holy Spirit is the creative, explosive power of God. Just like Jesus, we need the Holy Spirit activated and operating in our lives.

> *Being tempted for 40 days by the devil. And in those days He ate nothing, and afterward, when they had ended, He was hungry* (Luke 4:2).

— Faith Principal: —

+ Jesus fasted.

Fasting is a very powerful weapon in the spirit realm. When we fast and pray, we deny our fleshly desires and become very sensitive to the leading of the Holy Spirit. We need to learn to discipline our flesh, to put our flesh under submission to the Holy Spirit.

> *And the devil said to Him, "If You are the Son of God, command this stone to become bread." But Jesus answered him, saying, "It is written, "Man shall not live by bread alone, but by every word of God." Then the devil, taking Him up on a high mountain, showed Him all the kingdoms of the world in a moment of time. And the devil said to Him, "All this authority I will give You, and their glory: for this has been delivered to me, and I give it to whomever I wish. "Therefore, if You will worship before me, all will be Yours." And Jesus answered and said to him, "Get behind Me, satan! For it is written, "You shall worship the Lord your God, and Him only you shall serve." Then he brought Him to Jerusalem, set Him on the pinnacle of the temple, and said to Him, "If You are the son of God, throw Yourself down from here. "For it is written: "He shall give His angels charge over you, to keep you," "and, "In their hands they*

shall bear you up, lest you dash your foot against a stone." And Jesus answered and said to him, "It has been said, "You shall not tempt the Lord your God" (Luke 4:3-12).

— Faith Principals: —

+ He knew who He was (the Power of Authority).

+ He had studied the Scriptures before the trial came (the Power of the Word).

+ He responded with the Word and the Word only (the Power of the spoken Word).

+ He didn't just speak the Word; He lived the Word (the Power of Faith in Action).

Jesus was physically tired, and the enemy was playing on His physical weakness, just like he does with us. But because Jesus had a lifestyle of studying and living out the Scriptures, was filled with the Holy Spirit, and was led by the Spirit, when He was being tempted by the devil, He was able to stand firm and not compromise in His faith. He overcame every temptation by the Word of God. We too can develop a lifestyle centered on the Word of God, be filled with the Holy Spirit, and learn to be led by the Spirit in order to overcome in every situation.

After this difficult time of testing and proving in the wilderness, Jesus was released into the ministry in the power of the Spirit (see Luke 4:14). I believe that, before we are released into the ministry, we will be led by the Spirit into the wilderness, and satan will be allowed to tempt us to see if the Word is truly hidden in our hearts and if we are ready for the ministry. So when we find ourselves in the wilderness, we must keep our eyes fixed on Jesus and live by His example; then we too will overcome every temptation.

Now that we've seen what was the guiding force behind Jesus' faith-filled life, let's examine further in the next chapter how He applied faith principals to minister healing to the sick.

REVIEW QUESTIONS

1. What two faith principals guided the life of Jesus?

2. What two things do we need in order to walk in the realm of healing and miracles?

3. Why was Jesus able to stand firm and not compromise in His faith when He was being tempted in the wilderness by satan for 40 days?

CHAPTER 10

FAITH PRINCIPALS FOR HEALINGS AND MIRACLES

WE'VE LEARNED WHAT the guiding force was behind Jesus' faith-filled life. Now let's look at how He applied those faith principles to minister healing to the sick. To do this, we are going to go through the Book of Luke searching for one thing—*how did Jesus heal the sick?* There are 18 examples in Luke of Jesus ministering healing and deliverance. We are going to focus on the common faith principals that Jesus used consistently while ministering healing to the sick so that we can learn from His example. I believe God has these faith principals recorded for our benefit to equip us to go out and do as He did.

You will need your Bible for this study. First read the passages listed below, and then ask yourself, "What faith principals did Jesus use to heal and deliver the sick?" Faith principals are acts of faith that Jesus used when confronted with the pain and suffering of those around Him. Look also at how those being ministered to responded.

Before we jump into the passages from Luke, let's look at this list of 10 faith principals that are important for us to learn and activate in our lives. These are taken from the healing examples found in Luke, but it's helpful to outline them first before we discuss the individual passages.

— Faith Principals —

1. *The Power of the Word of God*

What is so powerful about the Word of God? Why can we be fully confident in its promises to us? The answer lies in *whose* word it is. It is the Word of the Lord. He is the reason behind the power of the Word. He is the great I AM (see Rev. 1:18). He's the way, the truth, and the life (see John 14:6). He's the Spirit of Truth (see John 16:13). He is not a man that He should lie (see Num. 23:19). He is the same yesterday, today, and forever (see Heb. 13:8). He is love (see 1 John 4:8). He's the Healer (see 1 Pet. 2:24). He's the Word of God in the flesh (see John 1:14), and it was signed, sealed, and delivered by the shedding of His Blood (see John 19:30). The Word of God is more than just mere words recorded on paper; it's a powerful blood covenant between Father God and us (see Heb. 13:20), and it's eternal (see 1 Pet. 1:25).

2. *The Power of Authority*

The power of authority goes hand-in-hand with the power of the Word. Jesus Christ is the Word of God in the flesh (see John 1:14). All authority was given to Him (see Matt. 28:18), and He gave us authority over all the power of satan and his wicked works (see Luke 10:19). Greater is Jesus Christ who is in us, than satan who is in the world (see 1 John 4:4). As Jesus is, so are we in this world (see 1 John 4:17).

3. *The Power of the Spoken Word*

Words have the power to create and to destroy. There is the power of life and death in the tongue (see Prov. 18:21), and we are to call those things that are not as though they already are (see Rom. 4:17).

4. *The Power of Faith in Action*

It's easy to say that we have faith, but it's when we put that faith into action that we truly believe. The Word teaches us that we are to be doers of the Word and not hearers only (see James 1:22).

5. *The Power of Faith*

Faith is not based upon feelings; it's what we stand upon when there are no feelings or when what we need to do doesn't make any sense. Rather, we do it because we know it's right. Faith is an actual substance; it's a real force. It will hold and sustain us. Faith itself in God and His Word is all the evidence that we need for our miracles to come to pass (see Heb. 11:1).

6. *The Power of the Healing Anointing*

There are moments in time when the presence of the Holy Spirit overtakes the natural realm, and many miracles and healings start manifesting all around and very quickly. Usually this is the case during healing crusades, after the Word of God has been taught concerning faith and healing. We can create an atmosphere that actually invites His holy presence onto the scene. As the Body of Christ is learning to cooperate and operate with the Holy Spirit, the power of His healing anointing is being released all around the world. Everyday believers with a passion for Him are doing great and mighty wonders in His name (see Luke 4:18-19).

7. *The Power of Praise*

We can create an atmosphere with the power of our words of praise and worship to the Lord that is actually desirable to the Holy Spirit. The power of true worship is irresistible to Him, and He inhabits or dwells in the presence of the praises of His people (see Ps. 22:3). This doesn't have anything to do with talent or technology, but has everything to do with the intentions of the heart. He knows when we are truly in love with Him and when we are really grateful for what He has done (see John 4:23).

8. *The Power of Agreement*

There is such a strong power released when two or more are in agreement that Jesus said that we can ask for anything according to the Word of God and the Father will give it to us. *Anything!* (See Matthew 18:19.)

9. The Power of Persistence

Persistence is necessary when pursuing the promises of God because the enemy is going to try to stop us from attaining them. We are not to be weak in the faith and faint or to give up at the obstacles that stand in our way. We are to be strong in the faith, take a firm grip on the promises of God, put our faith into action, and stand firm until our healing manifests (see Luke 18:1).

10. The Power of Compassion, Mercy, and Love

Faith is activated in the realm of compassion, mercy, and love. Everything Jesus did was from a pure heart of compassion, mercy, and love for the people. In order to walk in the realm of the miraculous, we need to have His heart of compassion, mercy, and love for people. These same characteristics need to be operating in our lives (see Matt. 9:36).

Now, that we understand what I mean by faith principals, let's look at the Scriptures listed below and find out what faith principals were activated in each situation.

— Luke 4:31-37: Unclean Spirit Cast Out —

Jesus went to Capernaum and was teaching the people the Word of God with such authority that the people were astonished with His words. One Sabbath a demon-possessed man cried out in the synagogue, and Jesus rebuked him and commanded the demonic spirits out of him. They obeyed Jesus' command, and the man was set free. The people were so amazed that they said amongst themselves, *"What a word this is! For with authority and power He commands the unclean spirits, and they come out"* (Luke 4:36).

Faith Principals:

+ The Power of the Word of God
+ The Power of Authority
+ The Power of the Spoken Word

— Luke 4:38-39: Peter's Mother-in-Law Healed —

Peter's mother-in-law was sick with a high fever, and Peter asked Jesus to heal her. Jesus stood over her and rebuked the fever. She was instantly healed, rose from her bed, and served them.

Faith Principals:

*   The Power of the Spoken Word
*   The Power of Faith in Action

— Luke 4:40-41: Many Healed on the Sabbath —

As the sun was setting one Sabbath, all those who had sick loved ones brought them to Jesus. He laid his hands on every one of them, and they were all healed and delivered.

Faith Principals:

*   The Power of Faith in Action

— Luke 5:12-16: Jesus Cleanses a Leper —

One day a leprous man saw Jesus and fell down at His feet, begging Him to heal him. He said to Jesus, *"Lord, if You are willing, You can make me clean"* (Luke 5:12). Jesus reached out and touched the leprous man, and He said to him, *"I am willing; be cleansed"* (Luke 5:13). The man was instantly healed.

Faith Principals:

*   The Power of Faith in Action
*   The Power of the Spoken Word

— Luke 5:17-26: Paralytic Forgiven and Healed —

One day Jesus was teaching, and the power of the Lord was present to heal. Some men brought a paralytic man on his bed, but there were so many people that they were unable to make their way to where Jesus was. However, they were persistent and lowered their friend down through the roof into the midst before Jesus. He saw their faith and said to the man, *"Man, your sins are forgiven you"* (Luke 5:20). The scribes and the Pharisees began to accuse Him of blasphemy. Jesus perceived their thoughts and dealt with their religious thoughts. And to prove to the scribes and Pharisees that He had the power to forgive sins, He said to the man; *"I say to you, arise, take up your bed, and go to your house"* (Luke 5:24). The man was immediately healed and left glorifying God.

Faith Principals:

+ The Power of the Word of God
+ The Power of the Healing Anointing
+ The Power of Agreement
+ The Power of Persistence
+ The Power of Faith
+ The Power of the Spoken Word
+ The Power of Faith in Action

— Luke 6:6-11: The Man with a Withered Hand —

Jesus was teaching again on the Sabbath in the temple, and there was a man with a withered hand. The scribes and Pharisees were watching closely, knowing what He would do, in hopes to accuse Him of breaking the Sabbath laws. Jesus knew what they were thinking, so He confronted their evil thoughts. Then He said to the man with the withered hand, *"Stretch out your hand"* (Luke 6:10). He did, and he was instantly healed.

Faith Principals:

+ The Power of the Word of God
+ The Power of the Spoken Word
+ The Power of Faith in Action

— Luke 6:17-19: A Great Multitude Healed —

The multitude of people came to hear Jesus and to be healed of their diseases, and others came to be delivered of demonic spirits. The whole multitude sought to touch Him because the healing power of the Lord was present, and He healed all of them.

Faith Principals:

+ The Power of the Word of God
+ The Power of the Healing Anointing
+ The Power of Authority
+ The Power of Faith in Action

— Luke 7:1-10: Centurion's Servant Healed —

A centurion sent word and presented his need to Jesus. Jesus began to make His way to his home. The centurion recognized Jesus' authority and responded with great faith. He sent word and said to Him, "*...But say the word, and my servant will be healed*" (Luke 7:7). His servant was instantly healed because there is no distance in the spirit realm.

Faith Principals:

+ The Power of Faith
+ The Power of the Spoken Word

+ The Power of Faith in Action

— Luke 7:11-17: Widow's Son Resurrected —

The day after the encounter with the centurion, Jesus made His way to the city of Nain. As he entered the city, He met a funeral procession. A widow's only son had died. Jesus was moved with compassion. He touched the coffin and said, *"Young man, I say to you, arise"* (Luke 7:14). The man sat up, began to speak, and was presented to his mother.

Faith Principals:

+ The Power of Compassion, Mercy, and Love
+ The Power of Authority
+ The Power of Faith in Action
+ The Power of the Spoken Word

— Luke 8:26-39: Demon-Possessed Man Healed —

Jesus met a man who was possessed with a legion of demons, who was naked and lived in the tombs. Jesus rebuked the demons, and they cried out to Him, begging that He would not send them into the abyss, but into a heard of swine. Jesus did so, and the possessed swine ran down the steep hill into the lake and drowned. The man was instantly set free, and the townspeople found him sitting at the feet of Jesus, clothed and in his right mind.

Faith Principals:

+ The Power of Authority
+ The Power of the Spoken Word
+ The Power of Praise

— Luke 8:40-42,49-56: Jairus' Daughter Raised —

Jairus fell down at the feet of Jesus and begged Him to come to his home to heal his only daughter, who was dying. Jesus started to make His way through the crowd, but was delayed by a woman who had an issue of blood. In that time, Jairus received a report that his daughter was dead. Jesus was not moved by the report and encouraged Jairus not to be afraid, but to believe and she would be healed. When they arrived at Jairus' home, Jesus permitted no one else to come into the house with Him except for Peter, James, and John and the girl's parents, and he made the mourners or the doubter's leave. Then He took the hand of the dead girl and told her to arise. She immediately came back to life and rose up from her death bed.

Faith Principals:

+ The Power of Faith
+ The Power of Authority
+ The Power of Faith in Action
+ The Power of the Spoken Word

— Luke 8:43-48: Bleeding Woman Healed —

A woman who had had an issue of blood for 12 years made her way through the crowd toward Jesus and said, "If I but touch the hem of His garment, I will be made whole." She came from behind Him, touched the hem of His garment, and was immediately healed. Jesus felt the healing power flow from Him, stopped, and asked, "Who touched me?" The woman stepped forward and admitted to what she had done, and Jesus turned to her and said, *"Daughter...your faith has made you well..."*

Faith Principals:

+ The Power of Faith

+ The Power of Faith in Action

— Luke 9: 37-42: A Boy Healed —

A man from the multitude cried out to Jesus, imploring Him to help his child. His son was demon possessed. He had asked the disciples to cast it out, but they could not. Jesus rebuked the disciples. As the man was still coming toward Jesus, the demon threw the boy on the ground and convulsed him. Jesus rebuked the demon, healed the child, and gave him back to his father.

Faith Principals:

+ The Power of Faith in Action
+ The Power of Authority
+ The Power of the Spoken Word

— Luke 13:10-17: Woman Healed of Infirmity —

Jesus was teaching in the synagogue on the Sabbath. There was a woman present who had a spirit of infirmity for 18 years; she was bent over and could not raise herself up. When Jesus saw her, He said, *"Woman, you are loosed from your infirmity"* (Luke 13:12). And He laid His hands on her, and she was instantly healed and glorified God. The ruler of the synagogue was indignant that Jesus had healed her on the Sabbath, but Jesus rebuked his hypocritical spirit. The multitude rejoiced for all He had done.

Faith Principals:

+ The Power of the Word of God
+ The Power of the Spoken Word
+ The Power of Faith in Action
+ The Power of Praise

— Luke 14:1-6: Man with Dropsy Healed —

Jesus went to the house of one of the rulers of the Pharisees to eat bread on the Sabbath. There was a man with dropsy. Jesus questioned the lawyers and the Pharisees about their religious laws and asked them if it was lawful to heal on the Sabbath. But they kept silent. Jesus took the man, healed him, and let him go.

Faith Principal:

+ The Power of Faith in Action

— Luke 17:11-19: Ten Lepers Cleansed —

Jesus met ten leprous men, and they cried out from a distance, *"Jesus, Master, have mercy on us"* (Luke 17:13). He said to them, *"Go, show yourselves to the priests"* (Luke 17:14). And as they went their way, they were healed. When one of the men saw that he was healed, he returned to Jesus and glorified Him with a loud voice. Jesus asked him where the other nine were, and said to him, *"Arise, go your way. Your faith has made you well"* (Luke 17:19).

Faith Principals:

+ The Power of the Spoken Word
+ The Power of Faith in Action
+ The Power of Praise
+ The Power of Faith

— Luke 18:35-43: Blind Man Receives His Sight —

A blind man was begging on the side of the road. He heard that Jesus was passing by, so he started calling out to Jesus to have mercy on him. He was told to be quiet, but he was persistent and cried out all the more, *"Son of David, have mercy on me"* (Luke 18:39). Jesus stopped and asked him, *"What do you want*

Me to do for you?" (Luke 18:40). The man said that he wanted to see. Jesus said to him, *"Receive your sight; your faith has made you well"* (Luke 18:42). He was healed immediately, and he followed Jesus and gave glory to the Lord. All the people who witnessed his healing gave praise to God.

Faith Principals:

+ The Power of Faith in Action
+ The Power of the Spoken Word
+ The Power of Faith
+ The Power of Praise

— Luke 22:50-51: Healing of Servant's Ear —

While Jesus was being betrayed and arrested in the Garden of Gethsemane, one of the disciples struck the servant of the high priest with the sword and cut off his ear. Jesus, even in the midst of His greatest trial, was moved by compassion, touched the man's ear, and healed him.

Faith Principals:

+ The Power of Compassion, Mercy, and Love
+ The Power of Faith in Action

As we see, Jesus never begged or pleaded with the Father that the sick be healed and delivered. He understood and walked in the Power of His Authority. He activated the Power of the Word and the Power of the Spoken Word. He used the Power of Faith and put the Power of Faith into Action. Even in the end, He activated the Power of Compassion, Mercy, and Love, which released the Power of the Healing Anointing. Those who received healing activated the Power of Agreement and the Power of Persistence. They put the Power of Faith into Action, and they glorified God with the Power of Praise.

My prayer is that we would all be encouraged to *dare to believe* that His Word is for us today. In the next chapter I am going to share one of the most powerful healings that I have ever been a part of. It's a very personal testimony. It's about our adopted son, Marcos, and how we raised him from the dead and believed for the recreation of severely damaged and dead organs inside his body. All things are possible if we *dare to believe!*

REVIEW QUESTIONS

1. What is so powerful about the Word of God?

2. Describe the Power of Authority?

3. What do spoken words have the power to do?

4. What power does the tongue possess?

5. How are we to call or speak things into existence?

6. If you truly believe the Word of God, what will you do with your faith?

7. Do feelings have anything to do with faith?

8. What is the only evidence that you need that your miracle will come to pass?

9. Whose power is behind the Healing Anointing?

10. What is happening all around the world with believers who have a passion for Him?

11. The Power of Praise doesn't have anything to do with talent or technology, but has everything to do with *what?*

12. There is such a strong power released when two or more are in agreement that Jesus said we can *what?*

13. What is necessary when pursuing the promises of God?

14. Everything Jesus did was from what type of heart?

15. In order for us to walk in the miraculous, what type of heart do we need to have?

CHAPTER 11

MARCOS

My husband, David, and I have been missionaries since 1994. One of our life assignments was to start a children's home in Guatemala, where we take in children of all ages who have been orphaned, abandoned, or abused. But this children's home isn't an ordinary children's home; it is a miracle center. This testimony is about one of those miracles that God brought into our lives.

Let's start at the beginning. There was a Guatemalan woman who was in a very desperate situation. She was single and had several children and did not have enough money to make ends meet. Yet she was about to give birth to another child. She did not know how to read or write; she washed clothes in the river and made tortillas for a living. Feeling desperate, she tried to abort her baby two times and failed. She then went to the hospital to have an abortion. Desperate people do desperate things, and they do not count the cost, the consequences, that others will pay for their wrong decisions. A Christian nurse in the hospital heard about her situation and talked to this woman. She told her that is a sin to have an abortion and that it was better to give the child to someone else to raise him. With the encouragement of this godly nurse, the woman made a quality decision, and that was how this precious child came to us. He was a beautiful, tiny, Guatemalan, baby boy. We named him Marcos.

Before I continue on with his story, I want to share with you a very important part of the story that happened two years prior to this time. During a time of extended fasting, the Lord had instructed me to start studying healing and nothing else at that time. He said that it was time for this part of my calling to begin. I read and studied and even fasted and prayed about what the Bible said concerning healing, along with reading the writings of other Christian healing evangelists and their life stories. The Lord had given me this assignment, and I took it very seriously. I'm so grateful that I was obedient. Only He knew what the future would hold for us and what was about to take place in our lives with Marcos.

During the first month of Marcos' life, he was normal and healthy in every way, but things were about to suddenly change for the worse. I remember working in the kitchen and watching my husband holding Marcos and playing ever so gently with him. That evening, I had fed Marcos his bottle, burped him, and changed him, and he fell asleep in my arms. It was now time for dinner, so I quietly laid him down on our bed and went to eat dinner. I was only gone for about 15 minutes at the most and went back to check on Marcos. When I entered the room, I looked at him and saw that he was barely breathing. I called my husband immediately to come to the room. He entered the room, and I said to him, "David, something is wrong with Marcos!" He took one look at him, grabbed him, and within a matter of three minutes, he headed out the door to the hospital.

These things I have spoken to you, that in Me you may have peace.
In the world you will have tribulation; but be of good cheer, I have
overcome the world (John 16:33).

At the children's home we had 18 children, and four of them were babies. I could not leave the children unattended, so I had to stay home. We lived in a village about 35 minutes outside of Guatemala City. Back then, we had no running water, the electricity was not the best, and we did not have a telephone line to our home. I had no idea which direction David had gone or what was happening with Marcos either.

I immediately called the other children in our home to pray for Marcos. They prayed the best they knew how, and then I went into our bedroom to pray alone. I prayed in the Holy Spirit or in tongues for a long time.

> *Likewise the Spirit also helps in our weaknesses. For we do not know what we should pray for as we ought, but the spirit Himself makes intercession for us with groaning which cannot be uttered. Now He who searches the hearts knows what the mind of the Sprit is, because He makes intercession for the saints according to the will for God. And we know that all things work together for good to those who love God, to those who are the called according to His purpose* (Romans 8:26-28).

I had no communication with David. All I knew to do was to pray in the Spirit, and I had prayed for several hours this way. All of a sudden, the Spirit of the Lord spoke to me in an audible voice, and He called me by my name. As the Bible says, *"My sheep hear My voice, and I know them, and they follow Me"* (John 10:27).

He said; "Becky, you need to come against the spirit of death over Marcos right now."

I did not question Him; I just did what He said to do. I said, "I rebuke the spirit of death over Marcos right now, and I release the Spirit of Life to flow into his body now in Jesus' name."

Then the Lord spoke to me again audibly and said, "Now, you need to speak to Marcos' spirit directly."

I don't remember anyone ever teaching me this, but I did not question it at all, and I heard myself say, "Marcos, I know that in the physical realm there is a distance between us, but in the spirit realm there is no distance. Marcos, I need you to start breathing on your own right now, in Jesus' name. Breathe! Breathe! Breathe!"

As it says in the Scripture, *"He sent His word and healed them, and delivered them from their destructions"* (Ps. 107:20).

I still hadn't heard anything from David. I just continued to pray and wait, but I now had a peace that surpasses all understanding. *"And the peace of God, which surpasses all understanding, will guard your hearts and minds through Christ Jesus"* (Phil. 4:7).

— Faith Principal: The Power of Faith —

+ I was already filled with the Word of God concerning healing.

+ There was great power being released from praying in tongues.

+ I had developed the ability to hear the voice of the Lord through relationship with Him.

+ I was obedient to do what He told me to do.

My husband returned to the house late that night, and the volunteer from the home who had gone with him to the hospital returned home to watch the children so that I could go with my husband to where Marcos was. I did not know what had happened with David, and he did not know what had happened with me either.

As we were driving down the road, David began to tell me what had taken place. He had decided to take Marcos to a hospital in the nearby town. Marcos' body was blue, and he was not breathing. (We were fighting against time; within four minutes the body starts to die without oxygen.) The first hospital he went to did not even have oxygen! Guatemala is a "developing nation," and they do not have all of the modern conveniences that the more modern nations have. The man at the hospital looked at Marcos and said, "Poor baby." My husband said sternly; "Tell me, where is there a hospital that has oxygen!" The man directed him to another private hospital a few blocks away. Maybe they could help.

At the second hospital, when the doctor saw Marcos, she grabbed him out of David's arms and ran. They put him in a small, make-shift oxygen tent and then worked and worked on Marcos, but it was too late. Finally, Marcos' blood and parts of his lungs came up through his nose and he was gone. The doctor looked at David and said she was sorry, but there was nothing else they could do for him. He was gone.

(Once while I was sharing this testimony, a Chinese doctor in the crowd came to me afterward in amazement at what he had just heard. He explained to me what medically had happened to Marcos. Because he went without oxygen for so long, his heart was pumping dry, and it caused great pressure within and made him burst or explode from within. He said, medically speaking, that it was impossible to resuscitate him in the natural.)

As they stood around him, overwhelmed with grief and in shock over all that had just taken place, something miraculous happened. Marcos, while lying in his blood and pieces of his lungs, having been pronounced dead, suddenly took a deep breath and came back to life! This happened at the same time that the Lord spoke to me in an audible voice, giving me instruction on how to raise Marcos from the dead, while I was praying in tongues in our bedroom and Marcos was lying in a hospital bed miles away.

> *But if the Spirit of Him who raised Jesus from the dead dwells in you, He who raised Christ from the dead will also give life to your mortal bodies through His Spirit who dwells in you* (Romans 8:11).

I wished the story had ended there, but we were about to face one of the toughest spiritual battles of our lives.

Marcos' story is a powerful testimony of faith in action. It's a testimony that defies the natural realm of understanding. It's about two ordinary people who chose to trust God and His Word regardless of the circumstances. The circumstances surrounding us were hopeless and impossible, but we serve the God of the impossible who gives hope to the hopeless.

And these signs will follow those who believe: In My name they will cast out demons; they will speak with new tongues; they will take up serpents; and if they drink anything deadly, it will by no means hurt them, they will lay hands on the sick, and they will recover (Mark 16:17-18).

Marcos was alive, but struggling. He had gone too long without oxygen. They diagnosed him with SIDS (Sudden Infant Death Syndrome). Because he had gone without oxygen for so long and then died, his organs were severely damaged. They did not know why, but moving him would cause him to have a severe convulsion, and he would die.

The little Guatemalan hospital where he was did all that they knew to do, but they were limited in knowledge and in resources, so we made the decision to hire an ambulance and have him transferred to Guatemala City, to the best and most expensive hospital in the city. The ambulance was nothing more than a form of transportation. We had Marcos lying on a pillow on top of a stretcher, with the ambulance worker holding onto a large tank of oxygen giving Marcos oxygen. I sat next to Marcos praying, with one of the older boys from the children's home, Antonio, in the back of the ambulance with me for support while David followed us in the car to Guatemala City.

When we arrived in the ambulance and Marcos was transferred to the Emergency Room, he again stopped breathing. I was there watching through the open curtain, and I spoke out and said, "No! In Jesus' name, you will live! You will not die! You will fulfill your destiny in Jesus' name!" And he started to breathe again. The doctors at this hospital are very well educated and trained. They ran many tests, but could not figure out what was happening. They had no hope for him and tried to convince us to let him die. We said, "No! We are Christians, and we believe in healing." Within 36 hours, the bill for this hospital was $6,000 USD, and we needed to find another hospital that we could afford.

One doctor who was working with Marcos understood our problem and offered us a solution. He not only worked at this hospital, but was also the head doctor of the Pediatric Intensive Care Ward in the main public hospital in

Guatemala City. He told us that he knew what we thought of the Guatemalan hospitals, but he promised us that he would make sure that Marcos was well attended to. So we took another ambulance ride. There were four nurses and a doctor in the ambulance with us to take a 20 minute ride from one hospital to the other. Again, when we arrived and Marcos was transferred to the Emergency Ward, he stopped breathing. I was standing there watching and praying through the open curtain. And I again said, "No! In Jesus' name, you will live! You will not die! You will fulfill your destiny in Jesus' name." He started to breathe again. He was then transferred upstairs to the Pediatric Intensive Care Ward.

David and I were allowed to see him twice a day, in the morning and in the afternoon. Every morning we would receive a medical report from the doctor. The first morning we received the following report. Because he had been without oxygen for so long and had died, his heart had been so severely damaged that he would not survive. We replied, "We are Christians, and we believe in healing. We cannot receive that report! We do not believe that God raised him from the dead so that he would die a few days later from heart failure. No!" And we laid our hands on his little body and commanded a new heart to be recreated and to function properly in Jesus' name.

The next morning the doctor showed us the heart monitor and said he didn't understand why, but Marcos' heart was now functioning normally. We had a new heart that was functioning perfectly! But because he had been without oxygen for so long and had died, his lungs were so severely damaged that he would never survive. We again replied, "We are Christians, and we believe in healing. We cannot receive that report! We do not believe that the Lord would raise him from the dead and heal his heart so that he would die a few days later from lung damage. No!" And we laid our hands on his little body and commanded new lungs to be recreated and to function properly in Jesus' name.

Several days passed, and the doctor told us that his lungs were doing well and that they were going to start to remove the tube that was connected to the respirator. It took a few days to remove, and the big test was to see if he would start breathing on his own. In the meantime, we continued to speak words full of life over Marcos. We called those things that were not as those they were (see Rom.

4:17). We told him that he was going to walk, jump, run, talk, sing, and play in Jesus' name. We always told him that he would live, that he would not die, and that he would fulfill his destiny in Jesus' name.

> As it is written, ("I have made you a father of many nations") in the presence of Him whom he believed—God, who gives life to the dead and calls those things which do not exist as thought they did (Romans 4:17).

After a few days of the doctors slowly removing the respirator tube, Marcos was breathing by himself! He had a new set of lungs that functioned perfectly! But now we faced another battle. The medical report that day was that because he went without oxygen for so long and died, his kidneys had been so severely damaged that he would never survive. His little body was so swollen, and he was now drowning in his own fluids and being poisoned by them as well.

> Now faith is the substance of things hoped for, the evidence of things not seen (Hebrews 11:1).

Our reply to this negative report was, "We are Christians, and we believe in healing. We cannot receive this report! We do not believe that God would raise him from the dead and give him a new heart and new lungs so that he would die of kidney failure a few days later. No!" And we laid our hands on his little body and rebuked the spirit of death and released the Spirit of Life and commanded new kidneys to be recreated and to function properly in Jesus' name.

The next morning, when we arrived to the hospital, the nurses came running out of the Intensive Care Ward toward us crying, but they weren't tears of sorrow, but of joy! They were so excited and told us that Marcos had been urinating like a faucet all night long! We had a new set of kidneys that functioned perfectly!

— Faith Principals: —

1. *The Power of Agreement*

+ We were unified in this battle.

2. *The Power of Faith in Action*

+ No matter what people thought, we laid our hands on him and released the power of the Holy Spirit; we spoke the Word over him.

3. *The Power of the Spoken Word*

+ We renounced every negative report

+ We spoke those things that were not as though they were.

+ We spoke words of life, recreation of body parts, and a hope for a good future.

+ We asked people of like faith to join their faith with ours for a miracle.

+ We did not report every negative detail, just what people needed to know.

+ We gave them specific prayer requests. "We need a new heart, new lungs, new kidneys that function perfectly."

In the Intensive Care Ward were many young children and babies who were in very critical condition. I remember one day, the doctor was instructing the other parents to stop crying over their little ones and to start doing what we were doing and speak positive things over their children. Even though they did not understand us, they saw that what we were doing was working.

> *Let your light so shine before men, that they may see your good works and glorify your Father in heaven* (Matthew 5:16).

When we take a strong position in the faith, many people will criticize us. During our fight for Marcos' life, they criticized us because they did not understand. But, if we will hold our ground and remain faithful and refuse to give up, regardless of the circumstances, we will see that very thing we desire from God come to pass. I often tell people, when it comes to faith, that we have to become stubborn like a mule—unmovable, unshakable—and regardless of what the situation looks like, we speak the Word of God into the situation.

Every day we would have to go to the basement of the hospital and go pay money to someone in an office for oxygen, medicine, and for whatever Marcos had need of, but to get to this office, we would have to pass by the mortuary. We were so unmovable in our faith that we would stop in front of the mortuary doors and point to them and speak to them! We would say, "No! You can't have him! He's not passing through your doors in Jesus' name!"

> *Death and life are in the power of the tongue, and they that love it*
> *shall eat the fruit thereof* (Proverbs 18:21).

The Nuns were always after us to baptize him, because they were afraid he was going to die. We said, "No! You may not touch him. He is not going to die in Jesus' name!"

I'm sharing with you what really happened so that you may be encouraged and dare to believe and trust God and His Word for your miracle. If you desire to live and to be healed, then you cannot be planning for a funeral just in case this faith thing doesn't work! If you are planning a funeral, then you're not standing in faith for a miracle. You are preparing for death, and that is what will happen, because that is where you are acting out your faith.

— Faith Principals: —

1. The Power of Persistence

+ We refused to give up.

2. The Power of the Spoken Word

+ We rebuked every negative word spoken over him.
+ We spoke what we needed into existence.

3. The Power of Faith in Action

+ We laid our hands on him and released the healing power of the Holy Spirit.

4. The Power of Authority

+ We rebuked the power of satan working against his life.

During this whole time, Marcos was on three different types of sedatives to prevent him from having convulsions. He was in a medically-induced comma state. He was unresponsive; he did not move, and he looked dead. But we continued to speak those things that were not as though they were. We spoke and sang words full and overflowing with life over him. We refused to be moved by our five senses and human reasoning. We chose to fix our eyes on the redemptive work of Jesus Christ.

> *Therefore take up the whole armor of God that you may be able to withstand in the evil day, and having done all, to stand* (Ephesians 6:13).

— Faith Principals: —

1. The Power of Faith

A few weeks into all of this, we were on our way to visit Marcos when our doctor called us on my husband's cell phone. I did not know what was being said, but I could tell that it was something serious. They had been slowly taking Marcos off of the three sedatives to prevent convulsions and had been testing him for brain activity. The bad report was that there was no activity in his brain, meaning he was brain dead. I heard my husband say to the doctor on the phone, "I do not believe that God raised him from the dead, gave him a new heart, new lungs, and new kidneys so that he would lie in a bed as a vegetable for the rest of his life. Run the tests again!"

We held each other's hands and rebuked the spirit of death that was fighting against him, and we commanded in the name of Jesus for a new brain to be rec-reated and to function perfectly in Jesus' name. We didn't say one word to each other. We got out of the car and walked toward the hospital. When we arrived at the hospital doors, the phone rang again, and it was our doctor.

He said he did not understand what was happening. Earlier that morning when they ran tests on his brain, there was no brain activity. He ran the tests again, just because we were friends; there was no other reason to do so. But now there was activity in his brain! We had a new brain! Hallelujah! David told him that we were at the hospital and that we would be up in two minutes. And we gave thanks to our God for what He had done for Marcos and for us!

— Faith Principals: —

1. *The Power of Persistence*

+ We were determined not to give up.

2. *The Power of Agreement*

+ We were united in this battle together.

3. *The Power of the Spoken Word*

+ We spoke what we needed into existence.

Marcos had been moved out of the Intensive Care Ward down to Interme-diate Care and then down to General Care. He now weighed a little over four pounds. You could see every bone in his cranial. He was so tiny and was now two months old.

We were tired; we had fought a very difficult battle. Remember, we were living in and running a children's home at the same time all of this was happening with Marcos. We had 18 children to tend to, and Marcos was one of those children. We would do what we had to do in the morning hours with all the children in the home. Then we would drive into the city to visit Marcos. Then we would return to the children's home. Then we would drive back into the city in the afternoon to be with Marcos again. Then we would return to the home again. The next day, we would start all over with the same routine. This battle was exhausting in every way, but we could not afford to let our guard down. The enemy (satan) was after his life, and we were standing in the gap for him.

David and I were in unity and were fighting for Marcos' life together. Regardless of how tired or worn down we felt, we did not allow one another to be weak in the faith or to speak faithless words over Marcos or the situation. We held each other up in the midst of the storm.

> *Two are better than one, because they have a good reward for their labor. For if they fall, one will lift up his companion. But woe to him who is alone when he falls, for he has no one to help him up. Again, if two lie down together, they will keep warm; but how can one be warm alone? Though one may be overpowered by another, two can withstand him. And a threefold cord is not quickly broken* (Ecclesiastes 4:9-12).

The long awaited day to bring Marcos home finally came. David had to go to another part of the hospital to sign the release forms. While he was doing that, I found an empty office and sat down with Marcos in my arms and was quietly thanking the Lord for Marcos' life and for all that God had done for him. *"Let the high praises of God be in their mouth, and a two-edged sword in their hand"* (Ps. 149:6).

Thinking the battle was over, I was starting to let my guard down when in walked a young doctor whom I had never seen before. I don't know how I knew it, but he had Marcos' file in his hand. He sat down at the desk, with the file covering his face, and never looked at me or acknowledged that I was in the room. Now generally speaking, it is customary in Guatemala to greet each other when you walk into a room, even if you do not know the people. This doctor did not greet me, but at that moment, I honestly did not care. I was just thankful for what God had done.

All of a sudden I heard this doctor say in an angry voice, "This baby will be blind!" At first, I felt confused and couldn't believe what I had just heard. I hesitated for a moment, and then I heard myself say to him, "Marcos is not blind, and he is not going to be blind in Jesus' name!" Then this doctor replied again, "This baby will be deaf!" I looked up at him hiding behind the file, and I said, "Marcos is not deaf. You can ask any mother on this floor. As soon as I walk in and greet the nurses, Marcos hears my voice and starts to cry. He is not deaf, and he is not going to be deaf in Jesus' name!" In a very nasty voice he said, "This baby will never talk!" I looked at him and I said, "Marcos has a voice, and he will learn to speak in Jesus' name!" And in a very strange voice he said, "He will never walk!" Now this mama was mad! I stood up with Marcos in my arms and I said, "He will walk in Jesus' name! And I'm taking my baby out of here now!" And I stormed out of that office, just fuming with disgust! I turned around and looked in the office, and there was no one in there! It was the devil himself trying one last time to plant a seed of doubt in my heart! *"You are of God, little children, and have overcome them, because He who is in you is greater than he who is in the world"* (1 John 4:4).

— Faith Principals: —

1. *The Power of Praise*

+ I thanked the Lord for what He had done for Marcos.

2. *The Power of Authority*

+ I didn't back down; I held my ground.

3. *The Power of the Spoken Word*

✦ I responded to every lie against Marcos with faith-filled words.

✦ And I sealed every response with the name of Jesus.

It's now the year 2011; nine years have passed since that very difficult time in our lives. Marcos walks, runs, jumps, and is strong and athletic. He is very coordinated, has great rhythm, and loves to dance. He hears and sees perfectly. He's bilingual (English and Spanish). *"For with God nothing will be impossible"* (Luke 1:37).

Since this time in our lives, we've been traveling the world sharing this powerful testimony of how great our God is and teaching others to *dare to believe!*

Marcos in the Hospital

I shall not die, but live, and declare the works of the Lord (Psalm 118:17).

— Letter from Marcos' Physician —

Juan Pablo Zaldana, M.D.

Guatemala, Guatemala

16 de marzo, 2011

Atendì a Marcos, el dìa 4 de agosto del 2002, a las 12:30 hrs, en el hospital Sanatoio El Pilar, quièn fuè referido de un hospital departamental de Los Aposentos, Chimaltenango, por haber presentado dificultad respiratoria y paro cardiorespiratorio de 5 minutos de duración. Marcos, fuè enviado a hospital El Pilar en muy malas condiciones generales, ya con 3 hrs del evento en el lugar departamental. Presentaba convulsiones tónico-clònicas generalizadas, dilatación pupilar (midriasis bilateral) sin respuesta a la luz. Fontanela tensa y llena, pulmones con sibilancias y estertores bilaterales. Se le inició medidas anti-edema cerebral, hipotermia, sin mejoría clínica, Por falta de recursos es enviado a hospital Estatal Roosevelt, en donde continùa con tratamiento y en ventilación mecánica por màs de 2 semanas, necesitando aminas vasoactivas.

Paciente presentò Necrosis tubular renal, en TAC cerebral con edema cerebral severo y hemorragia subaracnoidea severa.

Un electroencefalograma con actividad irritativa cortical difusa, de predominio frontal. Daño cerebral hipoxico isquémico severo.

El testimonio es que a base de la oración de todos y del tratamiento mèdico Marcos, salió intacto de toda la patología anterior, en este momento no necesita tratamientos para convulsiones. Por lo que creemos que es una intervención de Dios en la vida de Marcos y de todos los que estuvimos con èl.

Translated Letter from Marcos' Physician
(*with medical definitions added in italics*)

Juan Pablo Zaldana, M.D.

Guatemala City, Guatemala

March 16, 2011

I attended Marcos on August 4, 2002 at 12:30 PM in El Pilar Hospital, who had been transferred from a small private hospital in Los Aposentos, Chimaltenango, Guatemala. He was sent to El Pilar Hospital in very critical condition.

He was struggling to breathe, and went into cardiac arrest that lasted for five minutes upon arrival. Because his difficulties started three hours earlier, he presented general "tonico-clonicas" (*seizures*) His pupils were dilated without response to light; "bilateral mydriasis." His fontanela (soft spot) was tense and full[1] [*A tense or bulging fontanelle occurs when fluid builds up in the skull cavity or when pressure increases in the brain "increased intracranial pressure"].* He was wheezing and there was bilateral rattling in his lungs as well.[2] *[Wheezing and rattling sounds are abnormal breath sounds. Wheezing sounds are high-pitched sounds produced by narrowed airways, and rattling sounds in the lungs are believed to occur when air opens closed air spaces.]* We started Hypothermia Treatment as an anti-edema cerebral[3] *[induced moderate hypothermia initiated after severe traumatic brain injury (TBI) to reduce brain swelling]* without improvement.

Because the family lacked the financial resources, he was transported to the Roosevelt State Hospital, where I continued treatments.

He was put on an artificial respirator for more than two weeks, he needed vasoactive amines.[4] *[A substance containing amino groups, such as histamine or serotonin that acts on the blood vessels to alter their permeability or to cause vasodilation.]*

The patient presented tubular kidney necrosis,[5] *[Acute tubular necrosis (ATN) is caused by lack of oxygen to the kidney tissues (ischemia of the kidneys). The internal structures of the kidney, particularly the tissues of the kidney tubule, become damaged or destroyed. ATN is one of the most common structural changes that can lead to acute renal failure.]*

A CT Scan of the brain showed severe brain edema[6] *[swelling of the brain]* and severe subarachnoid hemorrhaging[7] *[A subarachnoid hemorrhage is an abnormal and very dangerous condition in which blood collects beneath the arachnoid mater, a membrane that covers the brain. This area, called the subarachnoid space, normally contains cerebrospinal fluid. The accumulation of blood in the subarachnoid space can lead to stroke, seizures, and other complications. Additionally, subarachnoid hemorrhages may cause permanent brain damage and a number of harmful biochemical events in the brain. A subarachnoid hemorrhage and the related problems are frequently fatal.]*

An electroencephalogram[8] *[a test to detect problems in the electrical activity of the brain]* showed irritated diffuse cortical activity from frontal predominance,[9] *[generalized whole brain volume loss]* and severe ischemic hypoxia brain damage[10] *[ischemic hypoxia— insufficient oxygen in tissues because of an inadequate blood supply].*

The testimony is that at the base of prayer from everyone and from the medical treatment, Marcos left intact from the previous pathology, and at this time doesn't need treatments for convulsions. We believe it is an intervention from God in the life of Marcos and from all of us who were with him.

Marcos, You Will Fulfill Your Destiny!

— Endnotes —

1. "Fontanelles – Bulging," *Medline Plus;* www.nlm.nih.gov/medlineplus/ency/article/003310.htm; accessed September 26, 2011.

2. "Breath Sounds," *Medline Plus;* www.nlm.nih.gov/medlineplus/ency/article/003323.htm; accessed September 26, 2011.

3. "Moderate hypothermia a safe treatment for traumatic brain injury in kids, Study," *Medical News Today;* www.medicalnewstoday.com/articles/23508.php; accessed September 26, 2011.

4. *American Heritage Medical Dictionary*, s.v. "vasoactive amine"; medical-dictionary.thefreedictionary.com/vasoactive+amine; accessed September 26, 2011.

5. "Acute Tubular Necrosis," *Medline Plus;* www.nlm.nih.gov/medlineplus/ency/article/000512.htm; accessed September 26, 2011.

6. *National Library of Medecine*, s.v. "cerebral edema"; dictionary.sensagent.com/cerebral+edema/en-en/; accessed September 26, 2011.

7. *Gale Encyclopedia of Medecine,* s.v. "subarachnoid hemorrhage"; medical-dictionary.thefreedictionary.com/subarachnoid+hemorrhage; accessed September 26, 2011.

8. "EEG," *Medline Plus;* www.nlm.nih.gov/medlineplus/ency/article/003931. htm; accessed September 26, 2011.

9. Mary Ann Liebert, Inc., "Diffuse Changes in Cortical Thickness in Pediatric Moderate-to-Severe Traumatic Brain Injury," *Journal of Neurotrauma* (Nov 25, 2008); www.ncbi.nlm.nih.gov/pmc/articles/PMC2747789; accessed September 26, 2011.

10. *McGraw-Hill Dictionary of Scientific and Technical Terms,* s.v. "ischemic hypoxia"; encyclopedia2.thefreedictionary.com/ischemic+hypoxia; accessed September 26, 2011.

CHAPTER 12

ANDRES

It was March 2001, David and I were caring for 12 children. Eleven were from the streets of Guatemala City, and the youngest was a baby boy who had been abandoned in a Guatemalan hospital. The baby had been teething and had not slept much that particular night—and neither had I. It was in the afternoon, and I was feeling exhausted. I asked the cleaning lady if she minded keeping an eye on the baby while I took a short nap, which was something I never did. She agreed, and I went to bed.

While I was sleeping, God gave me a dream. There was nothing angelic about this dream. I dreamt that a lady called me on the phone. She asked me how I was doing. I said I was just fine. She asked me what was new, and I told her that we were about to receive a family of five boys. Then I woke up with a joy within my spirit about receiving this family of boys. In the natural it was a crazy thought, because I had been feeling so tired from the night before.

Within five minutes, my husband David walked into our bedroom and said that the judge was on the phone and wanted to know if we would receive a family of boys. At first he had said no, but then thought he'd better run it by me and see what I thought. I was still kind of groggy when he came into the room and could hardly believe what I was hearing. I asked him how many boys were there, and he told me four boys. I looked at him and told him that I thought there were five. He looked at me and asked me what I was talking about. I quickly told him that I had just had a dream that we were receiving a family of five boys. He said he was going to tell the judge that we would take the boys. Within three hours a family of four very abused and severely neglected boys was standing at our door. The oldest was 9 years old, the second was 6 years old, the third was 18 months old, and the youngest was 6 weeks old.

Early that morning, the police had rescued them from a very abusive situation. The mother and grandmother were both alcoholics and were passed out on the floor and did not even know that the police had come and taken the children away. The police left a note. The oldest of the four boys had worked for a neighbor down the street. With the little money he made, he would purchase a bowl of cereal from a nearby food stand. He would give the 6-year-old brother the cereal to eat. The 18-month-old would drink the milk. And he would give the baby sugar water to drink, which is very common food for a baby among the poor people in Guatemala.

They were all very neglected and abused in every way. Not only were the mother and grandmother drunk all the time, but the uncles were too, and they mistreated these children as well.

Andres was the baby's name, and he was the sickest and weakest of all. Andres was very sick. The mother had been giving him alcohol and sugar water. His little body was full of scabies upon scabies. It took almost a year to rid him of these terrible things. But worse was the fact that he was addicted to alcohol, and we had to deal with alcohol withdrawals with him. His little body was literally screaming for alcohol. My husband and I took turns watching him during the nights. We had to force feed him baby formula with an eye dropper at first to keep it down in his system. We were both exhausted, but would do it all over again for him!

One month after the boys had been with us, I went to the courts to sign some paperwork for them. Before I signed, I was reading through the paperwork. I ran across another name of a child. I asked who he was, and they said that they had an older brother somewhere, and if they ever found him, they would send him to live with us as well. I immediately remembered the dream and thought to myself, *There are five boys!* I knew these boys had been sent to us by God.

I am going to jump ahead and give you some information about them. The oldest boy was found, and he did come to live with us, but ran back to a very abusive birthfather. The next two older boys ran back to their old situation too. These boys were so ingrained in their family's sinful system, and the abuse took its toll on them emotionally and spiritually, as well. Abuse was normal for them, and they equated it as love. I am confident that in time they will see the truth of what love is and isn't and that all that we seeded into them will come to pass. In the meantime, God brought the two youngest boys into our lives for many reasons. One reason was that we would become their adoptive parents. Now back to Andres' amazing testimony.

Andres had one physical challenge after another. He started having convulsions. Later we learned that this happened because, while he was in the womb, his birthmother drank so much alcohol that during the fourth through twelfth weeks of fetal development, the left and right sides of his brain did not completely form together. The tests showed black spaces between the two lobes. Because this had happened while he was in the womb, he was labeled with Fetal Alcohol Syndrome even though he did not have the facial features of a child born with FAS.

He was very delayed in his growth and abilities. Then he started to bang his head on the crib, spit, bite, scream, and tantrum for hours at a time. Mealtimes were extremely stressful for our large family, because as we would all try to sit and eat, he would scream at the top of his lungs, in his highchair, and refuse to eat. He only wanted to eat white things or things off the floor. He started spinning himself and his toys in circles non-stop. He did not learn to speak normally like our other toddler boys. He would say, "Mickey, Donald, Goofy," all day long. He could not look us in the eye. We brought him in for further tests, and they said he was autistic as well. They said that they could give him medication that would be more of a benefit for the mother than for him. We refused.

He was also born with one leg shorter than the other. He did learn to walk, but as he walked, he would have to swing his right leg around and wait to land on it, before he could take another step. As I said earlier, he was a child with many challenges, yet we loved him dearly!

In my journey to learn about physical healing, I would study and fast on the Word of God. I would journal everything I was learning and ask the Lord to reveal and teach me more concerning this. And He was very faithful and gracious to me. He wants us to understand His Word and learn how to apply it in our everyday lives. The children's home was the perfect place to learn to put into practice what His Word said concerning healing.

One morning while I was changing diapers on all our little ones, it was Andres' turn. I had finished changing his diaper and was massaging lotion into his legs when it dawned on me—I could minister healing to his short leg. That's exactly what I did. I straightened out his legs, held unto both his ankles and commanded, in the name of Jesus, the short leg to grow out and be even with the other one. Right in front of my eyes, our baby's leg grew out. I was so excited! I finished dressing him and stood him up on the floor, and he started walking as normally as could be. I called the older boys, who were studying with their teacher in the living room, to come and see Andres. I set him on the floor, and he started walking toward them. Everyone started applauding! It was exciting for the whole family to see.

Obviously, he had more serious issues than a short leg, but it was just the beginning of a long journey for us. His healing was a process, a progressive healing. It was not instant; it came little by little. But never-the-less, it was healing, it was miraculous, and it came from God.

As I mentioned earlier, as a toddler, he was developing some very aggressive behavior that was very different from the other children. He was starting to bang his head on his crib, spit, bite, and scream for hours at a time. This was very challenging and difficult to live with on a daily basis. There were days when David would come home and I would just be in tears.

One morning, while I was in the nursery with all the little ones, Andres was screaming away and becoming violent. In that moment the Lord spoke to me in a still, small voice, and I knew what to do. I took my authority in the name of Jesus, and I rebuked an autistic spirit within him. Immediately he stopped screaming and behaving violently and became quiet and peaceful. I picked him up and thanked the Lord. And we never had that problem again. He never screamed during mealtimes again, either.

Then we dealt with all of the other abnormal behaviors that went along with autism, one by one. We taught him to stop spinning himself and objects. We taught him to eat what was put before him. Yet he still could not look us in the eye or carry on a normal conversation.

Then one afternoon, while I was working in the kitchen, he walked into the kitchen and started a normal conversation with me and was looking into my eyes, too! He left the kitchen for a while to go play with the other little ones and then walked back into the kitchen and carried on the conversation where he had left off. It was a big day for him, to say the least! Praise the Lord! Every issue, one-by-one, was being healed.

Andres is a very a gifted little boy. He reads in English and in Spanish. His handwriting is beautiful. All he has to do is see a word once and he knows how to spell it. He just continues to grow and learn new things every day.

— Faith Principals: —

+ The Power of Authority
+ The Power of the Word
+ The Power of the Spoken Word
+ The Power of Faith in Action
+ The Power of Persistence

Andres is a Miracle Child!

CHAPTER 13

RICARDO

In 1998, David and I started taking boys from the streets of Guatemala into our home. We received a phone call from a fellow missionary about two young boys living on the streets. He wanted to know if we would take them. We prayed and knew we were to receive them. We drove down to the city and met the two energetic boys. The older one was 8 years old, and the younger one was 6 years old. The younger was named Ricardo, and this is his story.

Ricardo was a cute and quite, but very troubled little boy. He had been severely abused in every way. Before living on the streets, he lived with his very troubled and dysfunctional birthparents. When he was just a toddler, he saw his alcoholic, abusive birthfather try to burn his birthmother alive. Afterward, his birthfather was living on the streets with the older son.

Life was very brutal for little Ricardo, and it was about to get even worse. He was later abandoned by his birthmother on the street corner of a park in Guatemala City, where his older brother and alcoholic birthfather were living in a basement storage room below the park with many other street children and youth.

Considering the abuse from the alcoholic birthfather and the older street children, it's amazing that he survived. This helpless little boy was living in the midst of drugs, violence, and filth. His birthfather was in a drunken state all the time and was unable to care for him. At times Ricardo and his older brother would be locked up in a rented bar room for days at a time with no food or attention.

Now they were living with our family and were trying to figure out what it meant to live a normal and peaceful life. The daily struggles were tremendous, and our family was trying desperately to reach out to these boys with the love of God.

Ricardo would have horrible nightmares every night. We would find him screaming and clawing at the walls trying to escape from somewhere. He never would remember the terrifying dreams, but beyond all the hideous abuse and the nightmares, he had even worse problems. Six-year-old Ricardo was demon-possessed. The demonic spirits would throw this little boy into long fits of rage several times a day. It would take all the physical strength we had to get things under control and to prevent him from hurting himself and others.

During the afternoons, I would often hold him in my arms for hours at a time, sing to him, and rock him to sleep, knowing that this precious little boy needed to experience the love of a mother. Ricardo bonded with me before he did with David. He had a real hatred for his birthfather and took it out on David.

One morning I was home alone with Ricardo when all of a sudden he went into a demonic fit of rage. It lasted for a couple of hours. I was exhausted. He finally settled down, only to go into another rage that was even worse than the previous one. I had very little physical strength left. I just prayed in tongues.

Finally David returned home. He knew as soon as he walked in the house what was going on. He walked into the bedroom where we were, and we prayed in tongues together. The demonic spirit was outraged by our response, and it took both of us to hold this little boy down. We just continued to pray. I remember David was telling Ricardo that we loved him and that Jesus loved him. Ricardo covered his ears with his hands so that he wouldn't be able to hear. The situation became more and more intense. It's difficult to express in words, but all of a sudden a Gift of Faith (see 1 Cor. 12:9) came upon both David and me at the same time for Ricardo's deliverance. Our prayers became even more fervent, and we demanded that the demonic spirit release this precious child in the name of Jesus.

We were now in an even stronger and more difficult battle. But this was it; this was the moment that we had been praying and believing for. The situation was so intense and the demonic spirit was thrashing this boy all around, and he was screaming. All of a sudden, as we were holding him, I literally felt the demonic spirit with such a force come up from his belly out of his mouth, and as soon as it left him, Ricardo reached out his arms toward David and cried out, "Daddy!"

We burst into tears and were hugging one another, rejoicing over Ricardo's deliverance. Then we led him in a prayer of salvation, and he asked Jesus to come into his life to be his Lord and Savior.

— Faith Principals: —

+ The Power of Authority
+ The Power of Agreement
+ The Power of Faith in Action
+ The Power of the Spoken Word

That was 14 years ago. Ricardo has passed through years of many challenges, but he willingly gave it all over to the Lord and is free from hatred and unforgiveness. He is a godly, responsible young Christian man, and we are proud to have him as our son. For the sake of our children, let's *dare to believe!*

CHAPTER 14

SIPERONI

I HAVE HAD THE PRIVILEGE of ministering the healing power of the Holy Spirit to many people. It thrills my spirit to see people receive their miracle from the Lord. This testimony is about a young Maasai boy from Tanzania, Africa. Just mentioning his name brings me great joy.

David and I had finished teaching a three-day seminar about the power of the Holy Spirit in a very traditional Maasai Church. After the last service, a Maasai evangelist asked us if we could come to his village and pray for a child who could not walk. We agreed to go.

This young boy had been taken to witchdoctors who spoke their evil curses and chants over him, used their potions on him, and placed their trinkets on him, which opened him up to further demonic possession. Then he was taken to regular physicians, and they tried to treat a spiritual condition with physical means. In the end, he was worse off than before.

It was late into the evening by the time we arrived. As we drove into the village, we were met by a strong, evil, spiritual force. When we stepped out of the vehicle, we were surrounded by Maasai Warriors and others from the village. Many of the people were drunk, and everyone was curious to know who we were and what were we doing there. As we made our way through the people, we found 11-year-old Siperoni. This young boy could not walk upright. He crawled around on all fours and was not right in his spirit. Both David and I knew that we were dealing with a Nebuchadnezzar spirit (see Dan. 4).

As we sat outside of his family's hut, they brought the young boy to us. As soon as I touched him, the evil spirits manifested, and he began rolling all over the ground. The people in the village were standing around us, and a spirit of mockery was manifesting from a group of Maasai Warriors who were standing behind us.

I closed my eyes and asked the Holy Spirit what happened to this boy. What had caused him to be possessed? The Holy Spirit gave me a vision. I saw myself walking down a path through the fields to a wooden hut. This hut was nicer than the others in the area, and it had a wooden door that was locked. I saw my hand push the door open, and as I pushed the door open, I heard the Spirit of the Lord whisper to me, "The secret things." The door was wide open, and I saw this young boy wrapped completely in black cloth, and I knew in my spirit that he had been severely abused. As I saw these things, I was explaining what I was seeing to the boy with the help of an interpreter. I asked him if what I was seeing was true, and he stopped rolling on the ground to say, "Yes," and then continued to thrash around. I felt led in my spirit to get him out of this village, and my husband and the others confirmed this as well. We asked his mother if she would be willing to come back to the house that we were staying at, with Siperoni, so that we could minister to him the next day. She agreed.

The next morning, after breakfast, we started to minister to him. Several Maasai pastors came to visit us, and we asked them to pray in the Holy Spirit as we laid hands on him. All the pastors started to pray. There was another man there that was not praying, so I asked him to leave. When you're ministering deliverance and healing, you need to guard the spiritual atmosphere. Those who do not believe need to leave! So we joined our faith together and rebuked the evil spirits that were destroying and controlling him, and we commanded the recreation of his brain, spine, and nervous system. And we commanded anything else that had been damaged to be healed or recreated so that all the systems of his body would function together in harmony and he could walk.

We then put our faith into action and stood him up and commanded him to walk. He started to walk, but with great effort, and his body was jerking back and forth. We encouraged him in the faith and focused on the positive changes that were taking place. A few brothers were helping him to walk, and he was, but still with great effort. He grew very tired, so we sat him down in the chair to rest. He fell asleep for several hours.

I remember saying to our brothers that God would complete what He had started. We left to go minister somewhere else while he slept in a chair outside. After several hours had passed, we returned to the house. As we pulled into the driveway, I saw a young boy and asked everyone in the car, "Who is that? Is that Siperoni?" I immediately jumped out of the car and ran to him, and we both jumped up and down praising God! The others ran over to Siperoni, and we all rejoiced!

He shared with us that after we had ministered to him, he became very tired and slept for several hours. When he woke up, he stood up, and started walking normally! We were all filled with excitement and amazement that day. He not only walked, but was running, jumping, playing soccer, and having a wonderful time! The next day, he came with us to one of the public schools, helped us to hand out new shoes to the Maasai children, and testified what the Lord had done for him. Siperoni was contagious with the joy of Jesus!

The next day, a group of ladies from his village passed by the house on their way to a celebration. They decided to stop in and see Siperoni and his mother. They were astounded when they saw Siperoni. They were all crying and celebrating at the same time. They sent word to the village, and others from his village came to see him. They all agreed that this was truly the work of the hand of God! It was miraculous!

— Faith Principals: —

+ The Power of Authority
+ The Power of Agreement
+ The Power of the Spoken Word
+ The Power of Faith in Action

Our Maasai brother, the evangelist who had invited us to pray for Siperoni, said to us as we were leaving, "Look what the Lord has done through you, and now you are going to leave us."

We encouraged our brother that Siperoni's miracle was going to have a great impact on his very dark and lost village. After we left, another missionary went to the village and showed the *JESUS* film.[1] It was reported that 400-500 people showed up from surrounding villages because they had heard of Siperoni's healing and were saved! Praise Jesus! Signs and wonders point to Jesus; *dare to believe!*

Endnote —

1. *JESUS* film, *JESUS*, © 1979-2010, Inspirational Films, Inc. All rights reserved. The JESUS Film Project®, http://www.jesusfilm.org.

CHAPTER 15

OTHER HEALING TESTIMONIES

IN THIS CHAPTER I want to share a collection of divine healing and deliverance testimonies to encourage and strengthen our faith. I have included the faith principals that were put into action for each of these testimonies to help further cement these concepts into our spirits.

Once we hosted a group of college students who were visiting our ministry in Guatemala for a week. After we shared testimonies of our Lord's greatness, someone in the group made a comment that stuck in my heart. He said that it sounded as if miracles were happening in our lives all the time. He was right; they are, and they should be, because the creative, explosive power of God, the Holy Spirit, lives and resides within every believer. As we choose to reside in the habitat of His manifested presence, allow Him to teach us the Word of God concerning the redeeming power of the blood of Jesus, and activate that power by putting our faith into action, healings and miracles will start to manifest all around us.

Following is a list of the faith principals discussed earlier in Chapter 10:

— Faith Principals —

+ The Power of the Word of God

- The Power of Authority
- The Power of the Spoken Word
- The Power of Faith in Action
- The Power of Faith
- The Power of the Healing Anointing
- The Power of Praise
- The Power of Agreement
- The Power of Persistence
- The Power of Compassion, Mercy, and Love

And these signs will follow those who believe: In My name they will cast out demons; they will speak with new tongues; "they will take up serpents; and if they drink anything deadly, it will by no means hurt them; they will lay hands on the sick, and they will recover (Mark 16:17-18).

— Shouts of Joy —

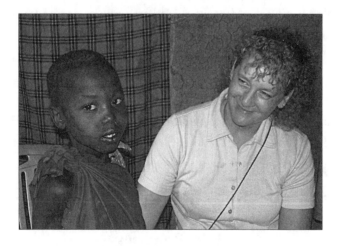

This little boy from Tanzania had been deaf since birth. I prayed over him, and he could hear instantly. Everyone present in that meeting, burst into shouts of joy for what the Lord had done!

Faith Principals:

- ✦ The Power of Faith
- ✦ The Power of Faith in Action
- ✦ The Power of Authority
- ✦ The Power of the Spoken Word
- ✦ The Power of the Word

— Tears of Joy —

One evening, while we were in Tanzania, a mother came with her 3-year-old daughter to where we were staying to ask us to pray for her little girl. When her little girl was a baby, she had been sick with malaria that had left her severely brain damaged. She was limp and motionless, and she could not stand or walk or even move. She could not hold her head up or even focus; her mouth hung open with a constant stream of drool. In the natural, the situation looked hopeless, but with

God all things are possible! After praying with her, I asked her mother to put her faith into action. I picked up the little girl and stood her up. I could feel her legs straighten out and the leg muscles strengthen, and she could stand up for the first time. The mother burst into tears of joy and received Jesus as her Lord and Savior. We encouraged her in how to continue believing for the completion of the miracle.

She started to walk back to her village, only to return about a half hour later to show us her daughter. The little girl was starting to take her first steps and walk! She was no longer limp or motionless; she could hold her head up and focus and could even respond to her mother! It was wonderful! We serve the God of the impossible and His name is Jesus!

Faith Principals:

- The Power of Authority
- The Power of Faith
- The Power of Faith in Action
- The Power of Agreement

— Gladys —

Several years ago, in a mining town in Tanzania, we were holding a three-day faith and healing conference. I taught three services a day and held a healing service in the evening. It was the last scheduled night of the meetings, and the expectancy was high. We praised and danced before the Lord together. I preached, and then we opened it up for ministry to the sick. Many people came forward to receive healing.

Our African brethren are a very lively group of people, and I love them for it! For some, it can be a little chaotic, but having lived and worked among so many children for so long, I've learned how to block out distractions, which helps me out in these situations.

I had assigned the team each a healing line to minister over, and we went to work. The worship team was singing their hearts out, and the people just kept on coming. That church building was packed out. Even all the chairs set up outside were full, and people were standing all over the place.

We had been ministering for quite a while when I noticed along one side of me that a group of pastors from the area was trying to minister deliverance to a demon-possessed woman named Gladys. This woman was known in the mining town to have been very dangerous. They dragged her to the meeting.

This poor tormented woman was thrashing all over the floor screaming. The pastors were trying to deliver this woman of demonic possession in the flesh. They were slapping and shouting and being very physical with her. I stopped what I was doing, walked over there, and told the pastors to stop what they were doing immediately! I told them that this was a spiritual matter and not a physical one. I knelt down and touched the woman, who began to scream, and the demons started speaking to me in Spanish! They do not speak in Spanish there. For whatever reason, the demonic spirits knew that I spoke Spanish. I rebuked them in the name of Jesus and told them to be silent! I cast them out of the woman, and the woman just laid there on the ground.

We were scheduled to be there for three days only, but ended up being there for one more service, the next morning. To my delight, when the choir marched up the aisle praising the Lord, Gladys was in her right mind, free from all demonic spirits, singing, and praising with the choir. She testified and gave God glory for her deliverance. This happened about seven years ago. To this day, she is free and praising Jesus!

Faith Principals:

- The Power of the Word
- The Power of the Healing Anointing
- The Power of Authority
- The Power of Faith
- The Power of Faith in Action
- The Power of Agreement

— Relieved and Grateful —

Right before I stood to minister in an outdoor campaign in Zambia, a young man made his way to the back of the platform, where we were sitting, to ask for prayer. He had suffered from a severe headache for seven months and could not find relief from the pain. I commanded his spine to be realigned and the pain and the swelling to cease in the name of Jesus, and I cursed any sickness or disease that had been attacking this body. Instantly, his headache was gone! This man was so grateful to God for his healing.

Faith Principals:

+ The Power of Faith
+ The Power of Authority
+ The Power of the Spoken Word
+ The Power of Faith in Action

— Stung Seven Times —

I prayed with a Guatemalan woman who had been stung seven times by a scorpion. Her tongue was swollen and paralyzed; her side and arm were in great pain, and she could hardly move them. After prayer, the intense pain was instantly gone, and that day everything returned to normal. We have been given authority over such things.

Faith Principals:

+ The Power of Faith
+ The Power of Authority
+ The Power of the Spoken Word
+ The Power of Faith in Action

— Healed and Unashamed —

In a village called Sonjo, Tanzania, where we held a conference, there was a teenage girl who had been deaf since birth. As I laid hands on her to pray, everyone was gathered around, including this girl's mother. This girl held her head down in shame and was uncooperative. I could literally sense unbelief around me. When I prayed with her, nothing happened, and I knew it was because of the unbelief that surrounded her. I spoke with the mother and asked her to come to the meeting the next day, and she said she would come. When it came time to lay hands on the sick, I came to this teenage deaf girl again. I looked at my friend, who was standing next to me, and told her to keep the mother busy. I took the young girl outside with me, where no one was watching. I stuck my fingers in her ears and rebuked the deaf spirit. Immediately, for the first time in her life, this young girl, who was so full of shame, could hear! Her smile said it all! The mother came outside, and I presented her daughter to her. The mother stood there in complete amazement at what the Lord had done for her daughter. He not only opened up her deaf ears, but he took away her shame, too.

I have learned through experience that there are times when we need to pray for a person alone. We need to create an atmosphere that is full of faith, because faith is a powerful force and so is doubt. Even Jesus kicked out the unbelievers when He raised Jairus' daughter from the dead in Luke 8:40-56.

Faith Principals:

+ The Power of the Word

+ The Power of Authority

+ The Power of Faith

+ The Power of Faith in Action

— Boneface Ng'ambi —

As David and I were traveling in an old, rented pickup truck from Chitipa to Karonga, Malawi, the driver would stop and pick up people along the way to earn extra money. The truck was so full of people and their wares that we could not even see who all was in the back. When we arrived at the bus stop in Karonga, we all started to get out of the truck. As I climbed out of the front of the truck, I was amazed at what I saw. The men in the back were all working together to lift this older gentleman, Boneface, out of the back of the pickup. It was a very difficult process because his left side was frozen, and he could not bend his leg and arm. He had suffered a stroke, which left him paralyzed on the left side. He and his daughter were on their way to see the witchdoctor in Karonga to ask for help. I asked to pray for him and he agreed. Within minutes, his arm and leg were loosed. I invited him to take a walk with Jesus. As we walked around the crowded bus stop, I started to witness to all those around about the goodness of our God. Glory to God, he walked out of the bus station on his own, praising Jesus!

Faith Principals: —

+ The Power of Compassion, Mercy, and Love

+ The Power of Faith
+ The Power of the Spoken Word
+ The Power of Faith in Action

— Angel —

One afternoon, in 2008, we received a family of nine children who were rescued from a drug house in Guatemala. All of the children had been severely abused and neglected, but there was one little boy in particular who had been neglected more than the rest, Angel. He was about 3 ½ years old, yet he weighed only 12 pounds and had been diagnosed with rickets. Rickets is a Vitamin D deficiency; the bones become very brittle and are easily broken. He could not stand, walk, or talk at all.

The first time I ever held this child was when the government brought them to our home. My heart was broken instantly with compassion, and the tears just flowed from my eyes when I lifted him out of the van. All I could feel were his sharp little bones. We prayed over him, we rebuked death and rickets, and we released life, healing, and creative miracles to flow into his tiny body. Within three months, he had gained over 20 pounds, was standing, walking, and running! He never broke one bone! And he quickly learned how to talk. We give God all the glory!

Faith Principals:

+ The Power of Compassion, Mercy, and Love
+ The Power of Authority
+ The Power of Agreement
+ The Power of Faith
+ The Power of Faith in Action

— His Mercy —

It was our last morning in Loliondo, Tanzania, and we were trying to pack up our things for the long trip back to Arusha, when a Maasai woman came to the home where we were staying. One of the brothers there asked if I could come out and pray for her. I asked her how I could help her, and she just gave me a blank stare. The others explained that she had been deaf and mute since birth. I motioned to her that I was going to pray for her. I stuck my fingers in her ears and rebuked a deaf and mute spirit and commanded her ears to be open. Within a second, she could hear! At first she was very frightened, but then her fear turned into joy. She was so excited that she ran back to her village!

I had a photo of her next to our computer and prayed for her throughout the year. When we returned to Loliondo, I asked a friend if she knew how this woman was doing. My friend told me that she was deaf again. I was so grieved in my spirit, and I knew that it had to be a spiritual problem with a deaf spirit and not a physical problem.

My heart hurt so much for this woman. I silently prayed and asked God to bring this woman back. On the last ministry day of the trip, we were traveling back to the house, and my friend quickly stopped the vehicle and said, "Becky, Look! Do you know who that is?" I was so astounded at God's goodness. I immediately rolled down the window, and she saw us and ran up to the window, motioning to me to pray for her. I stuck my fingers in her ears and rebuked the deaf and mute spirit that was attacking her. She could instantly hear once more! Then our Maasai brothers who were in the vehicle briefly told her that she could not be involved with witchcraft anymore and we drove away. I knew that if I had such a strong desire for this woman to be healed, our Heavenly Father must have desired for her to be healed even more.

Faith Principals:

+ The Power of Compassion, Mercy, and Love
+ The Power of Faith in Action

+ The Power of Authority

+ The Power of the Spoken Word

— Dana Borgschatz —

This young man was in a very serious car accident, and his knee had been seriously injured. He had had several operations already to try to repair the damage caused from the accident. Yet even after several surgeries, his knee would give out on him at anytime. He had about two years of surgery still to undergo to try to repair the damage from the car accident.

At the time, he was a college student from Minnesota and had signed up for a short term mission trip to come to Guatemala to volunteer with our mission, Vida Ilimitada (LIFE Unlimited) in Guatemala.

One morning I was teaching about faith and healing and sharing healing testimonies. After the teaching, Dana, along with a few other students, asked for prayer for healing. I ministered healing to him and asked him to put his faith into action. He immediately jumped up in the air and was instantly healed! In an instant, God had recreated this young man's knee! Glory to God!

When this group of college students returned to Minnesota, they testified in their home church about what the Lord had done. The word of their testimonies challenged the pastor, and later he called a group of his pastoral friends that he met with each month. He shared with them this testimony and how he felt that they needed to re-examine what they believed concerning healing, because there was no doubt that the Lord had healed Dana's knee.

A few months later, David and I were passing through Minnesota on our way to Africa, and we were meeting with friends who were committing themselves to pray for us while we were ministering in Africa. We received an e-mail from Dana explaining why he would not be able to attend the meeting. He said that since he was healed, he no longer needed to undergo two more years of surgeries, so he and his girlfriend were getting married! They would be on their honeymoon and hoped we would understand! God is good!

Dana's Story in His Own Words:

Toward the end of the week our hosts (David and Becky Dvorak) prayed for us for healing. Our hosts had noticed maturity in our team and that there was a need for healing physically, mentally, and spiritually. So I went up for healing of my knee that was injured in the severe car accident I was in on January 5, 2002. I began telling them that I had been through a lot already in the recovery from this accident and that God had brought me through it all. I told them that literally this knee was the last leg of my physical healing journey. You see, I had been consistently in and out of the Mayo Clinic ever since my injury, and the doctors there said that I would need to undergo arthroscopic surgery to repair the damage to my knee cap and ligaments.

So Becky had asked me if I believed that God could heal my knee, and I told them that God had started a great work in me, and I saw no reason why He wouldn't finish the great work He had started in me. I believed with all my heart that God would heal my knee. They then sat me down and began to pray over me. I began to close my eyes and they said, "Oh no, don't close your eyes; you're going to want to see this." I literally watched myself and felt myself be healed before my own eyes. When they finished praying over me, they said, "Well, you know your body better than we do, so do something you couldn't do before. Test it out." I tested out the knee playing soccer with the Guatemala boys, followed by a four mile cross country jog. I never would have even thought of playing soccer with my knee before, because it would have left my knee in one place and me in the other. The only thing holding me back in the jog was my wind. Wow! God is amazing!

Now confirmation of the miracle was to come with our return to Mayo Clinic for my pre-surgery consultation. Here they would take another look to make certain the decision that surgery was a must and would set the date, doctor, and time of surgery. However, when I sat up on that table, it didn't take them long to realize that surgery was no longer a concern for me. The expressions on their faces seem a bit baffled by it all. They had just told me a matter of weeks ago that surgery was just about a for sure thing. All they could say was, "Call it what you will, but unless something changes, I would no longer recommend surgery. There's just no need!"

God is amazing and He works in mysterious ways! Our Lord and Savior has no bounds, so open your heart and believe! You'll be amazed by the work He can do in you! **For the glory of our Lord and Savior, Jesus Christ!**

Faith Principals:

+ The Power of the Word
+ The Power of Authority
+ The Power of Faith
+ The Power of the Spoken Word
+ The Power of Faith in Action

— Stomach Cancer, Healed! —

Berta Yucute Pec is a wonderful sister in the Lord from Santiago, Guatemala. She had been suffering for eight long years and was finally diagnosed with cancer of the stomach. She dealt with great pain and could no longer eat. She weighed only 85 pounds. Her husband Romeo asked us to come and pray for her. David and I met with them one afternoon. We anointed her with oil and rebuked a spirit of death and the cancer in Jesus' name, and we released the Spirit of Life to flow through her body. We encouraged her in the faith and left her with some booklets about healing to study. Along with us, others were praying for her healing as well. With the support of many, Berta and her husband were strengthened in the faith to receive her healing from the Lord.

She was told by her doctor that her stomach was like melted plastic and that she needed to have surgery if she were to live. When she told him that she had been prayed over for healing, the doctor laughed at her and insisted that she have the surgery. They did not have the finances for surgery, but they had something much better; they had the Lord and His promise in the Word that she was healed. Now it was time for them to activate their faith and believe God for her miracle.

The Lord healed Berta, and she is free from cancer and pain, never having had surgery. Several years have gone by, and she can eat whatever she wants to eat and is strong and healthy! Our God is great! Berta and her husband and three children give glory to God for what He has done in their lives and pray for others for healing now as well. Berta says, "My healing is for the glory of the Lord!"

Faith Principals:

+ The Power of the Word
+ The Power of the Spoken Word
+ The Power of Faith
+ The Power of Faith in Action
+ The Power of Agreement

— Gloria —

Several years ago, after my husband and I and a team of young people were ministering in a church in Guatemala City, we invited anyone who needed healing to come forward. After we ministered to the people, the Lord highlighted to me a woman sitting in a wheelchair in the back of the church. The Lord told me to go and pray for her. As I made my way through the crowd to the back of the church, the woman was nowhere to be found. I finally found her outside by herself on the street. I went up to her and asked her if I could pray for her. She agreed. I asked her what she wanted, and she said that she wanted to walk.

This woman, Gloria, was 27 years old and had never walked before. When she was an infant, she had meningitis, and it left her paralyzed. Then she was operated on, and it made it even worse. She had been paralyzed from the waist down all of her life. As I laid my hand on her spine, I rebuked a spirit of paralysis and released the power of the Holy Spirit to flow through her spine. She immediately felt a warm sensation slowly moving down her spine. Her twisted, frozen joints were loosed, and her feet straightened out and were flat on the ground. She had feeling in her legs and could feel the ground beneath her feet. Movement and strength were restored as the power of the Holy Spirit continued to move slowly down her spine.

She started to stand up and sit down in her wheelchair. My husband and some of the team members assisted her in her first labored steps. I asked Gloria if she had family with her, and she said that her father was still inside the church. I sent someone to find him and the pastor so that they could witness what was taking place. God is amazing! God knew the desires of her heart, and He asked me to go and minister to her. I pray that this testimony will encourage us to go when He asks us to.

Faith Principals:

+ The Power of Compassion, Mercy, and Love
+ The Power of Faith

+ The Power of Authority
+ The Power of Faith in Action
+ The Power of the Spoken Word

— Joshua —

I was teaching in a Guatemalan Church from the Book of Joshua, and afterward, we prayed for people for healing. The day before we had been ministering in a church in Guatemala City and ministered to a woman named Gloria (the previous testimony). She had been paralyzed since she was a baby, and God did amazing things for her that day!

I had just finished teaching, and now it was time to pray for healing. One young mother came forward with her little 4-year-old boy who was in a stroller. This little boy had had meningitis when he was an infant, and it left him paralyzed. Like Gloria, he had never walked. His body was very twisted and distorted, and his legs were drawn up from the disease.

I prayed over the little boy and told the mama to put her faith into action. I picked up the sickly looking boy and stood him up. As soon as I did, I could literally feel his legs straighten out and his leg muscles strengthen under him. His feet were flat on the floor. I looked at this little boy in the eyes, and I asked him, "Do you want to go for a walk with Jesus?" As soon as I asked him this, he took a giant step forward! His mama started to cry, because he had never walked before. I held his hands, and we walked all around the church, giving thanks to Jesus! I later asked the mama what her little boy's name was. She replied, "Joshua!"

Faith Principals:

+ The Power of the Word
+ The Power of Faith
+ The Power of the Spoken Word
+ The Power of Faith in Action

— Frida Kogalo —

While we were ministering at an International Leadership Conference in Mbeya, Tanzania, a bishop and his wife from Ndola, Zambia, came to share a testimony with us in person. Three years earlier, when we were ministering in Ndola, Zambia, with this bishop, he had asked me to pray for his wife, who was suffering and dying of cancer. Instantly, after praying with her, all pain was gone. I told her that she would live and not die.

Four weeks later, she was scheduled for surgery, but before they operated, the bishop and his wife told the doctor that she had received prayer for healing. The doctor said that he did not believe in such things, but he said that if he did not find any cancer during the operation, he would not charge them for the operation, because he was sure that he would find the cancer. They agreed to have the surgery, but there was no cancer to be found.

This woman is full of life and sings for joy because her Lord has healed her from cancer! Several years later, she stood before an International Leadership Conference we were conducting in Mbeya, Tanzania, and testified in front of 3,000 people that she was healed from cancer and encouraged the people to *dare to believe* God!

Faith Principals:

+ The Power of Faith
+ The Power of Agreement
+ The Power of Authority
+ The Power of the Spoken Word
+ The Power of Faith in Action

— God Cares for the Little Things Too —

At our children's home in Guatemala, a little boy named Eddie lived with us for several years. When he came, his hands and feet were covered with many warts. Some were big and painful, and he was so ashamed of them. One morning he came to me and said, "Mom, these warts are hurting me." So I looked at him and said, "Let's pray that they disappear." After laying hands on the warts and commanding them to disappear in Jesus' name, I instructed him to speak to those warts every day, in the morning and in the evening, while he was changing his clothes, and to tell those warts to disappear in Jesus' name. The next morning he was so excited because all the warts were disappearing! Within a few days, every wart was completely gone, with no trace of scars.

I've heard people speak of big miracles and small miracles, and some would say that what happened to Eddie that week was a small miracle, but for him, that small miracle showed him how big God was and that He cared even for him and his need.

Faith Principals:

+ The Power of Compassion, Mercy, and Love
+ The Power of Authority
+ The Power of Faith
+ The Power of the Spoken Word
+ The Power of Faith in Action

— Get Out of the Boat —

One afternoon we were visiting the families in our village and sharing about Jesus. We came to one woman's home who was not interested in what we had to share, so she politely sent us to her parent's home. As we came up to the top of the hill and looked down at the home below, we were amazed at what we saw.

There at the bottom of the hill was an elderly man holding himself up by his arms between two long, horizontal poles that he had made. Eight months earlier, this man had fallen out of a tree and had broken his back and could no longer walk, but he had the desire to do so. Every day he would have his family members bring him out to the yard where he had made these two long horizontal poles.

There he would hold himself up by his arms and stare at his feet, but nothing happened until that afternoon when these white strangers unexpectedly showed up at his home.

When we saw him, we were moved with compassion for him. We introduced ourselves and asked him if we could pray for him for healing. As I stood before him between the two horizontal bars, I started to share with him about Jesus and how He desired to heal him. I asked him over and over again what he desired, and he said he wanted to walk again. I explained to the man just what I was going to do, and I instructed him to only say what I said. He was in agreement. His wife was so full of fear that something worse would happen to him that she ran into her house and hid.

I rebuked the paralysis and released the healing power of the Holy Spirit to flow through him. I instructed him to let go of the bars and hold on to my hands. He did. I said to him, "Let's go for a walk with Jesus." The man didn't even realize it at the time, but his feet started to move, and he started to drag his feet forward.

The funny thing about the whole incident is that this man was much taller than I was, and when he grabbed onto my hands, I had to do everything I could to hold his weight with my two arms. I was praying silently to the Lord to give me strength!

As I continued to walk with him, his legs started to get stronger with each step. But when we got to the end of his two poles, which was his comfort zone, he got frightened and walked backward toward where we had started from! He began walking forward and backward within a matter of a few minutes! We went back and forth like this for quite some time. All the while, his wife was peeking out of the window watching what was happening. Then David said to me, "Becky, he needs to get out of the boat!" Just like Peter had to get out of the boat to walk on water, so did this man.

While all of this was happening, I was thinking to myself, *Oh Lord, help!* At the end of the poles the ground dropped off, and if I stepped down there, my head would come up to his knees and the man would go tumbling down the hill! Oh my! The Lord surely has a sense of humor! David helped the man walk over to another flat area, and I held onto the man's hands. We started to walk around in a large circle. Each time around the circle, the man was getting stronger and stronger, and I started to witness to him about the love of Jesus and how good He was. His wife came out of the house and sat down by where we were walking, and I turned to her and asked her what she thought about all of this. She replied, "Can you pray for me too?" God is good!

Faith Principals:

+ The Power of Faith
+ The Power of Agreement
+ The Power of Authority
+ The Power of the Spoken Word
+ The Power of Faith in Action

— Gangrene —

Back in 1996, my husband and I were starting our ministry with the drug addicted street children in the main bus terminal in Guatemala City. One of the youth, Torre, hurt his foot, and it became infected with gangrene. He was already missing his little toe, and the infection was spreading.

We brought him to a private doctor, and he said that the disease had spread and that he would have to have his leg amputated above the knee. We did not have the finances to have him admitted into a private hospital, but we would find out that we had far more than money could buy. With the help of another missionary, Shari Vanderlin, we had him admitted to a public hospital, where he sat for two weeks without being treated. But before he was admitted, we prayed that his foot and leg would be healed.

David and I would visit him twice a week. His foot and leg were rotting away. The smell in that room was so foul. Torre would hold his foot off the edge of the bed so that the infectious material would drip on the floor. It was so bad!

Finally, after two weeks, they were going to operate and amputate his leg above the knee. They cleaned him up for surgery and wheeled him into the operating room. When the surgeon looked at his leg, he asked why he was there. They explained to him that he had gangrene and had to have his leg amputated. The doctor checked him out and said that he did not have gangrene and that they should take him out of the operating room! Torre knew that God had healed his leg.

Faith Principals:

+ The Power of Compassion, Mercy, and Love

+ The Power of Faith

+ The Power of the Spoken Word

+ The Power of Faith in Action

— "I Can Hear!" —

A man from Chitipa, Malawi, was deaf. He came forward during the outdoor campaign for healing. I stuck my fingers in his ears and rebuked a deaf spirit in Jesus' name and commanded his ears to be open and to hear. Instantly, he was healed. He stood to testify before a crowd of people that he was healed!

Faith Principals:

+ The Power of the Word

+ The Power of Faith

+ The Power of the Spoken Word

+ The Power of Faith in Action

— Run! —

In October 2008, we were doing door-to-door evangelism in Jocotenango, Guatemala, and inviting people to come to a faith and healing conference that we were holding in their neighborhood. We were also praying for any needs that the people had. As we were inviting people to come, a young man with a limp was walking down the street. The Lord told me to go and pray for him, so I walked up to him and greeted him and asked him if I could pray for his leg. He agreed and told me that he had been injured while serving in the military. I briefly prayed over him and told him to put his faith in action. He started bending his leg and had a big smile on his face. I told him to run, and he took off running up and down the street. The limp was gone; his leg was healed. I blessed him as he started to run down the street again! Amen.

Faith Principals:

+ The Power of Faith
+ The Power of the Spoken Word
+ The Power of Faith in Action

— Hands —

I remember one church service that my husband and I had ministered at in Minnesota. Before the service started, we were praying in our hotel room about that evening's service. As we were praying and seeking His direction, I started seeing hands in my mind's eye. I saw hands of all sizes—men's, women's, and children's hands. I also saw a woman in a beautiful white outfit standing to the side of me. I believed in my spirit that we were to pray for healing for hands that evening, and I wasn't sure what the woman in the white outfit was about.

That evening when we entered into the church, I noticed that the woman whom I seen in a white outfit was standing to my left. After my husband finished with the message, he called me forward, and I asked anyone who needed prayer for healing for their hands to come forward so that we could pray for them. I was astounded at the number of people who came forward for healing for their hands! And the woman in the beautiful white outfit came forward. This woman had had an accident, and her thumb had been smashed. She had been suffering with extreme pain in her thumb ever since the accident. If she touched her thumb, severe pain would shoot through her thumb.

As we prayed for these people for healing for their hands, many received their healings instantly. Then came the woman in the white dress. After I prayed for her, I told her to put her faith into action and do what she couldn't do before. *She looked at me and said, "Well, I couldn't do this!"* And she lifted up her arm and hit her thumb on the chair as hard as she could! The Lord had instantly healed her thumb, and she experienced no pain!

Faith Principals:

+ The Power of the Word
+ The Power of Faith
+ The Power of Agreement
+ The Power of the Spoken Word
+ The Power of Faith in Action

— The Baby Turned —

In Sonjo, Tanzania, several years back a couple came forward after the meeting for prayer. The wife was soon to give birth, but the baby was in the wrong position, and there was concern that they would have to do a cesarean. We prayed, the baby turned, and she was able to deliver the baby vaginally. My husband and I were invited to their home for lunch the next time we were in the country to celebrate the life and well-being of this child.

Faith Principals:

+ The Power of Faith

- ✦ The Power of Agreement
- ✦ The Power of Authority
- ✦ The Power of the Spoken Word
- ✦ The Power of Faith in Action

— Babies —

In 2008, I prayed for an Asian woman who had not been able to conceive a child for several years. Shortly after I prayed with her, she conceived and gave birth to twins, and she is very happy!

Another Asian woman in 2009 came to me for prayer to conceive a child. It had been three and a half years, and she and her husband could not conceive. We prayed together, and I gave her instruction on how to put her faith into action. Later, I received a praise report that she conceived a child. Amen!

A few weeks later, during the writing of this book, our daughter Annie and her husband Adam confided in us about their struggle to conceive a child. They went through the process of eight artificial inseminations without conception in two and a half years. The next step was to have an expensive operation with no guarantees of conception. They felt so discouraged. After the phone call that evening, I ordered a plane ticket and left Guatemala the next day to go to minister to them.

I encouraged them in the Word, laid my hands on them, rebuked the curse of barrenness, and blessed the fruit of her womb. We spent time together talking about the power of our words, and I instructed them on the importance of changing their negative speech and speaking those things that were not as though they were (see Rom. 4:17). I then told them to put their faith into action by choosing names, buying a few little baby things, dreaming about family vacations together, and doing things that would increase and release their faith to conceive a child. They did, and within a few months, they conceived a child. We were so excited to welcome our first grandchild into this world in 2010! With God all things are possible!

Faith Principals:

+ The Power of Faith
+ The Power of the Word
+ The Power of Agreement
+ The Power of the Spoken Word
+ The Power of Faith in Action
+ The Power of Persistence

— Plantar Fasciitis and Twisted Ankle Healed —

Six years ago Barb Cooper from Isabella, Minnesota, started experiencing pain with her ankles and feet. She says:

I was working long hours on my feet, standing 10-12 hours at a time. I developed plantar fasciitis in my foot, which was painful, and then four years ago, I twisted my ankle standing on my bed. I used arch supports, homemade braces, and any rigid boot I could to help support my ankles as they seemed really weak. This past year my ankles would get so sore that I had to ice them at night to get relief. I am an active person, and I cannot have this kind of limiting pain. I have had prayer of agreement a few times and have continued to speak life to my ankles and feet with some relief, but I wanted to be totally done with re-occurring incidents. So when Becky prayed for me at the meeting, I set my mind that this is it, I am going to have what I need. Since that time, I have had no pain, and I feel that my ankles have been strengthened. I am not limited to wearing certain shoes for support. I know I am free from this and continue to thank God for restoring me to full capacity. God is so good!

Faith Principals:

+ The Power of Persistence
+ The Power of the Word
+ The Power of Faith
+ The Power of Agreement
+ The Power of Faith
+ The Power of Faith in Action

— Healed of Hamstrung Calves —

My dear friend, Linda Ryan, had what is called Hamstrung Calves and was unable to bend and touch her toes or do many athletic activities. She even was unable to sit cross legged when she was a young girl. Linda had come with me to Tanzania, where the Lord led us to go and teach about faith and healing and pray for the sick. After the service one night, she asked me to pray for her legs. The Lord instantly healed them, and she could bend over and touch the floor with the palms of her hands for the first time in her life. Since then, she has taken hold of the message of faith and healing and is teaching others to pray for the sick. She has even started a ministry called Greater Works Ministries.

Linda says, "I was hamstrung for almost 50 years. It's been over eight years now since God healed me, and I still have the joy of being able to touch my toes.

I'm able to take long walks, work out at the gym, and run half a mile several times a week. God is good!"

Faith Principals:

+ The Power of the Word
+ The Power of Faith
+ The Power of Agreement
+ The Power of the Spoken Word
+ The Power of Faith in Action

— Life to Dead Bones —

One afternoon in Embu, Kenya, after we taught and ministered in a small village church, Pastor Duncan asked us to come and pray for a woman who was too sick to come to the service. We agreed. When we arrived at her home, we were met by her younger brother, who was full of faith. This man was ready for a miracle that day; as soon as we arrived, he started taking photos.

We walked into this woman's home. It was very dark, with a dirt floor, and this beautiful Christian woman was lying in a dirty bed and dressed with dirty worn-out clothes. Her body was all twisted and shriveled up; her arms literally were twisted around one another, her finger nails were growing into the palms of her hands, and her hands were frozen before her face.

This woman was completely paralyzed from the neck down. She was mentally alert and could communicate, but could not move. As we listened to her tell her story, we found out that her parents had died from this very disease and that, on the other side of the house, her older brother was suffering with the same disease.

One could not help but be filled with compassion and mercy for this woman. I laid my hands on her cold, stiff body, and I asked the Holy Spirit what to do. I heard the words, "Speak life to dead bones." I immediately rebuked premature death and spoke life to dead bones. The others (Linda Ryan, Christine

Lauterbach, and the pastors) continued to pray silently. I told the woman to put her faith into action and to do something that she could not do. That was an overwhelming request for her. So I suggested that she try moving her foot, but the Lord corrected me and said to tell her to move her little finger, which had been frozen in front of her face for many years. So I told her to move her little finger instead of her foot. She looked directly into my eyes, and I told her not to question it, but to just do it by faith. The woman moved her little finger for the first time in years! Within 20 minutes, we saw her arms that once were twisted around each other straighten out. We all were jumping up and down for joy! I told her not to stop and to continue doing what she was not able to do.

We then went to the other side of the house to pray for her older brother, who was lying in his bed crippled and paralyzed with the same disease. He had upper body movement, but from the waist down was unable to move. We ministered healing to him and saw his deformed legs straighten out and move. We encouraged him to continue to do what he was not able to do in the name of Jesus.

We did not have a lot of time, but returned to the other side of the house to where our sister had been. When we entered into her room, she was just all smiles and so excited! She said to us, "Look what I can do!" While we were on the other side of the house, she had taught herself to hold a bottle of soda and drink from a straw. She asked her other brother to bring food for her, and she taught herself to eat with a spoon all by herself. She removed the dirty, worn out sweater that she was using for a pillow, and she began folding and unfolding it for us. She was showing off for Jesus! It was wonderful! We encouraged her to continue doing what she had not been able to do.

Faith Principals:

+ The Power of the Word
+ The Power of Faith
+ The Power of Agreement
+ The Power of Authority
+ The Power of the Spoken Word

• The Power of Faith in Action

In the Book of Luke, Jesus met a man full of leprosy, and this man said to Him, *"Lord, if You are willing, You can make me clean."* Jesus reached out and touched the man and said, *"I am willing"* and the leprosy immediately left him (see Luke 5:12-13). We must be willing to go and reach out and touch someone today in the name of Jesus!

— Go! —

HIV/AIDS Booklets in Swahili and Maasai Languages

We were nearing the end our of ministry time in Nairobi, Kenya, and we were all physically tired. As I lay down to sleep that night, the Holy Spirit settled upon me, and I lay in bed weeping and interceding in the Spirit all night. The Lord spoke to me and told me to go and find the HIV Hospice in town and insist that they allow us to pray for the patients who wanted prayer and not to take *no* for an answer. I woke up the two ladies who were ministering with me (Linda Ryan and Christine Lauderbach), and we prayed the rest of the night together.

We left early that morning to go find this place. Finally we found it, but the administration did not want to let us in. I would not take *no* for an answer! I gave them a copy of a booklet that I had written and had translated into Swahili and the Maasai languages about HIV/AIDS, and they agreed to allow us to come in.

Our hearts were broken with compassion at what we saw. So many ladies were lying there dying in great pain and agony and all alone. We went to each room and stood in the middle of the room and shared a simple Gospel message with these ladies. We gave them the invitation to receive Jesus as their Lord and Savior and offered to pray with them for healing.

One of the ladies, whom I will never forget, was a Christian. She was in severe pain and just about to die. She laid there in a room full of strangers, she felt alone and abandoned, but she remembered what she had learned from the Bible and started to claim the promises of God. She prayed and asked God to send someone to pray for her. In God's great mercy and compassion for this woman, His child, He sent us to minister comfort and healing to her. As we laid hands on her, the pain was instantly gone. She stopped shaking and sat up in her bed, declaring the goodness of God.

We saw the compassionate mercy of God touch many of the women that morning, but I believe we were called by God to go to that place especially for our sister who was calling out to God in her time of need. Go!

Faith Principals:

+ The Power of Compassion, Mercy, and Love
+ The Power of the Word
+ The Power of Authority
+ The Power of Agreement
+ The Power of Faith
+ The Power of the Spoken Word
+ The Power of Faith in Action

— Johnny —

Late one evening, in September 2002, in Morogoro, Tanzania, Linda Ryan and I were sitting in the director's home of the hospital, waiting to make a late night visit in the women's ward. As we were sitting there, we had a divine encounter with a man named Johnny.

Johnny was infected with HIV and in the last stage of AIDS. He was tall, thin, and very weak. He also had a large bandage covering the left side of his face. An infection or disease had eaten a whole through the jawbone and face, and he could no longer eat. He asked for prayer for healing. We rebuked the spirit of death, rebuked HIV/AIDS and every infection and disease that was attacking and killing his body, and released the Spirit of Life to flow through him in Jesus' name. The Holy Spirit touched that man, and he was never the same again.

He stood up, went to the kitchen, and asked the director's wife to prepare him something to eat because he was so hungry. After a little while, he returned and carried our bags and things for us as he led us throughout the hospital to pray for the patients. Three years later, I received a report about Johnny. After that evening in the hospital when he was prayed for, he left the hospital and found a job and has been supporting his wife and children ever since.

Faith Principals:

+ The Power of Compassion, Mercy, and Love
+ The Power of Authority
+ The Power of Agreement
+ The Power of Faith
+ The Power of the Spoken Word
+ The Power of Faith in Action

— The Woman's Ward —

After we prayed for Johnny for healing from HIV/AIDS, he escorted us into the women's ward. I stood in the midst of the open ward and gave a short Gospel message of the saving grace of Jesus Christ and His healing power over all sickness and disease. I asked if there was anyone in the room who would like to receive Jesus as their Lord and Savior or prayer for healing. In the very back of the ward, two women raised their hands. We walked over to them and (with the help of an interpreter) asked them what we could do for them. The woman lying in the bed asked us to pray for the woman visiting her because she was deaf. I rebuked a spirit of deafness, and she was instantly healed. The other women in the ward were watching and started raising their hands for us to pray for them for salvation and healing. We went from one bed to another, praying against one serious illness after another. The presence of the Lord was in that place.

We returned to the hospital two weeks later and asked to visit the ladies whom we had ministered to before. We were told that the women were no longer there. The day after we prayed for them, they all went home healed! Praise the Lord!

Faith Principals:

+ The Power of the Word
+ The Power of Faith
+ The Power of Agreement
+ The Power of Authority
+ The Power of the Healing Anointing
+ The Power of the Spoken Word
+ The Power of Faith in Action

— Ana —

Ana came to our home several years ago in very critical condition. She had been in two children's homes prior to coming to ours. Her mother had died of TB, but we later found out that she had also been infected with HIV. Ana was two years old and only weighed 12 pounds. The other homes didn't realize that she had been suffering from HIV and TB. She was a very sick little girl.

We anointed her with oil and prayed over her. We took our authority over a spirit of death, over the HIV and TB, and over every other symptom that was attacking her body in the name of Jesus. Within five months she was a completely different girl. She had gained over 20 pounds and was undetectable, meaning they could not find the HIV in her blood. She was strong and healthy.

When she went for her doctor's check up, they were amazed when they saw Ana. They asked our workers just what it is that we do with our children. Our workers replied that we are Christians; we pray over the children, love them, and take good care of them. The nurse responded, "Well, there really is *life* at LIFE Unlimited!"

Faith Principals:

+ The Power of Compassion, Mercy, and Love
+ The Power of Faith
+ The Power of Authority
+ The Power of Agreement
+ The Power of the Spoken Word
+ The Power of Faith in Action

— A Sweet Sister —

One afternoon, while I was visiting an AIDS Hospice in Guatemala, I met a woman in the cafeteria. She had had a stroke earlier. As a result, her jaw was partially paralyzed, and it was very difficult for her to eat. I asked her if I could pray for her, and she agreed. Instantly her jaw was loosed, and she could eat freely again. Some would say that was minor in the whole of her situation, but it was the start of a relationship that lead her to Jesus.

Faith Principals:

+ The Power of Compassion, Mercy, and Love
+ The Power of Authority
+ The Power of Faith in Action

— Carlos —

In Guatemala, in our LIFE Unlimited Children's Home, we have a home especially for children who come infected with HIV called LIFE Tender Mercy Home.

In 2005, we received a 12-year-old boy named Carlos. Both his parents had been infected with HIV, and they both died of TB. When he came to us, he was in the last stage called AIDS. The HIV count in his blood was 250,000, which is over double the amount that they consider the last stage called AIDS (100,000). His level of defenses was all the way down to about 68. A healthy person's level of defenses is above 600.

Children infected with this dreadful disease usually live to be about 10 years of age. Carlos was now 12 years old. He was HIV positive, had an enlarged liver, had all the symptoms of TB, and had a large, freshly-stitched cut on his foot. He could not eat or drink, could not hold down water, had diarrhea, and was vomiting all the time. His young body was literally wasting away. This boy had been severely neglected, was dying, and had no hope for a future.

The situation looked very bad when he first arrived, but we prayed with faith in the God of the impossible. We rebuked the spirit of death, HIV/AIDS, TB, and every other sickness and disease that was attacking his weak body in Jesus' name, and we released the healing power of the Holy Spirit to flow into his body. The moment we prayed for him, his countenance changed. We began to speak words full of life over him.

The next four days we had to bring him to the doctors for more tests. One day, David was with him, and the doctors were confused about what they were seeing because the level of HIV in his blood was dropping. David testified that we are Christians, that we believe in healing, and that we had prayed for him. They thought he was in denial of the seriousness of the situation.

Carlos had to be tested for TB. I testified of God's healing power to the doctor and medical personal as they were preparing to put a tube down into his lungs for a sample. After they had removed the sample, the doctor came out and showed me the little bottle of liquid that they removed from his lungs. He pointed to the bottle and said, "This is TB." I responded, "No, he doesn't have it." We refused to accept his report. The test results came back negative, meaning *no TB!*

Every day was a new struggle, but we continued to build Carlos up in the Word of God. At first he was very weak, so while he lay in his bed, we had him watch Christian cartoons. The stories from the Bible were all new to him, and he would just watch them over and over again. We knew we needed to renew his mind with good things and start planting hope for the future.

He could barely walk, but we knew we had to get him up and exercise his faith. The older children in the home were a great help. Every morning the other children would do calisthenics, run and play a game of soccer with their school teacher. Even though he could not do jumping jacks or push-ups or run and play soccer with the rest, the older boys took turns holding Carlos up and walking him around the soccer field every day. And every day we saw his strength and hope return. It just blessed my heart to see the older boys pitching in to help him.

Within four months, he was declared undetectable, meaning they could not trace the HIV in his blood! When we received this report, I called Carlos to the kitchen, and when I told him, he leaped for joy! We both jumped up and down praising God! I asked him, "Who healed you?" He said, "Jesus!"

Carlos did not die as expected. They could not find the HIV in his blood, and even though he had all the symptoms of TB, they could not find it either. The swelling in his liver disappeared, and he started to laugh, run, and play with the rest of the kids. Now Carlos is full and overflowing with life. When his uncle saw him, he gave glory to God for what He had done for Carlos. When his uncle returned home, he told the other family members, and they didn't believe him, so they came to see for themselves, and they were utterly amazed! Carlos said to me, "I am very grateful to God for you and David; had you not taken me into your home, I know I would be dead. Thank you for all of your help."

Faith Principals:

+ The Power of Compassion, Mercy, and Love
+ The Power of Faith

- ◆ The Power of Authority
- ◆ The Power of Agreement
- ◆ The Power of the Spoken Word
- ◆ The Power of Faith in Action
- ◆ The Power of Persistence
- ◆ The Power of Praise

— Life Tender Mercy Home —

One night as I was praying and worshiping the Lord under the stars, God gave me a vision. I saw a two-story building that was being constructed. The outside of the building was not finished, but in the vision I went over the wall to the inside. The inside of the building was light yellow in color, and it was filled with an extreme peace and hope. As I was traveling around the inside of this building, I saw hospital beds, an emergency room, and other things that you would see in a hospital. Then I saw a very pale and sick child who was dying, and I saw my hand putting an oxygen mask over this child's face. I knew that I was ministering life and healing to this child. Then I heard God speak to me. He said to build a home for children born with HIV and that He would bring the children and heal every one of them.

My husband came home late that night, and I shared with him the vision. We prayed and sought God concerning this home, and we made the decision to trust God and to put our faith into action. David and a few of the older boys in the home started to dig the foundation for this home by hand; we sent a newsletter out to our partners, and before we knew it, teams of people came to build this home.

We knew we were to build a home and not just a building to house sick children. It was to be a place that would not be overshadowed with the fear of death, but a place of healing where these hurting children could be raised with dignity and hope for a future.

Every child we have received has come to us in a very desperate situation, most at the point of death. But we have no fear of death, nor do we allow ourselves to be consumed with it. It does not control our everyday life. We know our covenant rights with the Father through the blood of Jesus. We pray over them, and we speak words of life and not death. We install in each one a hope and a desire to live and to fulfill their destiny. And we have what we say. Our children in our home do not die. In other places, they are dying at an alarming rate. We fight for their right to live.

The name of our children's home is LIFE Unlimited. There is power in every word spoken, whether it is positive or negative. And we know every time we speak out the name LIFE Unlimited that we are actually declaring and producing life itself and a life without limits in Jesus Christ. *"And they overcame him by the Blood of the Lamb and by the word of their testimony..."* (Rev. 12:11a).

Faith Principals:

- The Power of Compassion, Mercy, and Love
- The Power of the Word
- The Power of the Healing Anointing
- The Power of Faith
- The Power of Authority
- The Power of Agreement
- The Power of Persistence
- The Power of the Spoken Word
- The Power of Faith in Action
- The Power of Praise

— In the Valley of the Shadow of Death —

It was the year 2005, and we were ministering in the hospital in Karonga, Malawi. The governor of the area invited us to come and minister to a loved one in the hospital. I remember being overwhelmed with such a strong compassion for the people suffering in this place. Most people were dying from HIV/AIDS. In fact, we could not escape the funeral processionals and the wailing and grieving people. So many were dying from this dreadful disease, and the people felt they were without hope. That day made a very strong impact on my life.

We walked into a small private hospital room and found the woman we came to pray for lying in her bed in a coma, no longer able to communicate with her family. There were several ladies in the room crying as they were trying to let her go.

I laid my hands on her body and rebuked the spirit of death over her and released the Spirit of Life to flow. I renounced every sickness and disease that was attacking and killing her body in the name of Jesus; then we left the room. The next day, we were returning to this hospital to minister to many others in this place. When we arrived, we were met by the family members of the lady we had prayed with the day before. They said that their sister was worse and asked if we could please come back and pray again. We agreed.

When we entered the room, the woman was in the final stage before passing on. I found a little stool and pulled it up to the bed so that I could be at eye level with this dying woman. My friend, Linda, was praying in the Spirit. Even though this woman could no longer respond, I knew she could still hear me. The spirit does not go into a comma; just the physical body does. I laid my hands on her bed, with my head resting on my arm, close to her head. I have learned to lean on the Holy Spirit and allow Him to direct my words. I heard myself say to her, "We were here yesterday and ministered healing to you, and today you are worse. At your family's request, we are here again today. They love you and do not want to let you go. I can see that you are walking down in the valley of the shadow of death. I am going to do the same thing, I did yesterday, but today you are going to have to choose to live."

This woman was just about to leave this Earth, and her family was in the room crying and hurting. In this hospital, there were no life support machines, as are in more modern countries. She was not even given morphine to ease the pain. She was laboring heavily to breathe those last few breaths. Her eyes were fixed firmly on the ceiling above her.

But when I said the words, "You are going to have to choose to live," the woman quickly grabbed my arm, slowly turned her head, and looked me firmly in the eye! I was so startled, I jumped in my seat! I immediately said to the family, "This woman has made her choice. She wants to live! Now, you are all going to have to stop grieving her death, stop planning her funeral, and only speak words of life and healing over her from now on." We hugged one another, thanked the Lord, and left to go pray for someone else.

Faith Principals:

+ The Power of Faith
+ The Power of Authority
+ The Power of Agreement
+ The Power of the Spoken Word
+ The Power of the Faith in Action

— The TB Ward —

As we were about to enter into the TB Ward in the Karonga Hospital in Malawi, we were told that over 70 percent of the people in there were also AIDS victims. It was like any other ward in East Africa—more patients than beds. Patients were sleeping anywhere they could find extra space on the floor; there was death and despair everywhere.

With the help of an interpreter, I stood in the middle of the open ward and gave a short Gospel message about salvation and healing. I asked if there was anyone there who would like us to pray with them for either. As usual, the patient in the back of the room raised a hand for us to come and pray. We made our way to the back of the room.

We were asked to pray for the first patient because she was deaf from high fevers. We prayed, and she was instantly healed. Everyone in the open ward saw what had just happened. While writing down the name of the first person, so that a local pastor could come and disciple her, we found out that she was related to our interpreter. We were called next to the opposite side of the room. When I asked what they needed, the second patient wanted prayer for the same thing. So we prayed, and she could immediately hear as well! From there, we went from bed to bed praying for whatever people had needed of.

One family asked me to pray for their little girl. She was about 13 years of age and was lying there in a comma. I laid my hands on her stiff, cold body. I rebuked the spirit of death over her and released the Spirit of Life. I commanded healing and recreation throughout her body. The little girl opened up her eyes, sat up, and drank a cup of water. The family rejoiced to have their little one back.

Faith Principals:

+ The Power of Compassion, Mercy, and Love
+ The Power of the Word
+ The Power of Faith
+ The Power of Agreement
+ The Power of the Spoken Word
+ The Power of the Healing Anointing
+ The Power of the Faith in Action

— You Are Most Welcomed Here —

In every AIDS Hospice that I have visited around the world, I have received the same response, "You are most welcomed here." I have met many precious people suffering in the last stages of HIV/AIDS. I have found the people to be very receptive to a visitor who truly wants to be their friend.

What do I do? I befriend the patients. I go in with an open heart, and I listen as they tell me their stories. I have never asked anyone how they became infected; they usually tell me, but I don't think it's necessary to know. I find small ways to show that I truly care. I read the Bible to them, give them a word of encouragement, pray for them, and lead them to Jesus.

> *"For I was hungry and you gave Me food; I was thirsty and you gave Me drink; I was a stranger and you took Me in; I was naked and you clothed me; I was sick and you visited me; I was in prison and you came to Me" Then the righteous will answer Him, saying, "Lord, when did we see You hungry and feed You, or thirsty and give You drink? When did we see You a stranger and take You in, or naked and clothe You? Or when did we see You sick, or in prison, and come to You?" "And the King will answer and say to them, "Assuredly, I say to you, inasmuch as you did it to one of the least of these My brethren, you did it to Me" (Matthew 25:35-40).*

> *Pure and undefiled religion before God and the Father is this: to visit orphans and widows in their trouble, and to keep oneself unspotted from the world (James 1:27).*

— The Truth Will Set You Free —

There was a pastor who was in great need in Nairobi, Kenya. We were ministering in Nairobi at a crusade, and a family came to us with a special request to come and minister to their father. This man had been a pastor for many years, but all of a sudden he lost his mind, and no one knew why. He had been this way for a long time now. When they heard we were in town, they asked us to come. We agreed to go.

As I was walking out of the doorway of the house where we were staying, a man met me in the doorway and in a very mocking tone said to me, "I know what you are going to do. You are going to command the demons in the name of Jesus to leave the man. It won't work!" I was shocked at what this man had just said to me, because he was a man of authority in the church. I wanted to give him the benefit of the doubt, so I asked him if I had heard him correctly or if, perhaps, his English wasn't very clear. He answered me and told me that I had heard him correctly.

I answered him immediately and said, "I'm sorry, but I disagree with you. The Bible says that we shall cast out demons in the name of Jesus, and that's what I intend to do." This man was very angry with me, and I believe jealous too that I had been asked to do this and not him.

As we drove across the city to their home, this man who had challenged me in the doorway continued to tell us that the only way to free this man was to speak all of these incantations over him and to do all of these rituals. He then took out these workbooks all about deliverance. He started to show us what was in these workbooks. What he was showing us was pure witchcraft. I just started to pray in tongues under my breath and asked God for wisdom.

When we arrived to their home, we walked up a flight of stairs, and this very confused man continued to try and convince me not to use the name of Jesus. Rather, the evil spirits that had control over this man were afraid of what was about to take place and were trying to get me to not use that all powerful name of my Jesus. We walked into the small home, and there was this pastor. He sat in a chair, completely out of his mind, and he moved his head up and down and from side to side saying in English, "Hallelujah. Praise the Lord."

I found a little stool, and I sat right in front of this man at eye level. I asked the ladies who were with me (Linda Ryan and Christine Lauderbach) to pray in tongues. As we were praying, I started to see a vision of some very gruesome witch-craft practices. I started to tell the pastor what I was seeing. His family immediately started asking why I was speaking to their father, since he wasn't in his right mind and couldn't respond to anyone. I ignored them and continued on. As I was asking this pastor if what I was seeing was correct, he would stop moving his head and look me right in the eye and say, "yes," and then continue shaking his head up and down and from side to side saying, "Hallelujah. Praise the Lord."

At first, I did not know what part this man had played in all of this, but as the vision progressed, I understood why I was there. The Holy Spirit, through the vision, revealed that this man's father had been a witchdoctor, and he had grown up in the midst of witchcraft and its ugly practices. He had tried to hide his past; even his own family did not know what had taken place in his life. But the memories just haunted him until he was consumed with fear and guilt. After all of this was out in the open, the Lord had me deliver a message of His forgiveness and deliverance.

As all of this was going on, the man who had challenged me in the doorway and who had tried to convince me to use witchcraft to deliver this man, started saying to the family that we needed to do all of these strange witchcraft practices. I ignored the man and continued on as the Holy Spirit led me. I told the pastor that the Lord had a final Word for him. It was a simple Word, "The truth will set you free." And we left.

I knew that the situation did not look good, but I knew in my spirit that we had done what we were supposed to do. Now it was up to this pastor to receive it or to reject it. We left the next morning to go and minister in Meru, Kenya, and the surrounding areas for the next five days. After five days of very powerful ministry, we arrived back to Nairobi late at night. We were leaving early the next morning for Tanzania. Thankfully, someone sent word to us where we were staying that this very special pastor had been completely delivered and had testified in the church that Sunday morning! The truth had set him free! Glory to God!

Faith Principals:

- The Power of Authority
- The Power of Faith
- The Power of Agreement
- The Power of the Spoken Word
- The Power of Faith in Action

— Like Electricity —

One evening after ministering, we were invited to pray for a sister in Jesus who was recovering from surgery in a hospital. While we were there, we were given the opportunity to minister to the others there. This was a large and very crowded, private hospital in Lilongwe, Malawi. As usual, I stood in the middle of the large open hospital room and gave a very brief Gospel message. Then I invited those who would like to receive Jesus as their Lord and Savior or who would like us to pray for them for healing, to raise their hands or indicate to us in some way. If people do not want us to come to them, we won't.

As I was speaking, a young man walked in and out of a small, private room in the corner, looking at me with urgency. As soon as I had finished, he called out to me to come quickly. I told the pastors and the ladies who were traveling with me to come, and we went into this small room. There we found a young Malawian woman, about 20 years old, dying from an asthma attack. Her family was standing around her bed waiting for her to die.

The young man was her brother. He said that they were Christians and asked if I could please pray for her. So I laid my hands on her body, and as soon as I did, her whole bed started to shake. I rebuked the spirit of death that was over her body and heard myself say, "And I release the Spirit of Life to flow through this body like electricity!" As soon as I had said these words, a power shot through my arm and threw me back against the wall! This girl's body started moving up and down, as if a wave of power was going through her body. Her legs immediately shot straight up in the air and then slammed down on the bed, and she jumped out of the bed completely healed! Glory to God!

She ran out of the room to use the bathroom! And the hands of every patient, but one, in that large hospital room went up for prayer for healing and to receive Jesus! Even the visitors were asking for prayer!

Faith Principals:

+ The Power of the Word

+ The Power of Faith
+ The Power of Authority
+ The Power of the Spoken Word
+ The Power of the Healing Anointing
+ The Power of Agreement
+ The Power of Faith in Action

— Lightning Bolts —

In September 2002, in Mbeya, Tanzania, I was teaching about healing when the anointing of the Holy Spirit came upon me very powerfully. I walked up and down the isle of this little church, and I heard myself speak out that if anyone needed healing in their physical body they should stand to their feet. With each word that I spoke, I could see lightning bolts flashing in my mind's eye. (I did not share this with the congregation.) As this was happening, a woman cried out in the congregation and later testified that as I was speaking she saw and felt lightning bolts hitting her as she stood up for her healing. Her back was instantly healed!

Faith Principals:

+ The Power of the Word
+ The Power of the Healing Anointing
+ The Power of the Spoken Word
+ The Power of Faith
+ The Power of Faith in Action

— He Flew Across the Platform —

We were ministering at an outdoor campaign in Ndola, Zambia. It was time to pray for the sick. A dignified looking man came up to the platform for prayer, but as I touched him, he went flying back on his backside several feet. I'll never forget the look on this man's face, as if I had done this on purpose! The ushers helped him to his feet, and he came again for prayer. As I laid my hands on him, he was instantly healed of a back injury. Only God knows why He had to do this to this man.

Faith Principals:

+ The Power of the Word
+ The Power of the Spoken Word
+ The Power of Authority
+ The Power of the Healing Anointing
+ The Power of Faith
+ The Power of Faith in Action

— Flies and the Eyes —

The Maasai are herdsmen, and they raise cattle. To protect the animals from the lions during the night, they keep the cattle between all the huts that are fenced in by a wall of thorn bushes. So there is a lot of cow dung, and there are thousands of flies. It can be quite a challenge at times having to fight off flies and minister at the same time. This was one of those moments.

While we were ministering in the entrance of a Maasai hut in Northern Tanzania, I had to put my flesh under, ignore the massive amount of flies, and press in to concentrate on what was before me. We were asked to pray for a precious lady with a growth on her eyeball. The woman was kneeling on the ground, and I laid my hand on her head. I started to take my authority over the growth, while at the same time moving up and down, not because the anointing was so strong, but because I had flies by the hundreds crawling all over me, and they had gotten into places where they just shouldn't be!

But when we are weak, He is strong! Right before our eyes, the growth on her eyeball rolled off and disappeared! Her brother was jumping up and down shouting praises. I just jumped right along with him! God is good. And He does have a sense of humor too!

Faith Principals:

+ The Power of Faith
+ The Power of Agreement
+ The Power of Authority
+ The Power of the Spoken Word
+ The Power of Faith in Action

— The Mute Shall Speak —

The Lilongwe Hospital in Malawi was over-crowded with patients lying on the floor because there was no more room. Death and hopelessness were every-where. Family members were screaming and wailing as they were mourning their dead. We were told the ambulance no longer was used to bring the sick to the hospital, but was used only to carry out the dead. At first it was difficult to know where to even begin, so I made the decision to go in a certain direction and just start tackling the situation head-on, going from room to room.

The rooms were filled and overflowing with patients. I would stand in the middle of the room and share a simple Gospel message of salvation in Jesus and offer them the opportunity to receive the Lord Jesus Christ as their Savior. Then I would share about the healing power of Jesus and offer to pray with anyone who wanted prayer. Many received Jesus, and almost everyone wanted prayer for healing. We went from bed to bed, laying hands on the patients, and watched God heal people.

We had been there all morning long, and it was time to leave. As we were leaving, we had to walk through rooms full of patients all needing miracles. One young man had been following us from room to room, and he asked me if I would please pray for his father. I agreed. His father had suffered from Malaria, and it had caused him to become mute. I quickly laid my hands on him in the name of Jesus and told him to open up his mouth and speak. Nothing happened! I then heard the Holy Spirit tell me to command the voice box to be recreated in the name of Jesus. So, I did, and I told him to open up his mouth and speak, and he did! Glory to God! Let's all take five minutes to pray with someone in need today!

Faith Principals:

+ The Power of Compassion, Mercy, and Love
+ The Power of Authority
+ The Power of Faith
+ The Power of the Spoken Word
+ The Power of Faith in Action

— Healed of a Brain Tumor —

In the year 2008, I was teaching about faith and healing at a meeting in Asia. Afterward, we prayed for the sick. In this meeting was a young man, about 20 years old, named Timothy. He had a brain tumor and was to be soon operated on for the second time. His friends raised money for him to have the surgery. His mother and father had come from the village into the city for the operation, which was scheduled for later that week.

After hearing my teaching about faith and healing, he came forward to ask for prayer for healing. As Linda Ryan and I laid hands on him, I saw a vision of a hand taking the brain tumor and squeezing the very life out of it. The vision was very graphic, and I saw everything inside of this tumor being squeezed out of it. I shared with this young man what I was seeing, and his faith was encouraged.

Timothy went to the doctors. They ran a CAT Scan and could no longer find the brain tumor; there was no longer a need for surgery. He went for another CAT Scan several months later, and again there was no brain tumor. God completely healed this young man, and he is now traveling and testifying of God's amazing grace and bringing encouragement to others. Praise the Lord! Timothy says, "Praise to our Heavenly Father! My parents are now a part of God's family. I have shared my testimony in my village. I am a new man in Christ."

Faith Principals:

+ The Power of the Word
+ The Power of Faith
+ The Power of Agreement
+ The Power of the Healing Anointing
+ The Power of Authority
+ The Power of Faith in Action

— He's the Witchdoctor —

In October 2009, I was teaching at our new LIFE Leadership Bible Training Center in the Serengeti Plaines of Northern Tanzania. It was the last day of the campaign, and we were holding an outdoor evangelistic campaign that afternoon. Before I was to stand and preach, I was walking around the perimeters of the people praying in the Spirit. As I was walking and praying, I saw an old Maasai man sitting on a pile of construction rocks. I felt impressed to go up to him and shake his hand and greet him. So I held out my hand and greeted him with a friendly smile and a hello in Swahili. I knew I had seen him before, but I did not remember who he was. It was now time to stand and preach. I preached about being redeemed from the curse of sickness and disease and ended with a few powerful short healing testimonies. I gave the altar call for salvation first and then for healing. Many people stepped forward for both.

As I started praying for people for healing, I prayed for the first lady in my line, and she fell over under the power of the Holy Spirit and was healed. I went to pray for the woman standing next to her. The old man whom I had greeted before the service started was standing next to her, and he accidently and very lightly bumped me. When he did, he went flying back in the air with such a force and landed flat on the ground, dead! Everyone standing around him stepped back to watch. I ran to the old man. I touched him, and he was cold and stiff as if he had been dead for quite a while. He was no longer breathing. I said, "Lord, help me. A man just died in the healing line!"

As I was kneeling on the ground beside him, I laid my hand upon his chest, and I rebuked the spirit of death over him in the name of Jesus and commanded life to return to his body. Nothing happened! I commanded; "In Jesus' name, breathe!" And he gasped for a breath. Demonic spirits started to manifest as he started to foam at the mouth and roll on the ground. A woman standing by me knelt down and said to me in English, "He's the witchdoctor!" I shouted, "Hallelujah!"

The Holy Spirit brought back to my memory what I had prayed earlier that morning. That morning, before we left for the training center, while Linda and I were praying, I heard myself pray, "And may all curses that are spoken against us bounce back on them, that they (the witchdoctors) would learn a lesson!" And I saw in my mind's eye what had just happened with this witchdoctor and how he literally bounced off of me and went flying back in the air, landing on the ground dead! I made my way through the crowd and found some Maasai pastors whom I trusted and asked them to minister to him in his own language, and I continued to minister to the others. *"You are of God, little children, and have overcome them, because He who is in you is greater than he who is in the world"* (1 John 4:4).

Faith Principals:

+ The Power of the Word
+ The Power of Authority
+ The Power of Faith
+ The Power of Faith in Action
+ The Power of the Spoken Word

— Henry Abdias Sinay —

Aldea Las Flores, Sumpango, Sacatepequez, Guatemala

In late November of 2008, Henry was run over by a large bus in his village. Someone ran to tell his mother; she came running and found her son lying on the road and in great pain.

The bus driver was fearful of the legal implications and tried to hide the fact that he had run the boy over. Thus, he lied to the mother and said that Henry had a bicycle accident. And because of the fear of vengeance, the people who witnessed the accident stood in front of Henry lying on the road and hid him as the police patrol passed by. No one would help this 13-year-old boy. They actually carried him further down the road, away from the bus, so that when the police drove by again they would find him, but not near the bus.

Henry's mother was able to get a hold of her husband by phone and tell him that there had been a serious accident and that he needed to come home immediately. His father arrived to find his son lying on the road all bruised, broken, and in tremendous pain. The bus driver again lied and told Henry's father that Henry had a bicycle accident. Those standing by knew the truth, but were too afraid to speak up.

The police patrol drove by again and found Henry and his family and took him to the emergency room in the back of the pickup truck. After the doctors examined him, the family was told that Henry's legs were broken in five different places. This was not the result of a bicycle accident.

I know as you are reading this testimony, a righteous anger is rising up within your spirit. This anger was to become Henry's father's greatest struggle. This wasn't just some stranger who ran over their son; it was a family member. It was Henry's grandfather, and to make matters worse, he lied to them.

As the days passed, in the midst of all of the confusion, this hurting family now had other challenges to fight. Fifteen days after the accident, gangrene had set in one of Henry's legs, and the prognoses did not look good. Surgery was scheduled, but this family did not have the money to pay for all of this. The father spoke to the doctor and told him that they were Christians and that they believed in healing. He asked if the doctor would give them a few days to pray and allow God to heal the gangrene. The doctor was against it and warned them that it was spreading really quickly. He said that if it was not treated, he would have to amputate above the knee. The father was firm in his convictions, so the doctor agreed and gave him three days. He had them sign a release form to protect the doctor from negligence.

Henry's mother and father washed the wounds continuously, and they kept their eyes fixed on the Lord and His promise of healing. As they washed his leg, chunks of flesh would fall off, but underneath the dead flesh was new, healthy flesh growing. It was a battle, but Henry was healed of gangrene and never had the surgery!

Both of his legs were set in casts, and the doctor told them that he would be in casts for a long time. Henry fought with discouragement and depression. The scene of the accident would play over and over again in his mind. He feared that he would never walk again.

It was draining emotionally and physically on the whole family. His mother was struggling physically to lift and carry Henry, and it was embarrassing for a 13-year-old boy to have to have his mother carry him everywhere, too. Finally someone lent them a wheelchair, and that helped to ease the situation a bit.

The time passed by slowly, and the conflict between family members grew more intense. Three lawyers were now counseling Henry's father to take legal action. I find it very interesting that Henry's father's name is Justo (Justice). And Justo was struggling with his convictions to forgive verses vengeance and getting even. He cried out to God to give him the grace and the strength to forgive, and in time, he did forgive and release his father-in-law from his wrong doing. This forgiveness was the key that released the confidence and faith for him to believe for his son's healing.

The months passed by, and one day, as Justo was seeking the Lord on behalf of his son, he heard the voice of the Lord say that Henry was already healed. Jesus already paid the price for healing at Calvary. We need to learn to activate that healing power in our lives, and that is what was happening with Henry and his family. The family took a bold step of faith and removed the casts from Henry's legs. In the natural, the results did not look good; the bones did not heal well. Henry could not stand or walk on his own. They lived in a mountain village, which made the situation even more challenging for him to move around. And the family was struggling and thinking that perhaps they should not have removed the casts early. His family did not have the resources to pay for corrective surgery, but they had something far better than a well-stocked bank account; they had a blood covenant with the Father that included healing, and they made a quality decision to trust the Lord for the completion of Henry's healing.

One evening, Henry's family carried him down the dirt road to our home to ask us to pray for his healing. David and I invited them into our living room. We spent a few minutes teaching them the Word of God and encouraging them with a few healing testimonies. Then we laid hands on him and commanded the bones, muscles, ligaments, tendons, and nerves in his legs to be healed and recreated and to function properly so that he could walk again in Jesus' name.

We looked Henry in the eye and told him that he needed to put his faith into action by doing what he could not do before. He started to bend his ankle, then his knee. Then he put his weight on his leg; then he started to lift his leg up and down until he was jogging in place on his own without the help of others. His mother was sitting on the sofa next to him, and she started to cry tears of joy. They left our home rejoicing as Henry walked down two flights of steps and through the field and down the rocky, dirt road to their home without their assistance.

Henry's mother says, "I am so thankful to God. He healed my son, and he walks again!" Henry's father learned that without forgiveness you cannot receive from God. And he says; "Great is the power of God! I will forever be grateful to Him. Like Paul says in Romans 8:38-39, 'Nothing can separate us from the love of God.'" And Henry wants the world to know, "God is good and powerful, and you can trust in Him. Look what He did for me. He healed me!"

Several months later, we had a group from Chicago, Illinois, with us, and we walked over to the village church that Henry's family attends and serves at. After the service, we invited those who needed healing to come forward so that we could pray for them. Henry's father came up to me to ask me to pray for Henry. I asked what was wrong with him. His father rolled up his shirt sleeve and showed me Henry's injured wrist and hand. I prayed over him and told him to put his faith into action. He immediately started to bend his wrist and open and close his hand. He was healed again! Amen!

Faith Principals:

+ The Power of Faith

+ The Power of Agreement

+ The Power of Authority

+ The Power of the Spoken Word

+ The Power of Faith in Action

— Let's Go for a Walk with Jesus —

This little Maasai boy could not stand or walk. We prayed and he walks!

This girl from our children's home could not stand or walk. We prayed and she walks!

This Maasai Mama's baby boy could not stand. As soon as I prayed over his legs, I felt a power shoot through his leg muscles, and he could stand up instantly!

Faith Principals:

- The Power of Authority
- The Power of Faith
- The Power of the Spoken Word
- The Power of Faith in Action

— A Little Boy with a Fever —

Late one morning, we went to pay a house call and pray for a sick man in Lilongwe, Malawi. As we entered the house, I noticed a little boy sick with a fever. I laid my hands on him and rebuked the fever and released the healing power of the Holy Spirit to flow through his body. He was instantly healed and went out to play.

Praying for the sick does not always have to take a long time, and it should not become a memorized formula either. We must develop a relationship with the Holy Spirit, learn how to recognize His voice, ask Him what to do, put our faith into action, and do it.

Faith Principals:

- The Power of Compassion, Mercy, and Love
- The Power of Faith
- The Power of the Spoken Word
- The Power of Faith in Action

— No Hepatitis! —

Our son, Jorge, was rescued from a very neglectful and abusive situation when he was 18 months of age; along with being malnourished, he was covered with scabies upon scabies. We were fighting to regain his health. He had all the classic symptoms of hepatitis. We prayed over his little body for healing. The doctors ran three different tests on him, and even though he had all the classics symptoms, they could not detect hepatitis or anything else in his system. From that moment on, he was fine. He gained weight and was strong and healthy. We as Christian parents have covenant rights with our Heavenly Father through the blood of Jesus to access the healing power of the Holy Spirit for the sake of our children. Faith-filled prayer works!

Faith Principals:

- ◆ The Power of Compassion, Mercy, and Love
- ◆ The Power of Faith
- ◆ The Power of the Spoken Word
- ◆ The Power of Faith in Action

— Arthritic Knee Healed —

Mirsa Santos from Jocotenango, Guatemala, came forward for prayer after the morning church service. I asked her what she needed, and she said she needed healing for her knee. She went on to explain that her knee was very painful and swollen all the time. She had a very difficult time climbing up and down stairs, sitting down, and standing up; her knee was in great pain all the time. She had been to the doctor before and was told that she had an arthritic knee and that there wasn't anything they could do for her.

I quickly showed her my knee that the Lord had healed several years ago, laid my hand on her knee, rebuked the pain and the swelling, and commanded a new knee to be recreated in the name of Jesus. She left the service still with pain in her knee, but the next morning when she woke up, she stood up and went about her daily business and didn't realize until later that the pain and swelling were totally gone. And she has been pain free ever since!

Faith Principals:

+ The Power of the Word
+ The Power of Faith
+ The Power of Authority
+ The Power of the Spoken Word
+ The Power of Faith in Action

— Twirling for Jesus —

One Sunday morning as we were entering the church, I stopped to greet Coni (her full name is Maria Consuelo Aleayaga de Cojielim from Jocotenango, Guatemala). I asked her how she was doing, and she replied, "Not well." I asked her what was wrong, and she said that she was feeling very dizzy and felt like she was going to fall over all the time. I hugged her and ministered healing to her. The following Sunday when I saw her, I asked her how she was doing. She gave me this big smile, lifted her hands to the Lord, started to twirl around in circles, and said, "I'm healed!"

Several weeks later, I asked her if I could share her testimony with you in this book and if she had anything that she wanted to share. Here is her testimony: "I am 76 years old and have had four strokes. The last one affected my balance.

I felt very dizzy, like I was going to fall over all the time. You prayed for me, and I am healed!"

Faith Principals:

+ The Power of Faith
+ The Power of Authority
+ The Power of the Spoken Word
+ The Power of Faith in Action

— Surgery Cancelled —

Mayrn de Sanchez from Jocotenango, Guatemala, had not been feeling well. She went to the doctor and was sent to have an ultra sound. They discovered that she had a growth. Further investigation showed that it was a tumor that needed to be removed immediately. Because she was receiving negative reports from the doctor and was told she needed to be operated on, she was fighting fear of cancer and premature death. Being a Christian, she turned to her brethren to pray for her.

One day, at the end of the service, she came forward for prayer for healing. I laid my hands on her and prayed, rebuking this tumor, cancer, and premature death that were attacking her body. She returned to her doctor for another ultrasound, and this time she received a good report and the surgery was cancelled. It's been over a year since then, and she is doing great and gives glory to God for healing her body!

Like many, Mayrn had received a negative and frightening medical report, but she chose to turn to God for divine healing, and she went to other believers for support when she was feeling weak in the faith. She received their encouraging words of faith to trust in God, and she received her healing. I think this is a beautiful testimony of the brethren joining their faith together and of a woman who dared to believe!

Faith Principals:

+ The Power of Faith

+ The Power of Authority

+ The Power of the Spoken Word

+ The Power of Agreement

+ The Power of Faith in Action

— No Distance in the Spirit Realm —

There is no distance in the spirit realm, as is evidenced by the next two testimonies.

As I was sitting at my desk in Guatemala, writing this book, I decided to take a short break and check my e-mail and Facebook. As I logged onto my page, I read the following prayer request by Amanda Jewel Rice in Las Vegas, Nevada, from the previous day.

> **Amanda Jewel Rice** is in a lot of pain. I threw out my back early this morning. Please pray for a miraculous healing!
>
> January 15, 2010 – 6:02 PM

There I was, writing this book about faith and healing, and found myself reading this prayer request for a miraculous healing. So I decided to be bold and write a response of faith back to her petition.

> **Becky Dvorak** Lay your hands on your back and command in the name of Jesus the vertebrae, disks, muscles, ligaments, tendons, and nerves to be realigned, and put your faith into action and do what you couldn't do before.

January 16, 2010 – 6:44 PM

> **Amanda Jewel Rice** I am healed!!! Thank you so much Becky!! I have never had the amount of faith as you have shown me until just now!! Praise the LORD!

January 16, 2010 – 7:21 PM

> **Becky Dvorak** Praise the Lord! I am sitting here writing my book on faith and healing, and it's filled with teaching and testimonies about healing. Can I add your testimony? Sweet!

January 16, 2010 – 9:20 PM

> **Amanda Jewel Rice** Please do! I would love to share my testimony. Also, I ran and carried heavy gallons of water up and down the stairs tonight!! This morning I could not even walk to the bathroom without having my hands pushing a hard pressure on my lower back!! I have been calling off from work for the past two days because I could not even walk in an upright position. I could not even bear to take a shower. When I saw your faith, I remembered when you were in Life Group at Pastor Eric's house and your testimony touched my heart. At first when I put my hands on my back and commanded the ligament and muscle back into place in Jesus' name, I could still feel the intense pain. Then, I re-read what you wrote. You said to put my faith into action, so I stood up and started moving my body around and felt an amazing and painless pop in my lower back... then I began to leap and jump and praise the Lord for His healing

power!!! I am so blessed to have known you! I always knew that there is healing in the blood of Jesus, and I have had faith, but have never put it into action right away. I would confess it with my mouth, but if I still felt pain I would assume that it was just because I did not have enough faith, when this whole time, I just needed to know how to put my faith into action. Praise the Lord! He is good! Thank you for your wisdom and encouragement.

January 17, 2010 – 4:36 AM

Isn't this a delightful testimony? I was brand new to Facebook. I hardly knew how to operate it, but when I read this request from this younger sister in the Lord, who I had met one time before in California, I put my faith into action. It took me less than one minute to write a response of faith to her request. She read it and did what she was told to do, and she was healed!

Faith Principals:

+ The Power of Faith
+ The Power of Authority
+ The Power of Faith in Action

Margie Wahing and I befriended one another via Facebook. We started getting to know one another and praying for one another's needs. One day, Margie wrote me asking for advice and prayer for a personal matter. As we were communicating back and forth, she mentioned that she had an ingrown toenail that became infected and was causing her a great deal of pain. I responded to her with a prayer of faith. Her initial response was not that of faith, but I wrote her back and encouraged her to trust God to heal her of this. I briefly taught her the power of her words and how to put her faith into action. She agreed, and the next morning it was completely healed! When all of this was taking place, Margie was in the Philippines, and I was in Guatemala. There is no distance in the spirit realm!

Margie says:

I was suffering for many days with an infected, ingrown toenail. I couldn't walk straight, couldn't go outdoors and hangout. I was also upset emotionally because of some personal matters happening in my life. I wanted to find some way to help myself forget about my problems. I had a lot of unanswered questions that were bothering me, but my toenail was in so much pain it was difficult for me to concentrate, and I wasn't able to sleep. The next day I just decided to stay home. I was sitting in front of my computer that night, checking to see who was online. It was great to see Becky online. I confided in her about my problem and mentioned to her about my toenail. She prayed for me for a complete healing. It was amazing! The next morning Jesus healed my toenail. It happened so fast! And not only did He heal my toenail, but He healed my broken heart as well. Amazing! He gave me an inner peace. He is alive! Wow! Jesus is my Healer! I was in a situation that forced me to seek His face. I asked Him to lead me back to Him, and now I am back in His arms. I am thankful for my friend Becky. I can see how God is working through her life. Prayer changes everything.

Faith Principals:

+ The Power of Faith
+ The Power of Faith in Action

— "OK, OK, I'll Put My Faith in Action!" —

Our 9-year-old son, Joaquin, had been playing ball with some of his friends when another boy jumped on him and hurt his back. That night, as he was getting ready for bed, Joaquin said, "Mom, my back still hurts." I prayed for his back and told him to put his faith in action and do what he couldn't do before. At first he kind of grumbled and complained, and climbed up to the top bunk. I said to him, "You can't expect anything to happen with an unwilling attitude."

He replied; "OK, OK, I'll put my faith in action." He stood up on his bed and started bending up and down, touching his toes. On the third time, he stood up and said, "I'm healed!" Then he laid down and went to sleep. Probably many of us have acted like our 9-year-old son and didn't want to cooperate, but afterward were glad that we did!

Faith Principals:

+ The Power of the Spoken Word
+ The Power of Faith in Action

— A Family Affair —

This is an amazing testimony of a family that united their faith in the Lord Jesus Christ and the healing power of the Holy Spirit for the glory of our Heavenly Father. Miguel Jerez from Pastores, Antigua, Guatemala, was not feeling well. After a series of aliments, many tests, and two surgery attempts, the root of the problem was discovered.

Miguel said:

> The doctors and the specialist came to speak with me one morning in my hospital room. They had discovered that there was

a tumor on the head of my pancreas. They were sure it was malignant, and they would need to operate immediately. They explained to me the seriousness of the operation and gave me a 20 percent chance of survival. If I survived the operation, they said I would then need chemotherapy and radiation treatment. These were very difficult words for me to swallow. I suddenly felt dizzy, my body felt cold, and I had a sour taste in my mouth. I had just received a death sentence.

When my parents arrived at the hospital, I shared with them everything the doctors told me. My mother responded with words of faith, and said that it didn't matter what the percentages of survival rate were, God is in control, and started quoting Isaiah 54:17, 'No weapon formed against you shall prosper...'

The people in the church were praying for a miracle for Miguel, and God continued to give the same words of encouragement to the family from Joshua 1:9, "Have I not commanded you? Be strong and of good courage; do not be afraid, nor be dismayed, for the Lord your God is with you wherever you go." Miguel and his family were all believers in Jesus Christ, and they knew that Jesus Christ could heal, but were not fully convinced that it was God's will to heal everyone, all the time, of all things. They struggled with fear after receiving such a negative medical report. Even though many people came to pray for them, they still lacked the confidence to stand firm in the faith for Miguel's healing. As a young man, Miguel had struggled with the fear of dying prematurely.

Miguel explains:

> During the next few days, we encouraged ourselves with the Word and by singing praises to our God. The doctor said that I could return to my home and be with my family for the month of December and then return in the beginning of January. I figured he wanted me to spend my last Christmas with my family. During the last few days in December, I was admitted to the emergency ward. It was the most difficult year my family had ever experienced.
>
> I was transferred to another hospital, waiting for another operation, but God was speaking so clearly to us about trusting completely in Him. In the midst of all that was happening, God gave me the following verse. Joshua 1:13, *"Remember the Word which Moses the servant of the Lord commanded you, saying; "The Lord your God is giving you rest and is giving you this land."*

The battle for Miguel's life was definitely raging! The doctors said that they needed to operate again and this time to remove his pancreas. They said that when he awoke from the operation he would then be a diabetic for the rest of his life, but at least he would be alive!

The family did not want this. Miguel didn't want to be a diabetic for the rest of his life, nor did he want to die prematurely. It was a very difficult battle; every report was so negative and without hope. Miguel had to choose life, and he had to choose divine healing. He had to choose to refuse to accept the negative medical reports. He had to choose to refuse to allow the physical manifestations in his body to dictate the final outcome. He had to choose hope instead of despair. He had to choose to dare to believe that God is who He says He is and that He will do what His Word says.

The family prayed that they would not have to remove his pancreas. After several hours, the surgeon came out and spoke with the family and said that he was not able to take out the pancreas because it was too close to one of his main arteries, and if they were to accidently cut it, he would bleed to death within five minutes.

The next morning, the doctors came to see Miguel and report what took place during the surgery. They said that all his organs looked really good, but that they were not able to remove the tumor and that they needed to find another type of treatment. Miguel was discouraged by the news.

One evening after this last surgery attempt, someone from the church came to their home and ministered to the family and encouraged them in the faith. He told them to open up their doors because His servants were going to start coming to minister to them.

Miguel's parents asked us to come and pray over Miguel. When we arrived, we found the family united, but struggling in the faith concerning healing. David and I listened carefully as they shared from their hearts. With the Word of God, we corrected a few misconceptions concerning healing, encouraged them with a few personal healing testimonies, laid hands on Miguel, and ministered healing.

We rebuked a spirit of premature death and commanded the growth to shrivel up and be gone. We released the Spirit of Life to flow into his body and declared that he would live and not die and that he would fulfill his destiny in the name of Jesus.

As we prayed, I saw a vision of a strong, mature oak tree whose leaves were changing color and starting to fall to the ground. I knew in my spirit that the interpretation was that Miguel would not die prematurely, that he would be healed and live to be a strong, old man.

After our visit, other servants of the Lord with the same healing message came in pairs and confirmed their faith in the healing power of the Holy Spirit. It reminds me of the story of Moses during the battle between the Israelites and the Amalekites (see Exod. 17:8-16). While Moses held up his arms with the staff in his hands, Joshua and the Israelites would prevail, but when Moses was tired and his arms would hang low, the enemy would prevail. So Aaron and Hur held up Moses' arms for him, and Joshua defeated Amalek and his people with the edge of the sword.

All of us who were standing in faith with the family for Miguel's healing were like Aaron and Hur, his family was like Moses holding up the staff during the battle, and Miguel was Joshua in the midst of the battlefield. And because the Body of Christ rallied around this family, they were able to hold up their staff (their faith in God and His promise of physical healing) so that Miguel was able to hold up his sword (the Word of God) and defeat that ugly spirit of cancer and death.

Once firm decisions were made, the healing power of the Holy Spirit started to manifest in his body. Seven days after the failed attempt to remove his pancreas and the tumor, the specialist called Miguel's mother with a wonderful report; "There is no cancer! There is not one cancer cell in his body!" And they never found a tumor, just some swelling, but no tumor!

Miguel concludes this testimony with these words:

God is doing great things in my life, and I pray that you can see that by reading this testimony. "*Behold, I will bring it health and healing; I will heal them and reveal to them the abundance of peace and truth*" (Jer. 33:6). I give God all the glory! His name is higher than any other name!

Faith Principals:

+ The Power of Compassion, Mercy, and Love

+ The Power of Faith

+ The Power of Agreement

+ The Power of Authority

+ The Power of the Spoken Word

+ The Power of Persistence

+ The Power of Faith in Action

+ The Power of Praise

— Luciana —

Luciana is a beautiful 85-year-old woman from Cahabon, Coban, Guatemala. She is a brand new believer in Jesus Christ and is learning who Jesus is and who she is in Him. She waited outside of our hotel where we were staying to ask me to pray for her. She has had a very difficult life and was full of arthritic pain, but not anymore! We prayed together, and she was instantly healed! Now, she is ready at anytime to meet her Maker, but she will leave this Earth like Moses did, full of strength and bringing glory to His name!

Faith Principals:

+ The Power of Compassion, Mercy, and Love
+ The Power of Faith
+ The Power of Authority
+ The Power of the Spoken Word
+ The Power of Faith in Action

— Victoria: Santiago, Guatemala —

Classes were done for the day, and Victoria was on her way home from seminary; as she was crossing the street, she was suddenly hit by a car. The doctor said she would not survive. Her Christian family prayed for a miracle. After lying in a coma for 20 days, she woke up, but the prognosis was not good. The doctor said she would remain in a vegetable state for the rest of her life. The family continued to trust God, and to the surprise of her doctor, she regained mobility and with help could walk. But all was not well with Victoria, physically she was very weak and unstable, she had suffered a severe brain injury, had constant dull head pain with sharp shooting pains, and had lost about 90 percent of her memory.

Months later, my husband and I were holding a five week faith and healing school in her church, based on the teachings found in this book. The first week we taught about being redeemed from the curse of sickness and disease (see

Chapter 1: "Redeemed from the Curse"). After teaching the Word, we gave an altar call for healing. Victoria, with the help of her mother, came forward.

As I laid my hands on her, the healing power of the Holy Spirit starting flowing through her brain and body. The constant pain in her head was instantly gone and so were the severe shooting pains. The next week came, and she walked up the isle without the help of others, and her memory had returned. Each week that we saw her, we could see a notable change in her physical body. No longer was she just walking up the isle, but she was now wearing high heels, too!

And to everyone's delight, her gift of music had returned, as well. Within three weeks she played a solo on her saxophone at an outdoor campaign with her father's Christian band, and at the end of the five week faith and healing school, she walked up to the pulpit with a grateful heart and sang; "How Great Thou Art" to Jesus Christ her Healer.

What Faith Principals Were Activated?

+ The Power of the Word.
+ The Power of Faith.
+ The Power of Authority.
+ The Power of Agreement
+ The Power of Persistence
+ The Power of the Healing Anointing.
+ The Power of the Spoken Word.
+ The Power of Faith in Action.

— In Just One Night —

One night, David was testifying to a few pastors that he had just met at a pastoral conference. One of the pastors asked him if we would hold a healing conference in his area. David agreed, and a meeting was scheduled for a few weeks later.

Our son, Joaquin, said to me during morning devotions, "Mom, I want to be a pastor when I grow up, so I think I had better learn how to pray for the sick now." So that week before the healing conference, we studied about healing from the Book of Luke. One day before the conference, our family traveled to Cahabon, Guatemala. It's a beautiful area with great needs, physically and spiritually, but we arrived fully expecting God to move mightily. For the next several days, both David and I taught on the healing power of the Holy Spirit, and we witnessed many miracles. We prayed for young and old alike, with our children praying along side of us.

One night, an elegant woman walked into the meeting and sat in the front row. After David was done preaching, he called the people forward for healing. I prayed for this woman, who had been suffering for years with severe abdominal pain and ulcers; she was instantly healed and gave glory to God.

We prayed for many hurting individuals and saw the Lord touch them in such a special way. We prayed for numerous couples in the Church with troubled relationships. Numerous alcoholics repented and gave their lives to the Lord. Infertile couples came forward for healing to conceive. Severely injured backs, shoulders, necks, and knees were healed, as well as fevers and infections. It was a glorious night.

The next evening, we held a healing crusade in the local stadium. A local Christian band ministered in song, and then I taught about being redeemed from the curse of sin, sickness, and disease by the blood of Jesus Christ. After the people were convinced by the Word that it was God's will to heal everyone, of everything, all the time, I gave an altar call, asking anyone who wanted to receive Jesus Christ as their Lord and Savior to come forward, and we led them in a prayer of repentance. Then a call for healing was given; David and I, our children, and our team from the host church went to work and started ministering healing to a thousand or more people who came forward. Here are two short testimonies.

As I was ministering healing in the midst of the crowd, I was asked to pray for a blind, elderly woman. I laid my hands over her eyes, rebuked a spirit of blindness over her, and commanded that her eyes be recreated in the name of Jesus. I spoke to the eyes—that they would first see light, then the outline of objects, and then colors. Then her vision would be restored to perfect. I told the woman to put her faith into action and to open up her eyes and tell me what she saw. She said that she could see light, but nothing else. I explained to her how I had prayed, and I told her to open up her eyes again and tell me what she could see. She then could see the outline of me standing in front of her. I asked her what the color of my dress was, and she answered correctly, red.

Then I held up my hands in front of her and asked her to tell me how many fingers I was holding up. She said that she could not see my fingers, but could see the rings on my fingers. Then she started to see my fingers. Her vision continued to get clearer and clearer. At the end of the night, when the crowd had left, this woman was sitting on a chair thanking me for praying for her because she could see. I explained to her that it was God who healed her and led her in a prayer of thanks to Him.

A paralyzed woman was carried on a chair to the meeting that evening, and she sat in the front row. She was one of the first people I ministered to. She went out under the power of the Holy Spirit and was set free. Now she walks. Jesus set her free in spirit, soul, and body. We ministered to over a thousand sick people that night until midnight, and the healings were amazing and great in number. Afterward, the people in that stadium broke out in dance, celebrating what the Lord had done! All glory goes to our Lord Jesus Christ!

Within the next few days, family groups that were saved and healed at the healing conference came to see the pastor of the host Church, asking him to disciple them in the Word. In just one night with the Lord, the young Church grew to full and overflowing. They actually had to extend the roof of the building into the parking lot to accommodate for all the new members. What more could we ask for? God did a mighty work in our midst!

The next morning, we ministered healing at the host's Church service and made a few home visits in the afternoon. It was late Sunday afternoon and time for our family to start the seven-hour journey home. Because we were all so tired, we decided to spend the night at some bungalows by the river in a nearby village and get an early start the next morning for home, but God had other plans for us.

On the morning of the outdoor healing service in the stadium, I had shared Marcos' amazing testimony on the local radio station that reaches the nearby villages. Well, the community that owned the bungalows where we were staying had heard the radio program, and one of the families wanted us to come and pray for their very sick mother.

This woman had been fighting severe pain for five years straight. They had tried it all—visiting medical doctors, purchasing medicine, even paying for the witchdoctor to come and see if he could make her well. All their efforts failed, and the family did not have the resources to continue to pay for medical treatment and medicine. That night we walked over to their hut to meet the family and minister healing to this woman named Rosa.

We found Rosa lying in great pain in a hammock in the dark, smoke-filled hut with her family standing all around her. Listening to their story, we all realized that the first and most important miracle that this family needed was the salvation that is only found in Jesus Christ. After some teaching, the whole family prayed and received Jesus as their Lord and Savior. Then we ministered healing to Rosa while she was lying in her hammock. The whole evening was very interesting as most of the family did not speak Spanish and our Spanish needed to be translated into the local dialect. After we ministered the healing power of the Holy Spirit into Rosa's body, we asked her to put her faith into action and do what she could not do before. Very slowly, the family helped her out of the hammock, and she started to move her feet, bend her knees, and touch the floor. Then she started to walk around the hut. She had been healed in Jesus' name!

The next morning, while eating breakfast, we asked her son how she was doing, and he said she was up and doing great! Amen!

Faith Principals:

+ The Power of the Word
+ The Power of Faith
+ The Power of Authority
+ The Power of Agreement

+ The Power of the Healing Anointing
+ The Power of the Spoken Word
+ The Power of Faith in Action

— Can We Pray for You? —

The other day, David and I and our five boys walked down to the store to buy some pop to drink. When we arrived, I asked the owner of the store (an elderly, Guatemalan woman) how she was doing. She replied; "Oh Sister, my back and shoulder hurt so much. I can't handle it." I asked her if she would like us to pray for her. She said; "Please pray." So, David and I and the boys reached over the counter, laid our hands on her, and rebuked arthritis, pain, and swelling, commanding her back to be realigned in the name of Jesus. She was instantly healed.

Such an encounter is called a divine appointment from God, and we can all have them if, we will listen and obey Him.

Faith Principals:

+ The Power of Compassion, Mercy, and Love
+ The Power of Faith
+ The Power of Agreement
+ The Power of the Spoken Word
+ The Power of Faith in Action

CHAPTER 16

CHILDLIKE FAITH

THIS TESTIMONY HAPPENED to me back in January of 2003. We had been on the mission field in Guatemala for nine years at that time. I had been told that I was going through early menopause, but I was misdiagnosed for about five years. What I found out on January 13, 2003, was that I had a prolapsed uterus that was pushing into my intestines, I had infected ovaries, and I had a growth of some sort. Doctors told me that I needed to have immediate surgery. The next morning, I walked to the operating room, climbed up onto the table, and had a total hysterectomy and exploratory surgery. I woke up several hours later, not having had been given any form of pain medication, and was suffering with extreme pain.

I left the hospital about three days later, though my digestive system was not working. A week into the ordeal, my system still was not working. All I was being given was an over-the-counter pain reliever every four hours, and it was not helping at all. At nighttime, the pain became so intense. The only way I could escape the pain was to pray in tongues until I fell asleep.

After the surgery, I spent a week with some very dear friends of ours in the city before returning to the children's home. It was the fourth night after the surgery, and the pain was so intense that I honestly felt I was going to lose my mind. I listened to worship music and prayed in tongues until I fell asleep. Later that night, I was awakened by the Holy Spirit calling me by name in an audible voice.

He said, "Becky!"

I answered, "What?"

He said, "You need to come against four spirits coming upon you right now."

I asked, "What are they?"

He answered, "A spirit of death, a spirit of cancer, a spirit of gangrene, and a spirit of infections."

I laid my hands on my abdominal area, I rebuked each one of these evil spirits by name, and I released the Spirit of Life to flow through my body in the name of Jesus. The next thing I knew, it was morning.

The next night, the pain was even more intense than before. My system was still not working, and I think the pressure was making matters worse. I lay in that bed crying because the pain was so intense. I again turned the worship music on and started to worship the Lord and pray in tongues. As soon as I started to do this, the Lord gave me a vision. I call this vision "Childlike Faith."

In this vision, I saw myself in the form of a little girl. I came walking from behind the throne of God into the throne room. I didn't walk through a magnificent, guarded entrance, but from behind the throne. I didn't understand until years later why that was, but it was because I didn't need to enter in. I was already in His presence. The atmosphere of this place resonated with a very tangible love, compassion, mercy, and peace. There were angelic beings all around, but I didn't even care that they were there. I wanted and needed my Heavenly Father. Not one of the angelic beings stopped me or asked me what I was doing there. Everyone seemed to know who I was and why I was there. And in fact, it was the most natural thing for me to be in there. No one stopped me to give me any type of instructions or directions, I knew where I was, and I knew what to do.

I saw myself in this vision as a little girl in a pink dress with red shoes, just like I was when I was a little girl, and I climbed up a very large throne, onto the lap of the Father. I never saw His face, but I was climbing up into His lap, just like a child does with her earthly father. As I reached His lap, I stood up and wrapped my little arms around His neck, and both in the vision and in the natural realm, I heard myself cry out to God and say, "Daddy, I need You!"

As soon, as I spoke these words, He took me back into time. Now I saw myself as I actually was, an adult woman in my pink pajamas, standing next to a very tall angelic being. As I was standing next to him, I looked in front of us and saw a large arm with a whip in hand. I saw this whip crack down hard on the back of Jesus. I could see and hear the whip as Jesus was being whipped. I saw Jesus kneeling beside a post that He was tied to, while He was being whipped. The whole time He was looking directly into my eyes. My eyes were fixed on His eyes, and I held out my hand to Him and started walking toward Him. As I reached out to touch His face, He blurred the vision of His face and spoke to me in an audible voice and said, "Becky, you could not stand to see My face at this point in time. By My stripes you are healed; now rest in Me." Then He continued to speak to me about the next ministry trip to Tanzania that was scheduled in five months. He said to be at peace and assured me that I would be ready to go and minister.

About two days later, we received the test results of the growth that they had removed, and it was benign. I give glory to God, because I know He healed me. There is healing power in His manifested presence. Why did I have the surgery? Because that's where my faith was, at that point in my life, but God in His great mercy met me where I was at. Since then, I have strengthened my faith in the Word, as the following testimony shows.

— Immediate Surgery—No! —

One night, I was not feeling well and quickly became very ill. I could feel my kidney on the left side and was experiencing a lot of back pain. My husband looked at my back and said it was very swollen on the left side. I went to a doctor to see what was wrong with me. They sent me to have an ultrasound done, and it showed that my right kidney was enlarged and the shape was abnormal. Since the body has a mirror effect, all of the symptoms were on the left side, even though the problem was actually on the right side. I had to fast for about 12 hours and prepare for further testing for the next day.

I became so violently ill that night; I was vomiting and was fighting such a strong fever that our bed was literally shaking. David became frightened, and I was too out of it to know what was really happening. I know that I prayed to God for His help. I rebuked the spirit of death over me in the name of Jesus. It was a rough night, but by His grace, I made it through. The next morning tests showed that I had a kidney stone blocking my urethra tube, close to the bladder, which had caused my urine to back up into my right kidney. They said that I needed to have immediate surgery. I said, "no!"

Within two days I was on an airplane headed for Minnesota from Guatemala to attend my niece's wedding, and from there I was to fly to Tennessee and then to the East Coast to speak in a few churches in Connecticut and Virginia and then back to Guatemala.

I had prayed that this stone would either supernaturally dissolve or that it would break up into very tiny pieces and that I would not feel it pass. The doctors had filled me with fear and said that I needed immediate attention when I was in the States and to be prepared because I would be falling on the floor in great pain when the stone passed. I had to face the fear of pain, but chose to put my trust in God. Only once did I feel a little tinge of pain when I was in Virginia. I had to face that fear of pain again. I went into the restroom, I took my authority over the situation, and I commanded it to dissolve and to pass without any pain. I was straining my urine in a strainer like the doctor had instructed me, because I was supposed to bring him the stone, but I never found one. God is the great physician, He healed me, and I never had that problem again. Glory to God!

— Typhoid Fever —

David and I live in Guatemala, and we also travel around the world. During the year 2001, I had traveled in Nigeria, the United States, and Mexico, and I had contracted typhoid. I don't know where I contracted it, and I didn't care at the moment either. I just knew I had it and was very ill.

This was my third bout with the wicked illness! I was in level four (which is the worst level of typhoid). I was vomiting and had diarrhea at the same time. I was fighting very high fevers, my head was pounding, my bones and muscles were screaming with pain, and I held onto my abdominal area and cried because the pain was so bad. I went to a small Guatemalan clinic to get shots of vitamins for four days straight, but it didn't seem to help. I would just lie in bed and cry.

I reached a point where I thought I could not handle it anymore, and I asked the Lord to take me home. That was when I heard His voice, and He said to me, "Get up and get dressed!" There was no mistaking His voice. I tried to get up, but I couldn't because I was so weak. Then I heard Him say it again, "Get up and get dressed!" I slowly slid out of the bed and crawled to the dresser and got dressed. I opened up the bedroom door and walked down the long hallway to the kitchen.

When our workers saw me, they scolded me and told me to get back into bed! I said; "No!" And from that moment on, I regained my physical strength and never had typhoid symptoms again. Jehova-Rapha is my Healer and my strength!

— Blessings Shall Overtake You —

I was born again and baptized with the Holy Spirit when I was 18 years old, in May of 1979. As a baby Christian, in 1980, I could not get enough of the Lord and His Word. I would read and study the Word and fellowship with the Lord all afternoon. My life started to evolve around Him. As a baby Christian, I did not know much about healing. I had heard some fabulous testimonies, but I didn't understand that it was for me, too. Nevertheless, I was consumed with His love for me and spent my days with Him.

I had a few warts on my left hand. They were not very big, but I did not like them. One day I looked down at my hand, and they were completely gone. I never had anyone pray over them. I did not know to pray over them myself either. They were just suddenly gone, and I know they disappeared because I was in the habitat of His manifested presence. *"And all these blessings shall come upon you and overtake you, because you obey the voice of the Lord your God"* (Deut. 28:2).

I was so in love with Him (and I still am), and I was in His Word, learning to live according to His ways. I was diligently listening and obeying Him, and because of it, His blessing of healing came upon me and overtook me. He removed those warts from my hand, even though I was not seeking healing, but because I was seeking Him.

— Healing Through Communion —

Many years ago when I was a young Christian, in the early stages of learning about faith, I had become very ill with a fever and a bad throat infection. We were short on money, and I couldn't go to the doctor. After a month of fighting this sickness, I was feeling worse than before. One Sunday night at church, while we were taking Communion, I asked the Lord to heal me, and He did. I was instantly healed. No one laid hands on me; I went directly to God, my Healer. We as Christians have a blood covenant (through the blood of Jesus Christ) with the Father that cannot be broken, and healing is a part of the blood covenant.

> *In the same manner He also took the cup after supper, saying, "This cup is the new covenant in My Blood. This do, as often as you drink it, in remembrance of Me"* (1 Corinthians 11:25).

— Laying on of Hands —

In 2003, I had injured my back and was in great pain. However, I was scheduled to go to Africa for a couple weeks to teach the Word of God. My husband was the only person who knew about this problem. I didn't speak of this condition to anyone else. I had prayed and made the decision that I would trust the Lord to heal my back. He created my back, and He was able and willing to heal it, too.

One evening, in Rural Mbeya, Tanzania, I was ministering healing by the laying on of hands to many people. The line of people seemed to grow in number as the evening went on, and I stepped back to take a break, just for a moment. As I did, I heard the Spirit of the Lord say to me, "Lay your hands on your back."

I replied; "Oh yes, my back!" And the Lord instantly healed my lower back. That severe pain never returned again. Praise the Lord! We shall lay hands on the sick and they shall recover (see Mark 16:18). This includes ministering over our own bodies, too!

— Progressive Healing —

In 2003, as I was stepping off the bus to cross the road to preach at an outdoor evangelistic campaign in Lilongwe, Malawi, when my foot touched the ground, an excruciating pain shot through my right knee. As I crossed the road, my knee became stiffer and stiffer, along with many other strange and painful manifestations on my body. Most of what I was experiencing was a manifestation of the Gifts of the Spirit (see 1 Cor. 12:8)—a Word of Knowledge of the needs of certain people in that meeting. Everything during the meeting disappeared as I ministered to the people with those particular problems, except for one thing, the knee pain.

By the time I made it back to Guatemala, my knee was rubbing bone on bone. I remember sitting down at the table next to my husband, and he looked at me and asked, "Was that your knee I just heard?" It was indeed what he heard, but I continued to speak to my knee to be recreated in the name of Jesus. And my knee slowly got better and better as the days went by until it was completely healed. No longer does bone rub against bone. He not only is my Healer, but He is also my Re-Creator!

My knee is perfectly fine today. Since then, the Lord has brought others to me in healing lines with the same problem, and I show them my knee and testify, and they receive an immediate healing in their knees. Let's not only receive healing into our bodies; let's multiply those same healings for the glory of our Lord (see Gen. 1:28).

I did not allow my five senses or the pain to dictate my confession, but rather my confession of faith in His promise dictated and brought forth my creative miracle for my knee. "By His stripes I am healed" (see Isa. 53:5).

— Cursed at Its Very Root and Seed —

In 2008, I had a mole growing very quickly on my body, and it became peppered with black spots. I didn't think it was a good thing to have, so I laid my hands on it and cursed it at its very roots and seed. David and I left for Tanzania, Africa, for a few weeks. While we were there, I noticed that the mole was drying up and had started to detach itself from my body. When we arrived back to Guatemala, I was getting dressed in my pajamas. I looked down and saw that the mole was almost completely detached. As I went to touch it, it fell off in my hand and I was now holding a small pile of grainy, sand-like material in my hand. I brushed it out of my hand and thanked the Lord! I used my authority in the name of Jesus and the power of the spoken word, and what I spoke came to pass.

— New Arches —

Living and working in a children's home for so many years had taken a toll on my physical body, especially my arches. I was battling with a lot of pain in my feet and in my legs. I continued to speak faith-filled words over my arches and continued about my daily routine as a mama to many.

One day I was studying my Bible on the plane to Nashville, Tennessee. The next morning, I knew I would be standing and teaching at the morning service. My arches were in a lot of pain, and I silently quoted the Word of God over my arches again.

The next morning after the service, some of the people wanted to pray for me. They all circled around and started to pray. I closed my eyes, and I felt someone's hands touching my feet as they were praying over me. When they were all done praying, Heidi Lamberg started to share with me that as she was praying, she saw in her mind's eye a picture of my feet. She didn't know why she saw my feet, but decided to pray for them. I told her that I knew why she saw my feet and told her the healing that I was standing in faith for. And my arches were healed that day!

Since then, the Lord has also brought numerous ladies with painful arches to me for prayer. I show them my arches and testify, and they receive their healings immediately!

This is an example of the multiplication principal in Genesis 1:28. I am putting my faith into action and multiplying healing for arches.

— Chose to Testify —

In May 1982, David had a serious back injury at work. He and his co-workers were trimming a large tree when a rope slipped, and an 8-inch round limb on a 50-foot rope went swinging and hit David in the lower back. It sent him flying through the air and onto the ground. He had seriously injured his lower back and kidneys. He fought with severe back pain for numerous years. He had to literally slide out of bed every morning, and he wondered if there would ever be a day when he would not feel pain in his back. He used to meditate on Heaven and try to imagine a life with no pain. Several years later, he went forward for healing at a healing service, was miraculously healed, and was free from pain.

A few years later, after the morning church service, David went to talk to the pastor because he felt impressed to share his testimony of how he was healed. While he was waiting to talk to the pastor, he noticed that his shoe lace was untied. As he bent down to tie his shoe, a severe pain went through his lower back. He thought to himself, *How can I testify? I am no longer healed?* But he spoke with the pastor anyway, and the pastor said that he had heard from God, because he was planning on having a night of testimonies from the congregation at that evening's service.

He spent the afternoon on the couch in severe pain and in turmoil because he was to share his healing testimony in front of the congregation that night. But he made a decision that he was going to share his testimony no matter how he felt.

That evening, in severe pain, he sat on the front row waiting for his turn to share his healing testimony. The pastor finally called him up to the altar. He slowly stood up, and as he walked up the steps to the altar he was once again miraculously healed. Now he had two amazing healing testimonies to share, the healing testimony that he had originally planned on sharing, and now a second healing testimony about how the enemy tried to steal his first testimony, but he did not allow him to do so. It was an amazing testimony that encouraged and taught us that we have authority over all the attacks of the enemy. Twenty-five years later, he has been pain free in his lower back!

— Having Done All, Stand —

"Therefore take up the whole armor of God, that you may be able to withstand in the evil day, and having done all, to stand" (Eph. 6:13). One afternoon in Guatemala, David was working outside and walked into the house with major back pain. When he removed his shirt, his spine was in a very distinct "S" shape, and he was in great pain. I laid hands on his back, and we prayed for healing. We saw no real immediate changes, but we knew that we had done what the Lord teaches us in His Word to do.

And these signs will follow those who believe; In My name they will cast out demons, they will speak with new tongues; they will take up serpents, and if they drink anything deadly, it will by no means hurt them, they will lay hands on the sick, and they will recover (Mark 16:17-18).

David and I stood on the promise of God that, if we believe, we shall lay hands on the sick in Jesus' name and they will recover. Within a few hours, his back returned to normal and all pain was gone. Glory to God!

— Are You Healed? —

Back in 1979, we were new believers attending Jesus People Church in Minneapolis, Minnesota. The pastor made an altar call for healing. David had a problem with his shoulder and could not lift a few pounds without severe pain in his arm. He wasn't sure why he had this pain, other than the words of his father resounding in the back of his memory, "I hope you don't have pain like this when you grow up!" His father had injured his rotary cup and lived with great shoulder pain.

David went forward to be ministered to for healing. When he returned to his seat, we asked him if had been healed. David said that he didn't know, because he was too afraid to lift his arm to find out! We told him to lift his arm. As he put his faith into action, he lifted his arm and was instantly healed. About two weeks later, the pain started to return. For the next several days, he had to fight to hold onto his healing. He kept on confessing; "In Jesus' name, I am healed!" And the pain ceased and never returned again. He called those things that were not as though they were (see Rom. 4:17).

— Poison Ivy —

For many years David had struggled with a severe allergic reaction to poison ivy. He would have to go to the hospital as a child to receive special medical attention because he would be so swollen from it. But, in his early 20s, as a young Christian, he was growing in his faith and had been learning about healing.

It was around 1980, and David was working for a company doing tree trimming and removal. Because of his experience with roping limbs down, he had been called out to do a special tree. The tree was growing over a green house, and they couldn't get a truck into the back yard, so it had to be climbed manually.

When David arrived, he saw that the entire yard had been covered with poison ivy. The problem was that the ropes he would be using would be contaminated with the oil from the poison ivy plants, which would get all over him. He remembers exactly what he said: "I curse you in the name of Jesus! I command you not to have an effect on my body!" And he's never had a problem with poison ivy since!

He exercised his authority over the curse in the name of Jesus and used the power of his words to control the situation. We have been given dominion over every living thing on this Earth, and that includes allergic reactions to poison ivy (see Gen. 1:28).

I could continue to write testimony after testimony of God's marvelous healing power. I count it such a privilege to be able to testify of His marvelous acts. I pray that these testimonies have stirred our hearts to *dare to believe* that Jesus Christ is who He says He is and that He will do exactly as His Word says!

CHAPTER 17

COMMISSIONED
TO HEAL

THE OTHER DAY, I was walking down the street and a woman from the church that we attend in Guatemala stopped and asked me if God would heal an unbeliever too. I answered, "yes." Let's look to the Scriptures for proof.

> *Now when the sun was setting, all those who had anyone sick with various diseases brought them to Him; and He laid His hands on every one of them and healed them. And demons also came out of many, crying out and saying, "You are the Christ, the Son of God!" And He, rebuking them, did not allow them to speak, for they knew that He was the Christ* (Luke 4:40-41).

It says that Jesus laid hands on every one of them, and healed them—not just those that professed to believe in Jesus, *but every one of them!*

I have visited numerous hospitals filled with sick and dying people. As I went from bed to bed praying for the patients, I never denied healing from people because they didn't profess Jesus. In fact, I have seen the compassion of God move very powerfully over the lost, and after they receive their healing, they have been ready to confess their sins and receive Jesus Christ as their Lord and Savior.

One time, after we ministered to the sick in Malawi, the pastors traveling with us said to each other, "She even asks the Muslims to renounce Mohammed!" I was surprised at their response. We do not just want people healed; we want them saved. Healing is a tool that the Holy Spirit uses to prove Himself to the lost, especially to those who have not been taught about Jesus. It has become a method of evangelism that my husband and I teach others around the world. We call it *Spirit-led evangelism*, which results from a daily life of being led by Him.

What are our motives for praying for the sick? Is it because we want others to see that God is moving through us and our ministry? Do we want others to think that we are super-spiritual or superior over them? Are we in it for financial gain or position? These are wrong motives. Jesus, on the other hand, was moved with compassion to heal the sick. Compassion is love in action. We can develop within us His heart of compassion for others, and when we do, we will start to see healings manifest all around us. *"And when Jesus went out He saw a great multitude, and He was moved with compassion for them, and healed their sick"* (Matt. 14:14).

Recently, David and I and some friends were walking down a nature trail along the Cahabon River in Champuey National Park, in Guatemala. Our five boys were running ahead of us. We happened to stop and chat with a man who was hired to guard and tend the trail. The man shared with us about a serious accident he had while swinging on a rope swing into the river. His hands slipped off the rope before he swung out into the river, and he came crashing down onto the large rocks below. He was very seriously injured. He broke his leg in several places, and it did not heal well. As he was telling us this story, I heard the voice of the Lord say to me, "Pray for him."

After he finished telling us about the accident, I asked him if we could pray for him for healing. He agreed, and we all prayed. I asked him to put his faith into action and do something he couldn't do before. He put his weight on his leg and squatted low to the ground with no problem or pain. With tears in his eyes, he thanked the Lord. This healing opened up the door for us to minister into his personal life.

God wants us to care about people the way He does. He loves this man, and He knew that he was in a lot of pain physically and that he also needed prayer for other matters. God wanted him free from pain, and He was waiting for someone to notice him, to care enough to take a few moments and step out in faith and minister healing to him. That's having a heart of compassion for others and put loving into action.

Have I discovered a key to walking in the power of the Holy Spirit with signs and wonders following? It is amazing how many times I have been asked this question in one form or another by others. Yes, I have found a key to walking in the power of the Holy Spirit with signs and wonders following, but I am *not* the only one who has discovered this. Anyone you see walking in the miraculous realm has discovered the same thing as I have. The whole key to walking in the miraculous realm is spending time and developing a relationship with the Holy Spirit. He is the Lord of miracles; the miraculous is His terrain. And as we have discussed throughout this book, the entrance into this miraculous terrain is by residing in the habitation of His manifested presence. We can walk in this realm if we choose to get to know Him and obey Him. *"Finally, my brethren be strong in the in the Lord and in the power of His might"* (Eph. 6:10).

We, as believers, have all been commissioned to minister healing to the sick. Jesus, standing in the synagogue, read from the Book of Isaiah, the following prophesy about Himself.

> *The Spirit of the Lord is upon Me, because He has anointed Me to preach the gospel to the poor. He has sent Me to heal the broken hearted, to preach deliverance to the captives and recovery of sight to the blind, to set at liberty those who are oppressed, to preach the acceptable year of the Lord* (Luke 4:18-19).

It's easy to think, *But that was Jesus; He was God.* But we must remember, as we discussed in Chapter 2, that the amazing miracles Jesus did on this Earth, He did in the strength of a man. He did not cheat and use His God powers. Jesus was always about doing His Father's business, winning souls, and multiplying the Kingdom of God. In these next few verses, Jesus commissioned the 12 disciples to go out and heal the sick.

These twelve Jesus sent out and commanded them, saying... "And as you go, preach, saying, 'The kingdom of heaven is at hand.' Heal the sick, cleanse the lepers, raise the dead, cast out demons. Freely you have received, freely give (Matthew 10:5a,7-8).

We may be tempted to elevate the 12 disciples as special ones chosen by God to carry on the work of the Lord. Yet, the 12 disciples needed more help to carry out the work of the ministry, because the Lord also appointed 70 others to minister healing to the sick.

After these things the Lord appointed seventy others also, and sent them two by two before His face into every city and place where He Himself was about to go (Luke 10:1).

Obviously, there were many more sick people than the 70 could reach, because after Jesus rose again from the dead, He made a point of commissioning all who believe to go out and minister healing to the sick.

And these signs will follow those who believe; in My name they will cast out demons; they will speak with new tongues; they will take up serpents; and if they drink anything deadly, it will by no means hurt them; they will lay hands on the sick, and they will recover (Mark 16:17-18).

In James, the Church receives further instruction about ministering healing to the sick.

Is anyone among you sick? Let him call for the elders of the church, and let them pray over him, anointing him with oil in the name of the Lord. And the prayer of faith will save the sick, and the Lord will raise him up. And if he has committed sins, he will be forgiven. Confess your trespasses to one another, and pray for one another, that you may be healed. The effective, fervent prayer of a righteous man avails much (James 5:14-16).

Jesus also said that those who believe in Him will do even greater works than He did! When He went to be with the Father, the Holy Spirit and His creative, explosive power was given to us.

> *Most assuredly, I say to you, he who believes in Me, the works that I do he will do also; and greater works than these he will do, because I go to My Father* (John 14:12).

> *But you shall receive power when the Holy Spirit has come upon you; and you shall be witnesses to Me in Jerusalem, and in all Judea and Samaria, and to the end of the earth* (Acts 1:8).

I know that the thought of ministering healing in the name of Jesus can be rather intimidating for some, but we need to remember that we do not go alone. The Holy Spirit, who lives and resides inside of every believer in Jesus, is the One working in and through us. Let me share a personal testimony of what happened the first time I ministered healing to someone.

Back in 1991, in Guatemala City, we were going door-to-door sharing about Jesus and inviting the people to an evangelistic campaign that we were holding in their neighborhood. At one home, the people already were Christians, so I asked them if there was anything that I could pray with them about. They said "yes" and asked us to wait. The interpreter and I sat down in their one room home and waited. Soon afterward, they returned with a little girl who had been deaf since birth and could not speak.

I did not know much about healing back then, but I laid my hands on her anyway, and I rebuked a spirit of deafness and commanded her ears to be opened, and immediately she could hear. Her first word was, "Hallelujah!" I share this testimony because sometimes people think they can't pray for people because they do not know enough about healing. But here is a powerful secret. If we know Jesus as our Lord and Savior, we have what it takes to pray for the sick. His name is Jesus, and He is the Healer!

And as we will see in the next chapter, signs and wonders, divine healings and miracles point to Jesus.

REVIEW QUESTIONS

1. Would God heal an unbeliever?

2. Where is there an example of this in Scripture?

3. What are wrong motives for praying for the sick?

4. What is compassion?

5. When we develop hearts of compassion, what will we start seeing?

6. What is the key to walking in the power of the Holy Spirit with signs and wonders following?

7. What is the terrain of the Holy Spirit?

8. As believers in Jesus Christ, what is one of the things we have all been commissioned to do?

9. In what strength did Jesus minister all the amazing miracles while He was on this Earth?

10. According to Mark 16: 17-18, what signs will follow us if we believe?

11. According to John 14:12, what type of works will we do if we believe?

12. Who is the Healer?

13. By whose power does healing manifest in us or through us?

CHAPTER 18

SIGNS AND WONDERS POINT TO JESUS

THIS STORY IS ABOUT a man named, Ray. Ray suffered the loss of his mother when he was just a young boy, and he was raised by his father and eventually a step-mother. He also had an older brother who he never learned to get along with.

Later on in life, he met and married a sweet woman and had three beautiful children and later nine wonderful grandchildren, but he was not happy, and he blamed those around him for his unhappiness. Something in his life was missing, and he looked for what was missing in all the wrong things. He was an alcoholic for most of his life, but never received any help for his problem.

Having fostered and raised many hurting children—most of them have been boys—I've always told them that until they deal with all the hurt, rejection, and pain in their lives, they will forever be little boys trapped inside big men's bodies; this was the case with Ray.

His family tried to reach out to him, but his bitterness chased them away. I believe he knew that he had failed his family, and all the guilt and shame just continued to increase. He carried a very heavy burden. Then one day his sweet wife past away, leaving him even lonelier in life.

One hot August day in 2005, David and I were in the States on our way to Tanzania, Africa, and our daughter and her husband, Annie and Adam, were visiting with us for the weekend. We decided to pay a visit to David's father, Ray.

When we pulled up in the driveway, the living room curtains were drawn and the lawn and flowerbeds were overgrown. We decided to weed the flowerbeds for him before we went inside the house. Ray saw what we were doing from the window and came outside to get us to stop, but we insisted that we were going to weed the flowerbeds for him. In a way, it softened his heart to receive his family for a visit.

Visiting him was always an uncomfortable event for everyone. But when we entered the house, he offered all of us a bottle of pop, and we sat down in the living room together for a chat. We did of course have to turn the volume on the television down so that we could hear one another!

As we were chatting, I heard the Lord say to me, start testifying to him about the miracles in Africa. I was shocked! I knew how hardhearted he was toward us and the decision we had made many years ago to be missionaries. But I knew I had heard the Lord speak to my spirit. So I started to testify to him about many different miracles. David, Annie, and Adam couldn't believe what I was doing. I continued to testify and didn't leave any details out; before I knew it, I was witnessing to him about how great God is. Ray was listening to every word. He was actually sitting on the edge of his chair, leaning forward and wanting more.

As I continued to testify, I heard God say, "Ask him if he wants to receive Jesus in his heart." So I boldly asked him if he would like to receive Jesus as his Lord and Savior, and he answered, "Yes." I wanted to make sure he understood what I had asked him, so I asked him again, and explained it further to him, and he answered, "Yes."

I led him in a prayer of salvation. He asked the Lord to forgive him for all of his sin and asked the Lord to come into his life and be his Lord and Savior. As soon as he finished praying, he said, "It's gone! It's gone! The heaviness is gone!" He was so excited and so free. He hugged every one of us and told us for the first time that he loved us!

There was no doubt in our hearts about what had just happened. We only felt sad that we could not be there to disciple him. We left for Africa, and when we returned to Guatemala, David's sister, Cheryl wrote us an e-mail saying that Ray had changed. He was softer than he was before, and he wasn't angry all the time, but she didn't understand why. She also said that his pastor was coming out to his home and reading to him from the Bible. We were thrilled to hear the report. It wasn't until several years later that David told Cheryl about the day their father was saved. He received the Lord on August 8, 2005. We had been praying for his salvation for 25 years, and at His appointed time, through our obedience and the words of our testimony, he received the Lord!

Signs and wonders are powerful, and they point to Jesus. If we will surrender to the Lord and use them for His glory, we'll lead many to the Lord. Trust in Him, and *dare to believe!* Whether our family, our friends, our neighbors, or those we consider strangers are in need of divine healing, God has provided an ark of promise for those of us who would believe.

REVIEW QUESTION

1. To whom do signs and wonders point?

CHAPTER 19

THE ARK
AND HIS PROMISE

I WOULD LIKE TO END with one last chapter about the faithfulness of God to keep His promises to us. This last word of encouragement came to me in the form of a vision while I was on a ministry trip in East Africa. My heart had been broken for all the people who were suffering and dying from the dreadful disease HIV. As I was interceding for the people and for a mighty move of the Holy Spirit to break out in that land, I saw a simple vision of the ark. There was a warm and inviting fire inside the ark, and those who believed in Jesus Christ were sitting securely around this little fire, with all of their needs met, while a fierce storm was raging all around them outside the safety of the ark.

Genesis 6 records the account of Noah and the Ark. The Earth was filled with evil and all forms of corruption, and God was going to send a flood that would destroy all of humankind and every living thing on the Earth—except for one man, his family, and a group of animals—to clean the Earth of such physical and spiritual filth.

Noah was the only righteous man left on the Earth, and he found favor in the eyes of the Lord. The Lord gave him exact instructions on how to build an ark. This ark would become the salvation for him and his family, and they would be used by God to replenish the Earth. It would become the only safe place left on all the Earth, and it would be for a man who dared to believe God when all others laughed and mocked him to scorn. He appeared to everyone who knew him to be the foolish one. Yet, this did not stop him from obeying the voice of the Lord, and he constructed the ark according to the word of the Lord that he heard. Despite all the criticism, this man remained faithful and did as he was instructed.

— Faith Principals that Guided the Life of Noah: —

- He was a just man.
- He was blameless and a man of integrity.
- He walked with God.
- He obeyed God.

In Genesis 7, we read how Noah, his family, and the animals came into the ark, and after they had entered, the Lord shut the door. The foundations of the great deep were broken up, and the windows of Heaven were opened, and it rained for 40 days and 40 nights. A grave storm was raging, and they could hear the reports of death screaming all around them, yet they remained safe inside the ark.

Just as the ark was their salvation, today the ark represents our redemption through the blood of Jesus Christ. He is the only way to salvation; there is no other way, but through Him. *"Jesus said to him, 'I am the way, the truth, and the life. No one comes to the Father except through Me'"* (John 14:6).

In Genesis 8, we see the deliverance of Noah and every living thing that was on the ark with him.

> *Then God remembered Noah, and every living thing, and all the animals that were with him in the ark. And God made a wind to pass over the earth, and the waters subsided* (Genesis 8:1).

The wind God made to pass over the Earth represents the Holy Spirit. And it was by His power that the miracle they needed was released on the Earth. The power of that wind continues to be released for us as well. No matter what we have need of today, His wind is blowing.

In Genesis 9:12-17, we read about the sign of the promise, the rainbow, and how God set this beautiful bow of colors in the sky as a reminder for perpetual generations to come that He would never again destroy all flesh with a flood.

One time, when I was a little girl, my parents, my four older brothers, and I were standing in the front yard looking up at a beautiful rainbow that had freshly painted the sky after a summer rain. As my family was standing in the warm, wet grass, gazing up at the rainbow, I heard for the first time about the true meaning of the rainbow. This was probably the first lesson I had been taught about the faithfulness of God to keep His promise. And hence forth, it has become an encouragement to me that He is not only faithful to this promise, but to all His promises in His Word. *"Let us hold fast the confession of our hope without wavering, for He who promised is faithful"* (Heb. 10:23). *"Jesus Christ is the same yesterday, today, and forever"* (Heb. 13:8).

Why did I choose to end this book with this story? Regardless of the storms raging all around us, despite the grievous death reports given to us, no matter how much we are ridiculed and mocked, the wind of His Holy Spirit has been released and is blowing throughout the whole Earth looking for people to show Himself strong through. He remains faithful and ever true to keep His promises to us, and He has given us instruction in His Word on how to enter into His ark of healing. The question remains, "Will we enter in?" God promises us, *"'For I will restore health to you and heal you of your wounds,' says the Lord..."* (Jer. 30:17). *Dare to believe!*

REVIEW QUESTIONS

1. Who was the only righteous man left on the Earth?

2. What did this man find?

3. What was he instructed to do?

4. Despite all the criticism, what did he do?

5. What were the faith principals that guided the life of Noah?

6. Just as the ark was their salvation, what does the ark represent for us?

7. What does the wind that God made to pass over the Earth represent?

8. What is the significance of the rainbow?

9. What was the lesson that I learned as a little girl about the rainbow?

10. Why did I choose to end this book with this story?

ANSWERS TO REVIEW QUESTIONS

— Chapter 1: Redeemed From the Curse —

1. mirror image
2. authority
3. His authority and dominion on this Earth
4. God
5. Serving God, by serving people
6. their identity in Christ
7. The habitation of His manifested presence
8. The curse entered, perfect became imperfect, the process of deterioration and degeneration began, and eventually Adam and Eve died.
9. A plan to redeem people to Himself
10. The word *redeemed* means "to save from a state of sinfulness and its consequences, recover ownership of by paying a specified sum, to set free, rescue or ransom."

11. Unmerited favor

12. satan, comes to steal, kill, and to destroy

13. Sickness and disease steal, kill, and destroy you and your loved ones.

14. Jesus came to give us life and life more abundantly.

15. Heath and healing are two good and perfect gifts.

16. *Blessing* is something promoting or contributing to happiness, well-being, or prosperity.

17. The key to manifesting the blessings of God is by abiding, dwelling, and actually residing in the habitation of His manifested presence.

18. We believe and receive the blessings of God by faith.

19. A *curse* is "to bring evil upon or to afflict."

20. List the seven ways Jesus shed His Blood for us.

    1. The great drops of blood He sweated in the Garden of Gethsemane

    2. The plucking out of His beard

    3. The stripes He received

    4. The crowning of thorns

    5. The nailing of His hands

    6. The nailing of His feet

    7. The piercing of His side

21. Jesus became the curse for us.

22. As a man

23. His Holy Spirit is the manifested glory of His presence within us.

24. An eternal blood covenant

— Chapter 2: Healings and Miracles —

1. By the Gifts of the Holy Spirit and by activating your own faith

2. The Gift of Faith is a Gift of the Holy Spirit. It's a special faith given as the Holy Spirit wills to receive a miracle.

3. Gifts of Healing are a Gift of the Holy Spirit, given as the Holy Spirit wills to minister healing to others.

4. The Working of Miracles is a Gift of the Holy Spirit, given as the Holy Spirit wills to work out a miracle by the power of the Holy Spirit working through you.

5. Miracles are instant, physical changes start to take place instantly. Progressive Healings are progressive in nature. They do not happen suddenly or all at once, but little by little, but they are still miraculous.

6. The more common methods of healing in the Bible are the laying on of hands, anointing with oil, the power of faith, the power of the Word of God, the power of the spoken word, obedience, and prayer cloths.

— Chapter 3: Resolving Doubts and Questions —

1. The truth is the best way to handle premature death. It allows for a healthy closure in the midst of a difficult situation.

2. We will come to our graves at an old age, having lived strong and healthy lives, and then He takes our breath away.

3. The leprous man was asking a sincere question concerning God's will to heal, while the other is a statement of doubt and unbelief.

4. Doubt and unbelief

5. Our confession

6. He had to clean the temple of sinful and religious dealings. Like

Jesus cleaned the temple, we too need to clean our spiritual temples of sin by repentance, so that the healing power of the Holy Spirit can flow freely in our physical bodies.

7. A spiritual problem

8. Aaron and Hur climbed to the top of the mountain with Moses, they set a stone under his head, and they held up his arms during the battle. Because they supported Moses, Joshua won the battle with the edge of the sword. Like Aaron and Hur, we need to support one another (climb to the mountain top with them and hold up their arms during the battle) by encouraging them to stand on the Word (set a rock under Moses) against sickness and disease and to be willing to fight the battle with them and for them by using the power of the Word of God (the edge of the sword) against sickness and disease.

9. The filthy garments that were removed from Joshua the High Priest represent the old sinful nature, the rich robes that he was then clothed with represent the salvation by the blood of Jesus Christ, and the placing of the clean turban upon his head represent the transformation of the mind of Christ. For us this means that our old, sinful nature has been redeemed by the blood of Jesus Christ at Calvary and that we need to renew our minds with His mind or with the Word of God

10. Deliverance and healing in spirit, soul, and body

11. Amazingly enough, many people act like that puppy. God miraculously heals them, gives them a second chance to live life, but they take His mercy for granted and return to dangerous habits and sinful behaviors, only to have a worse thing come upon them, and it costs them their lives.

12. He feared his living testimony and the power it had to win souls.

13. Someone who has moved against God and His Word, is weak in relationship with God, has not taken the time to study the Word,

has carelessly strayed away from the Body of Christ, is dabbling in the things of the world, and is no longer living the Word.

14. A spirit of fear

— Chapter 4: How to Receive Healing —

1. You need to be fully convinced that it is God's will to heal you all the time and of everything.

2. You need to be humble, you need to seek, you need to press into His presence, you need to be fully persuaded, you need to judge God faithful, you need to be obedient, you need to put your faith into action, and you may need to find support.

3. Study the Word of God. Focus on the Word of God and not on the symptoms. Stand firm in your faith on the Word of God.

4. Doubt and unbelief

5. By faith in God and His Word

6. Submit to God and resist the devil; draw near to God, be patient, and remain strong in the Lord.

— Chapter 5: The Blood and Our Testimony —

1. By the blood of the Lamb and by the word of our testimony

2. First, you need God's presence on the scene; next, you need to start to speak that miracle into existence; then, you need to be patient and wait for it to manifest; after the manifestation of your miracle, you see and enjoy the goodness of God.

3. Our words either create or destroy, and there is the power of life and death in the tongue.

— Chapter 6: A Special Rod —

1. Our special rod is the spoken Word of God put into action, or the active, spoken Word of God.

2. We do.

3. We first cast out our special rod by the power of our confession. And then we need to act accordingly to those words that were spoken.

4. If you are in a battle against life and death and you choose life (see Deut 30:19), you not only speak words of healing and life, but you also put your faith into action and plan and act like you are going to live.

— Chapter 7: Power From on High —

1. The Holy Spirit

2. The Holy Spirit is the creative, explosive power of God.

3. Power from on high

4. The Holy Spirit prays through us the perfect will of the Father in every situation.

5. Praying in tongues edifies, encourages, strengthens, or builds up the one praying.

6. It says that the promised Holy Spirit is to you, and to your children, and to all who are afar off, meaning this is our inheritance for generations to come.

7. The evidence that someone has received the baptism of the Holy Spirit is that they will start to speak in tongues.

8. By asking the Father

— Chapter 8: A Special Touch —

1. As she touched the hem of His garment, she came into the very presence of His being, and she no longer saw Him as just the Great Healer, but as the Messiah. And she reached out and touched Him for who He was and no longer for what He had. She touched the very center of His Spirit, and not for what was in His hand. She received the revelation of who He was and saw that He was the only one who could save her, deliver her, and yes, heal her.

2. When we reach out and touch Jesus in this manner, we come into the habitation of His manifested presence, and something wonderful happens. We touch Him, we touch His presence, and we become united with His presence.

— Chapter 9: Faith Principles in Jesus' Life —

1. Faith Principals that guided the life of Jesus:

    A. Jesus was filled with the Holy Spirit.

    B. He was led by the Spirit.

2. We to need to be filled with the Holy Spirit and learn to be led of the Holy Spirit.

3. Because Jesus had a lifestyle of studying and living out the Scriptures, was filled with the Holy Spirit, and was led by the Spirit, when He was being tempted by the devil, He was able to stand firm and not compromise in His faith. He overcame every temptation by the Word of God.

— Chapter 10: Faith Principals for Healing and Miracles —

1. The answer lies in whose word it is. It is the Word of the Lord. He is the reason behind the power of the Word.

2. The power of authority goes hand-in-hand with the power of the Word. Jesus Christ is the Word of God in the flesh, all authority was given to Him, and He gave us authority over all the power of satan and his wicked works.

3. To create and to destroy

4. The power of life and death

5. As though they all ready existed

6. You will put your faith into action.

7. No!

8. Faith in God and His Word is all the evidence you need for your miracle to come to pass.

9. The Holy Spirit's power

10. They are doing great and mighty wonders in His name.

11. It has everything to do with the intentions of the heart.

12. Ask for anything according to the Word, and the Father will give it to you.

13. Persistence

14. A pure heart of compassion, mercy, and love for the people

15. We need to have His same heart of compassion, mercy, and love for people.

— Chapter 17: Commissioned to Heal —

1. Yes

2. Luke 4:40-41

3. Wrong motives for praying for the sick include: wanting others to see that God is moving through us and our ministry, wanting others to think that we are super-spiritual or superior over them, or wanting financial gain or position.

4. Compassion is love in action

5. We will start to see healings manifest all around us.

6. The key to walking in the power of the Holy Spirit with signs and wonders following is spending time developing a relationship with Him.

7. The miraculous is His terrain.

8. We've all been commissioned to minister healing to the sick.

9. In the strength of a man.

10. We will cast out demons, speak with new tongues, and take up serpents; if we drink anything deadly it would not harm us, and we will lay hands on the sick and they will recover.

11. We will do even greater works than Jesus did if we believe.

12. Jesus Christ is the Healer.

13. By the power of the Holy Spirit

— Chapter 18: Signs and Wonders Point to Jesus —

1. Signs and wonders point to Jesus.

— Chapter 19: The Ark and His Promise —

1. Noah

2. He found favor in the eyes of the Lord.

3. To build an ark

4. He remained faithful and did what he was instructed to do.

5. Faith Principals that guided the life of Noah:

1. He was a just man.

2. He was blameless and a man of integrity.

3. He walked with God.

4. He obeyed God.

6. The ark represents our redemption through the blood of Jesus Christ. He is the only way to salvation; there is no other way, but through Him.

7. It represents the Holy Spirit.

8. It is a sign of the promise of God for perpetual generations to come, that He would never again destroy all flesh with a flood.

9. That God is faithful to keep His promise

10. I chose to end this book with this story because, regardless of the storms raging all around us, despite the grievous death reports given to us, no matter how much we are ridiculed and mocked, the wind of His Holy Spirit has been released and is blowing throughout the whole Earth looking for people to show Himself strong through. He remains faithful and ever true to keep His promises to us, and He has given us instruction in His Word on how to enter into His ark of healing.

FAITH ASSIGNMENTS

THE PURPOSE OF THESE faith assignments is to build up or strengthen your faith in God and His Word concerning healing—that God is willing and able to heal and deliver all who come to Him and that He wants to use you for His Kingdom purposes.

— Faith Assignment #1 —

1. Pray the following prayer:

    Dear Holy Spirit,

    I ask You for Your help in changing the way in which I speak. Help me to hear every negative and faithless word that comes out of my mouth, and teach me a new way to speak that would bring You glory and honor and cause Your power to be released over my life. I surrender my tongue to You this day.

    In Jesus' name I pray, amen.

2. Listen to the words that you speak.

3. Today, with the help of the Holy Spirit, start to change your negative, faithless words to words of faith and power in Christ

Jesus. This is not as easy as it sounds. It is a daily habit that must be formed in order to walk in the miraculous.

— Faith Assignment #2 —

If you, or someone you know who is willing to cooperate with you, has a mole or wart, do the following: Using godly discretion, lay your hands on the mole or wart and curse it at its very root and seed and command it to dry up and fall off in Jesus' name. Do this every day, several times a day, until it is gone. Then testify of the power of God after it is healed, and find someone else with the same problem and pray for them, too.

— Faith Assignment #3 —

If you, or someone you know who is willing to cooperate with you, has a damaged knee, do the following. Using godly discretion, lay your hands on the knee and speak the following: "In Jesus' name I rebuke the pain, swelling, and damage to this knee. I command this knee to be recreated, healed, and free from pain and swelling. I command it to function perfectly." Then put your faith into action and do what you could not do before. Allow the person receiving decide how best to put faith into action. It's that person's body, not yours! It may take time, but continue to speak healing over the knee, remembering that words have power to create or to destroy, until the total healing manifests. Then testify and find someone else with a bad knee to pray for again. Don't stop; every time you see someone with a bad knee, ask if you can pray for healing.

— Faith Assignment #4 —

If you, or someone you know who is willing to cooperate with you, has a bad back, do the following. Always remembering to use godly discretion, lay your hands on the spine, and command in Jesus' name that the vertebras, disks, muscles, ligaments, tendons, and nerves be realigned and that all pain and swelling is gone. Command the back to be completely healed, recreated in Jesus' name. Put your faith into action, and do what you couldn't do before. It's very important that you allow the person receiving to decide how to put faith in action. It's that person's body, so that person gets to decide. You do not have to rush people. It may take time, but continue to speak words of healing. After the healing manifests, testify, and always be willing to pray for others who have bad backs.

— Faith Assignment #5 —

Because the greatest sickness that exists is a spiritual condition, a lost soul condemned to hell, pray that God will lead you to people who need to hear the Good News that Jesus Christ loves them so much that He gave His life for them so that they could be forgiven, set free from the pain and suffering on this Earth, and have eternal life with Him. Put your faith into action and lead someone to Jesus Christ.

— Faith Assignment #6 —

Go visit someone who is sick and hurting; encourage that person with the Word of God concerning healing, share a testimony of God's healing power, and ask if you can pray for that person. Ask that person, "What would you have the Lord do for you?" Put your faith into action.

— Faith Assignment #7 —

Pray to God and ask Him for divine appointments, ask Him to lead you to people who are willing and wanting someone to pray with them. When He shows you someone be bold, speak out, and allow God to use you mightily on a daily basis. Put your faith into action and make this a lifestyle.

— Faith Assignment #8 —

Invite a few friends over for a Bible study in your home. Go through this book together, put your faith into action, and pray for one another. Allow God to show Himself strong in your midst. He will confirm His Word with signs and wonders.

WE WOULD LIKE TO HEAR FROM YOU

If you have received physical healing after reading this book and would like to share your testimony with us, please send us an email at:

daretobelieve@lifeunlimitedmin.org

LIFE UNLIMITED MINISTRIES

Please pray for David and Becky Dvorak and Family

LIFE Unlimited Ministries

Website: www.lifeunlimitedmin.org

Blog: http://beckydvorak.wordpress.com/

E-mail: life@lifeunlimitedmin.org

If you would like us to come minister at your church, e-mail us at the address above.

If you would like to support a child at the LIFE Homes in Guatemala on a monthly basis or if you would like to support a student at the LIFE Leadership Institute in Tanzania with a Bible and curriculum, please go to our Website and click on donations for further instructions.

Proceeds from this book will be used around the world to help translate, publish, print, and distribute this book, corresponding curriculum, and Bibles so that others less fortunate can be equipped to overcome life's adversities in the name of Jesus Christ by the empowering of the Holy Spirit for the glory of our Heavenly Father.

ABOUT BECKY DVORAK

BECKY DVORAK WITH HER HUSBAND, David, have been full time missionaries under Mutual Faith Ministries Int'l since 1994 and have been living by faith and serving Christ in Guatemala, Central America. Together they founded and established LIFE Unlimited Ministries—Guatemala, where they have developed the LIFE Homes for the orphaned and abandoned children of Guatemala, and the LIFE Tender Mercy Home, a home of healing for children who are in the healing process from HIV. They also teach the Body of Christ how to live a Spirit-led life, and they conduct faith and healing schools and campaigns throughout Guatemala.

In the year 2000, Becky started traveling to East Africa teaching, preaching, and ministering a bold message of faith and healing to the lost and dying people of that land, with great signs and wonders following. She has witnessed God's amazing grace for the nations, and with a mother's heart has since nurtured people groups around the world in the Word of God, and in the ways of His Spirit.

David and Becky are developing LIFE Leadership Institute in Northern Tanzania, where they are equipping the Maasai tribe and surrounding tribal people in the Word and the ways of the Holy Spirit.

Becky and David have been married for over 32 years. They raised their three biological children on the mission field, who are now grown and happily married. They are adopting five boys from their children's home in Guatemala, who they now home-educate and are raising for God's service. They are also enjoying their first three grandchildren.

In the right hands, This Book will Change Lives!

Most of the people who need this message will not be looking for this book. To change their lives, you need to put a copy of this book in their hands.

> *But others (seeds) fell into good ground, and brought forth fruit, some a hundred-fold, some sixty-fold, some thirty-fold* (Matthew 13:8).

Our ministry is constantly seeking methods to find the good ground, the people who need this anointed message to change their lives. Will you help us reach these people?

> *Remember this—a farmer who plants only a few seeds will get a small crop. But the one who plants generously will get a generous crop* (2 Corinthians 9:6).

EXTEND THIS MINISTRY BY SOWING
3 BOOKS, 5 BOOKS, 10 BOOKS, **OR MORE TODAY,**
AND BECOME A LIFE CHANGER!

Thank you,

Don Nori Sr., Founder
Destiny Image
Since 1982